# War and Women across Continents

# WAR AND WOMEN ACROSS CONTINENTS
## AUTOBIOGRAPHICAL AND BIOGRAPHICAL EXPERIENCES

*Edited by*

Shirley Ardener, Fiona Armitage-Woodward
and Lidia Dina Sciama

berghahn
NEW YORK • OXFORD
www.berghahnbooks.com

First published in 2016 by
Berghahn Books
www.berghahnbooks.com

©2016, 2018 Shirley Ardener, Fiona Armitage-Woodward and Lidia Dina Sciama
First paperback edition published in 2018

**Library of Congress Cataloging-in-Publication Data**
A C.I.P. cataloging record is available from the Library of Congress.

**British Library Cataloguing in Publication Data**
A catalogue record for this book is available from the British Library

ISBN 978-1-78533-013-1 (hardback)
ISBN 978-1-78533-825-0 (paperback)
ISBN 978-1-78533-014-8 (ebook)

# Contents

# Illustrations

# Women's Autobiographical and Biographical Experiences of War across Continents

## An Introduction

**Shirley Ardener**

The volume we offer here is concerned with contemporary issues. It reflects our anxieties about the spread of social conflict – even extreme violence – throughout the world today and our awareness of the fragility of peaceful existence. To see beautiful cities turned into rubble in this digital age, with its global economies, its international institutions, while social media cut across international, social and ethnic boundaries, is almost unbelievable. Sitting comfortably at home watching the devastation shown on TV we cannot believe our eyes. Commentators struggle to explain today's news stories by references to past events, before the modern technological wonders of our twentieth century existed. We can say that the past interprets our present for us; it is always with us. It is there as a warning and as an inspiration. And we come to realize that our present is a heritage for the future. When grand events dominate, their impact on individuals is overshadowed. The everyday disturbances to people, the personal tragedies and the ways they are overcome get lost in the thunder of events. So, as well as considering ongoing events, this book looks at former times, as reflected in the narratives of women experiencing conflict. For example, through their voices we learn from women in the jungles of the Cambodia-Thailand border, along the canals of Venice, in the hills of Rwanda and in the harsh terrains of Afghanistan.

There are multiple visions here – held by women who see themselves, or who are seen by others, as victims or heroines, as liberators or oppressors, as indigenes or refugees. In one lifetime a woman may pass from being one to another, perhaps several times over. A 'liberation movement' to some may be an 'insurgency' to others. Apparently benign acts, such as policies to prevent soil erosion, may trigger turmoil or worse, as was the case in Cameroon before Anlu (a women's revolt), and in Kenya before Mau Mau. Not all Kenyans supported Mau Mau, though they may have shared its ultimate objectives. It depends on who is counting.

We should note that the emphasis in this book is not on institutions, political parties or policies, nor is it primarily focused on the historical causes of conflict; rather it is placed on named persons, on family, on those with whom they interact, for good or bad, in specific contexts. The authors report on what people tell them, and they consider the ways women's actions have impacted on life today as memories cascade down to the present, sometimes bearing with them unexpected outcomes. They show how women on active service are still coping, and contributing, in today's war zones.

In 2013, Sharon Macdonald (p. 217) wrote 'Some pasts loom especially large in both official and popular memory within Europe. That of World War II is perhaps the largest and loomiest, and ... far from fading, its public marking is increasing.' Given this interest, it is fortunate that, just before the Second World War began, members of the British public were invited to record their daily activities in diaries which they deposited in the newly established Mass Observation programme. Continued and expanded throughout the Second World War to include the day-by-day thoughts of men and women at the front, these archives are now a treasure trove offering insights into the life and times – good and bad, simple and complex, amusing and horrifying – which our elders experienced.[1]

Indeed, in June 2014 the media of the United Kingdom, as elsewhere, was flooded with recollections as Europe and America celebrated the seventieth anniversary of the D-Day landing in Normandy on 6 June. At such events uniforms come out of wardrobes, young men fly the flags, heads of state and politicians parade. Former foes stand ceremonially side by side in France; their seemingly casual encounters offering them opportunities to negotiate political boundaries and citizens' rights from very changed positions. Did memories of the politics preceding the Second World War and the cruelties of combat bear upon their thoughts as they discussed today's boundary disputes in Crimea?

Following the celebrations for D-Day, attention has since moved to an earlier conflict, the First World War (1914–1918). The extensive coverage in British newspapers, and on television programmes, has been reflected in the public response, notably at the display of ceramic poppies, emblems of the renewal of life on the battlefields, which attracted over four million viewers to the historic Tower of London. The public interest in the past is not merely an expression of nostalgia, nor of heart-rending sentiments. It is because the past offers heroic accomplishments to be cherished, as well as burdens to regret. At the same time the past is refigured as elements are forgotten or revived, especially when claims to prestige and, perhaps, to natural and political resources arise. While acknowledging that traditionalist forma-tions, like military anniversaries, have their place, we cannot fail to note the relative absence of women in the parades. To balance this somewhat, we bring to the fore here how women, in military and in civil society, cope with conflict by their deportment under great stress, their survival strategies, each in her own way and particular circumstances, so that we may identify with them, perhaps learn from them. The chapters that follow open our eyes, both to unfamiliar histories and to ongoing current affairs that we read about in the newspaper or see enacted on TV. We may wonder whether we would manage as well as those women whose lives we discuss here, should events put us into similar circumstances.

Since this book focuses on the experience of particular women who have been chosen by the authors, rather than by complicated random selection processes, no attempt is made to generalize or to come up with syncretized statements. While commonalities are of interest, it is often the *differences* of women's everyday lives that fascinate us. It is the contrast between the actu-ality of the 'common woman' in uncommon places, times and events that appeals. Given the limited number of cases here, and their diversity over time and place, not to speak of cultures, it would be inappropriate to con-flate them. Consider the many millions affected by wars since the outbreak of the Second World War in Europe.

Many thousands of wise words are available in books and articles on the methodology of collecting and analysing field data and written narratives, which are accessible to readers, should they wish to take advantage of them. As most of the authors here are social anthropologists, we can note that nearly thirty years ago, the chapters in Anthony Jackson's *Anthropology at Home* (1987) discussed in depth the positioning of the anthropologist writing on his own and others' cultures. Therein, in her subtle disentanglement of the information gathering and analysing process, Marilyn Strathern (p. 20) warns us that 'Ultimately, the use anthropologists make of their data is for ends of their own making.' The same could perhaps be said of those proffer-ing autobiographical material.

Jumping the years, Helen Callaway and Judith Okely's edited collected essays *Anthropology and Autobiography* (2009: xi) also remind us that 'fieldwork, the process of writing and the creation of the final text involve a series of choices which depend on the selective interests of the ethnographer: monographs, often presented and read as definitive and timeless, are in fact selective and historically contingent.' Another helpful discussion has been given to us recently by Sharon Macdonald. 'Building, upon a [schema] developed by Edwin Ardener (1989: 26) ... which had a more sophisticated list of levels involved in the structure of history', Macdonald (2013: 55) lists a number of dimensions in her book (*Memorylands; Heritage and Identity in Europe Today*, 2013).[2]

Besides *multitemporal* considerations, studies of narratives may also be *multisited* (Marcus, 1998). Segalen and Zonabend (1987), quoting Levi-Strauss, say that 'there is one essential datum in our societies: they are *multidimensional* ... we have to take account of the emergence of the state, the church, the role of economics as it connects with kinship or becomes autonomous from it.' Michael Rothberg (2009: 3) considers 'memory as *multidirectional*: as subject to ongoing negotiations, cross-referencing, and borrowing; as productive not private'. From other recent anthropological literature on methodology we can pick out the following books whose titles are suggestive: *The Ethnographic Self as a Resource: Writing Memory and Experience into Ethnography* (Collins and Gallinet 2010), *Up Close and Personal: On the Peripheral Perspectives and the Production of Anthropological Knowledge* (Shore and Trinka 2013) and *Understanding Cultural Transmission in Anthropology* (Ellen, Lycett and Johns 2013).

The implied message in works of this kind is that, before approaching biographical and historical materials, to avoid the dangers of subjective and textual misunderstandings, readers should undertake a course in how to interpret them. Most social anthropologists, like those in other academic disciplines, are aware of this literature. Taken too literally, perhaps none of us should attempt to deal with narratives! To do so we have to risk the dangers of leading ourselves and others astray. Readers lacking the time and the will to follow suit will draw their own conclusions as they enter the worlds of the women in these pages.

Regarding the authors' 'positionality' we may note that the authors did not all know each other when they did their fieldwork. They had different life trajectories and ethnicities – English of Dutch descent, Italian, German, Kikuyu, Welsh and English. Three writers were fortunate since – in one case her mother (Jaschok), another her aunt (Clarke) and a third her mother-in-law (Sadan) – had left written autobiographical accounts. One of our authors (Davies) could draw on her letters home to her mother. Of course, books, articles and records in the form of news reports and other publications were also available. Some of our authors were writing in retrospect; some were still engaged in the field. Janette Davies was a participant witness (in Cambodia) of the events described; Rachel Grimes is still a participating member of the British Armed Forces. Moreover, several authors undertook their work in difficult, even dangerous, situations (see Davies and Grimes).

Despite the geographical and temporal spread, and the cultural diversity, some points of congruence among the narratives emerge as they touch common or parallel concerns. Three places studied had colonial and postcolonial pasts. In two of these we find women suing the British government for money – for different reasons. Fear of or actual sexual abuse, although not a main focus here, is referred to in the studies of a German woman's flight across Europe, of the experiences of Kenyan women during Mau Mau, and of problems encountered by some war correspondents. Three chapters concern displaced women. Three of the studies introduce women who, at great risk, carried guns under the gaze of the enemy.

With such matters in mind, the material can be considered in more detail, broadly in chronological order. First, the recollections of the three women who endured the Second World War intrigue us. Thus the chapter by Lidia Sciama who, born and brought up in Venice (and still a resident), tells us of the exploits of a courageous, well-born young lady carrying guns under German eyes to her partisan father. Sciama brings wartime Venice to life; she shows how the atmosphere changed as the war proceeded and that its likely outcome began to have an effect on German (and Venetian) morale. She reflects upon on how today young Venetians are re-evaluating the period of foreign occupation, and the part women played in the resistance. This exercise is paralleled in another chapter by Tabitha Kanogo's account of the way women's activities in Mau Mau in Kenya, and the crimes committed against them, are being revalued.

Lidia Sciama's account of confronting Nazi soldiers coexists with Marieke Clarke's story of her aunt Ank's brave involvement in the Netherlands, when she gave shelter to a beleaguered Jewish family. Both had close face-to-face relations with an overpowering enemy. The Dutch family have naturally held their memory of those days close. Ank Faber-Chabot's heroic actions were finally acknowledged in Israel after the war. Any effect the war has had on Dutch feelings towards Germany today, whether or not we take into account friendships that cut across national boundaries, is hard to calculate. It was said that the wartime experience of Greek families made negotiations with Germany for bail-out loans during the sudden credit crunch in Greece's national budget in 2009 all the more difficult to swallow. Indeed it was said that Greece's counterclaims against Germany for compensation for wartime deprivations were in the minds of many Greeks. And so the effects of the Second World War linger on ...

It is salutary that we also give space here to the suffering of a German woman, Hildegard Jaschok, as described by her daughter Maria. As the Second World War neared its final climax, Hildegard, who was living in Silesia, a German-speaking component of Poland, was warned by the departing German soldiers about the Poles who were arriving from further East; she was advised to make haste away in the opposite direction. For women, there is not much worse than chaos. The lack of order, the overreaching fear of personal violence, the problems Hildegard faced as she tried to keep her family group together (mother, two children and young servant) is vividly portrayed. This is a story that still has an impact on her daughter and other members of her family. It is a reminder that women on both sides of a conflict suffer. There are no winners here. Hildegard's story raises the question of how women (just as men) choose when to speak, what to repress or omit and when to be silent. There is much more to be said about the unspoken, and why speech is sometimes seen as inappropriate, see, for example, the work on 'muted groups'.[3]

As an exhausted post-war Europe licked its wounds and struggled to adjust to new realities, countries and regions in other areas of the world, which were also affected by the parts their people played on battlefields, began to flex their muscles. This was especially so in what was quickly redefined as the British Commonwealth, rather than the British Empire. During the war colonial recruits had become world travellers; for example, Igbo men from Eastern Nigeria and other West Africans found themselves fighting the Japanese in Burma. As a result, many were awakened to new possibilities. Anticolonial liberation movements already smouldering were uplifted by the post-war breeze. So it was that in Burma a movement closely associated with Aung San, father of Aung San Suu Kyi began. In many former colonies not only were there nationalist groups based on colonial boundaries, but internal 'tribal' nationalisms were also generated. In India and Pakistan, there were devastating upheavals as the two split up. Later, it was the Igbo who, unsuccessfully, fought other Nigerians and died for 'Biafra'.

In Burma it was the Kachins and Karens who became caught up in active struggle. We have in this volume an account by Mandy Sadan of how the Kachins, one of the many semi-autonomous ethnic groups that make up Burma, struggled for political recognition. Kachins had filled a significant role in Britain's armed forces in the Second World War, becoming soldiers on the payroll of the UK government, the men receiving pensions as they retired. This wartime experience meant that they were well equipped for armed liberation struggles, against not only colonialism but also against those they were opposed to within Burma. The Kachin State still has a structured uniformed and armed force, and is still asserting its identity in modern Burma (now Myanmar). Sadan, whose mother-in-law is a Kachin, shows how women contributed to the endeavours of both the colonial and nationalist forces. Moreover, she confirms the presence of the past, for the Second World War lives on today in the claims of former colonial Kachin soldiers, and by widows of serving men, to the payment of UK pensions.

Across the oceans, Africa, as already noted, was also stirring in the post-war period. In Kenya the activities of Mau Mau – defined by the colonizers as insurgent but by others as liberating – has been well documented. Mau Mau was a phenomenon particularly associated with the Kikuyu and related peoples who then numbered about one million, although some Embu, Meru and others of the many peoples of Kenya joined them. The country was traumatized, as people took sides or were caught up in the colonial system of administration and counter-insurgency practices introduced by the British; thousands of Kenyans, mainly Kikuyu 'loyalists' and Christians, and a small number of white residents, lost their lives. There is a considerable literature available, some of it from the pen of Tabitha Kanogo, herself a Kikuyu. Here, while she looks over her shoulder at past activities, Kanogo is primarily concerned with contemporary attitudes and assessments within Kenya of that period. As Sciama does here for Italy, and Sadan for Burma, Kanogo looks at how women fare in today's public perceptions of those men and women who were activists in their day. In Venice, Rangoon (aka Yangon) and Nairobi, women's roles are being re-evaluated by historians, including, of course, those of a feminist disposition. And, in all three contexts, the women are not happy: they feel undervalued. And they are protesting about it and even seeking government compensation. While in Burma, military widows appeal for British pensions, in Kenya former Mau Mau activists claim financial compensation for past atrocities during the colonial period – with considerable success.

Some twenty years after the troubles of Mau Mau, millions of men and women in Cambodia suffered badly at the hands of Pol Pot. One of our authors, Janette Davies, arrived over the border into Thailand in the refugee camps set up by the military to house people who (like Hildegard in Germany) had run for their lives to Cambodia from their homelands in Thailand. We are given a vivid eyewitness account – as noted, a participant's account – of how men and women, both carers and sufferers, coped with the hardships, with their painful memories, and how they began to regenerate their lives. A trained midwife with wide medical experience in Bolivia and Bangladesh before becoming a social anthropologist, Davies has been able to use her letters home, and other documentation, to enhance her memories of those dark days. Dark they certainly were but, to quote from Davies, the new babies brought a sense 'not of death but of life'. Her chapter, like so many others in this book, describes the interaction, the clash of cultures, between autochthonous peoples and incomers from overseas, be they from military or humanitarian organizations.

Hannah Spens-Black switches our attention to dramatic events in Africa when she describes the activities of women in the Rwandan Patriotic Front (RPF). Spens-Black arrived in Rwanda three decades after Davies' arrival in Cambodia in order to meet the men and women who had been involved in the RPF. She was inspired by the stories of a number of notable women, only to discover 'not only how they had experienced war but also the social stereotypes they had to contend with in order to participate'; patriarchal echoes from Kenya ring in our ears here! And we begin to see how the women interviewed by our authors in various parts of the world at different times have common concerns. For example, the Kachin women took loyalty oaths when joining their paramilitary association (the KWA), as in like fashion the Kikuyu and Rwandan women were sworn to secrecy in their fields of protest, while today the British women soldiers promise loyalty to their Queen and country.

Which brings us to the three final chapters, to this millennium – the 2000s. First Glenda Cooper, a journalist herself, looks at the role of women war correspondents, especially those reacting to the so-called Arab Spring in North Africa. Cooper notes that 'during the time of the Libyan revolution of 2011 the first three reporters into Green Square, Tripoli, were women'. They resented being treated as 'phenomena' by the rest of the media, seeing this as patronizing. As Cooper explains, there was a woman correspondent as long ago as 1898, there were well-known women reporters during the Second World War and there have been ever since, so their presence in Libya should not have been so surprising. All the same, such women had problems. Cooper herself draws on the memoirs of correspondents to give us a useful insight into the obstacles placed in the way of women war correspondents and the imaginative tactics used to overcome them.

Journalists, of course, come into contact with army personnel. They have more freedom of expression than the latter, upon whom they sometimes depend for access and information. It is appropriate that Mathew Hurley gives us a study of British women in the structures of NATO. He gives voice to four women serving in different parts of the NATO structure based in Europe. In the opinion of these women, men 'view warfare and provision of security, differently from women'. As one of them put it, 'the inclusion of women challenges traditional understandings'. Hurley's interviewees draw our attention to the different spatial awareness of women and men, and to the contrast in a war zone between street and home, and the violence within each. Hurley also draws out views on the different 'competences' of men and women.

It is fortunate that, for our final chapter, we can turn to Rachel Grimes who speaks to us with authority as a major in the British Armed Forces. She draws upon scholarly works as well as army reports and statutes as she critiques for us the army structures and the military objectives in Afghanistan, Grimes has 20 years' experience travelling between war and conflict zones from hot spot to hot spot in Europe, Asia and Africa. These first-hand experiences and her discussions with military colleagues add authenticity to her descriptions of life on army air transport, and of what women bring to the British Army's Counterinsurgency Operations.

Finally, we are grateful to the authors of the following chapters, which we commend to you; but most of all we thank the women whose voices reverberate through the book. With all the caveats, the editors believe that the diverse collection of texts give plenty to think about.

## Notes

1. Historians have already raided them: the prize-winning collections of excerpts from wartime diaries made by Simon Garfield (2004, 2005 and 2006) have been bestsellers. They remain startling reading today. Max Arnold's book (2004) is also composed of interleaved diary extracts. He drew largely on recordings in the Imperial War Museum made mainly by British men and some women, most of whom were in the British and Commonwealth armed services. Two popular illustrated histories of the Second World War include those by Janice Anderson (2009) and Raynes Minns (first published 1945) the latter of which has been through seven editions.

2. Macdonald takes a *multitemporal approach* which, she says, is not only about how the past is referred to in the present. She also identifies:
   (a) ways in which events, persons or whatever, were perceived and experienced at the time;
   (b) ways in which events or experiences were encoded at the time, i.e. how they were materialized or documented. Both (a) and (b) may also involve attention to historiography – that is, to the ways historians may have perceived and recorded events, and to notions of time and change (including perceptions of past, present and future);
   (c) ways in which past traces survive over time, including attention to why these and not others may endure and to the structuring of historical evidence (as text, trace, material, verbal account and so forth) at different moments in time;

(d) ways in which past events and experiences are perceived, experienced, used and recast today, including the notions of time, change, identity etc. that are implicated.

3. Much has been written on the silencing of people, including on 'muted groups' (see E. Ardener 1975 and Shirley Ardener 2005).

## Bibliography

Anderson, J. 2009. *Women of the War Years: Women in Britain during 1939–1945*. London: Futura.

Ardener, E. 1975. 'Belief and the Problem of Women' in S. Ardener, *Perceiving Women*. London: Dent.

Ardener, E. 1989. *The Voice of Prophecy and Other Essays*. M. Chapman (ed.). Oxford: Blackwell.

Ardener, S. 2005. 'Ardener's "Muted Groups": The Genesis of an Idea and its Praxis' in *Women and Language* 128(2).

Arnold, M. 2004. *Forgotten Voices of the Second World War*. London: Ebury Press.

Callaway, H. and J. Okely (eds). 2009. *Anthropology and Autobiography*. London: Routledge.

Collins, P. and A. Gallinet. 2010. *The Ethnographic Self as a Resource: Writing Memory and Experience into Ethnography*. Oxford and New York: Berghahn Books.

Ellen, R., S. Lycett and S. Johns. 2013.*Understanding Cultural Transmission in Anthropology*. Oxford and New York: Berghahn Books.

Garfield, S. 2004. *Our Hidden Lives: The Remarkable Diaries of Post-War Britain*. London: Ebury Press.

——. 2005. *Private Battles: How the War Almost Defeated Us*. London: Ebury.

——. 2006. *We Are at War...* London: Ebury.

Jackson, A. 1987. *Anthropology at Home*. London: Tavistock.

Macdonald, S. 2013. *Memorylands: Heritage and Identity in Europe Today*. Abingdon, UK: Routledge.

Marcus, G. 1998. *Ethnography through Thick and Thin*. Princeton, NJ: Princeton University Press.

Minns, R. 2012 [1945]. *Bombers and Mash: The Domestic Front 1935–45*. London: Virago

Rothberg, M. 2009. *Multidirectional Memory: Remembering the Holocaust in the Age of Decolonization*. Stanford: Stanford University Press.

Segalen, M. and F. Zonabend. 1987. 'Social Anthropology and the Ethnography of France: The Field of Kinship and Family', in A. Jackson (ed.), *Anthropology at Home*. London: Tavistock.

Shore, C. and S. Trinka. 2013. *Up Close and Personal: On the Peripheral Perspectives and the Production of Anthropological Knowledge*. Oxford and New York: Berghahn Books.

Strathern, M. 1987. 'The Limits of Auto-anthropology', in A. Jackson (ed.), *Anthropology at Home*. London: Tavistock Publications, pp. 16–37.

**Shirley Ardener** (BSc(Econ) London, MA status Oxford, OBE), has carried out many years of fieldwork (until 1987 with her husband, Edwin) in Nigeria and in Cameroon, where she is still involved with the University of Buea and the National Anglophone Archives that she set up with Edwin. She was the Founding Director of the Centre for Cross-Cultural Research on Women (1983–1997), now International Gender Studies at Lady Margaret Hall. She is also a Research Associate at Oxford's Institute of Social and Cultural Anthropology. Books she has edited and contributed to include *Perceiving Women* (1975), *Women and Space* (1981), *Swedish Ventures in Cameroon* (2002) and *Changing Sex and Bending Gender* (2005).

# 1

# The Resistance of Francesca Tonetti in German-Occupied Venice 1943–1945

## Lidia Dina Sciama

We will glorify war – the world's only hygiene – militarism, patriotism ...
Beautiful ideas worth dying for, and scorn for woman ... We will destroy
the museums, libraries, academies of every kind, will fight moralism, feminism, every opportunistic or utilitarian cowardice.

> (*Manifesto of Futurism*, an inspiration to fascists!)

## Introduction

In a lively and detailed autobiographical narrative, Francesca Tonetti
describes her wartime experiences under German occupation, from
September 1943 to May 1945. A strong theme in her book is her dramatic
transition from adolescence to maturity, as she had to face responsibilities
and take decisions that would have been quite unthinkable in peacetime. I
too experienced war in a very direct and personal way, but I was then too
young to follow and understand its strange events.[1]

After the war, as I was naturally keen to know how life in Venice
was under Nazi occupation, I was lucky to meet some of the people who,
just a few years older than myself, had fought for the city's Liberation –
among them Francesca Tonetti. During several meetings at friends' houses
in Venice, and holidays in Abano and in Puglia, an awareness that those

years had had a strong impact on our lives implicitly led to mutual interest and understanding, but neither of us was disposed to speak much about the war. However, like many people with comparable experiences, Francesca did write and speak about the past many years later (1970, 1994).

Before I turn to her narrative, I shall introduce a brief account of events that took place before and during the German occupation of Italy – and more specifically Venice.

## The Context

Benito Mussolini entered Parliament in 1921. After his March on Rome in October 1922, the opposition was violently repressed, and after the fascist murder of socialist MP Matteotti in 1924, Italy's Parliamentary Democracy came to an end. Friendship between Italy and Germany, developed through-out the 1930s, led to the Rome/Berlin Axis Alliance of 1939 (also joined by Japan in 1940). Italy entered the Second World War on 10 June 1940. To fulfil Mussolini's dream of empire, Italian troops first fought in Africa; they conquered British Somaliland in August 1940, but held it for only a few months, as it was soon taken back by the British. The Italians were defeated in Greece, France and both East and North Africa. But their worst losses took place in the Russian campaign (Hitler's 'Operation Barbarossa'). In the battle of Stalingrad, from August 1942 to February 1943, the Italian 8th Army lost 20,000 soldiers, 60,000 were captured and many died in captivity. By 1942, as losses on the Russian front had a devastating effect on the population, Italians had had enough of the war; the Futurists' celebration of 'militarism and patriotism' had had its day.

After the Allies landed in Sicily on 10 July 1943, members of the fascist Grand Council advised Mussolini to resign (25 July). He was arrested by *carabinieri* and spirited away to an isolated place in Abruzzo: Italians believed that the dictatorship had come to an end, but their newfound freedom only lasted for forty-five days. As the Allies advanced up the peninsula, and, on 8 September, the new head of state, General Badoglio, announced that an armistice was signed, in no time at all, the Germans invaded Italy. The army was disbanded; about 100,000 Italians continued to fight alongside the Germans, while those units that were able to join the Allies fought alongside them as a 'co-belligerent'. But 710,000 men were transported to Germany as slave labour. To escape that fate, large numbers of soldiers, left with no orders or instructions by their officers, abandoned their uniforms and weapons. They were helped by the population, who sheltered them and gave them civilian clothes; many of them would eventually join the Resistance.

Meanwhile, Mussolini, rescued by a German commando, was forced by Hitler to set up a new fascist state, the 'Italian Social Republic of Salò' with its own army, the 'Esercito Nazionale Repubblicano' or 'Black Brigades'.

## The Germans Arrive in Venice

After Italy's ill-fated armistice with the Allies in September 1943, German forces poured into Italy through the Brenner Pass. They arrived in Venice mainly by sea, while some frighteningly low-flying airplanes dropped large numbers of leaflets signed by the new 'National Fascist Government', urging the population to collaborate with the German forces. The leaflets were then followed by bombs aimed at a number of ships, as they were trying to leave the port in the hope of joining the Allies in the southern Adriatic. Venice's historical centre was not considered a 'useful' military target, while Marghera's industrial area was spared because it would have been valuable for the war effort.

Because the Venice port had so far been relatively safe, several ocean liners, as well as hospital ships were anchored there. One luxury liner, the *Conte di Savoia*, was repeatedly attacked by German planes and left near Alberoni, completely burnt, like a ghostly reminder, until the end of the war. Venetians, who until then had not come into direct contact with war, were shocked at the sight of a procession of half-naked wounded soldiers, their tattered clothes soaked in oil and blood, struggling to land at the city's embankments from a German patrol boat; they were deeply angered when armed Germans did not allow them to assist the wounded and help them to reach the navy hospital.

Meanwhile a German general demanded the surrender of all the city's military authorities and establishments, threatening to carry out some violent reprisal against the civilian population, if his orders were not complied with. As two German submarines had ominously reached Saint Mark's basin, he also threatened to order the destruction of ships that continued to arrive from Fiume and from the Balkans. Large numbers of Italian soldiers and pupils from a naval academy were thus held hostage in their own ships, fearing they would be blown up, or at best sent to some labour camp in Germany or Poland, had a compromise not been reached.[2] Some Italian officers were advising their soldiers to obey German orders, while a Venetian colonel, seeing that there was nothing he could do to help his men, committed suicide (Bobbo 2005: 70).

As the situation in the ships was deteriorating, the population did their utmost to help; it was at that time, under those distressing and dramatic

**Figures 1.1 and 1.2.** 'We soon learnt how to use our weapons.' Courtesy of the National Association of Italian Partisans (ANPI).

circumstances, that women and men began to work together to offer some relief to the starving and dejected soldiers. Under threat of German fire, they approached the ships in their rowing boats to bring the men water, medicines and food. For those who had already been transferred to sealed cattle trains about to leave for Germany or Poland, some of the women who were committed to helping, instructed students to bring paper and pens, so they could send a note to their family (G. Milner, personal communication; Bobbo 2005: 63–69).

## Francesca Tonetti

Francesca Tonetti was then in Venice – a full participant and keen observer of the disastrous events of the German invasion. Her autobiographical book, *The Wind of Quarnero* (1994, *Il Vento del Quarnero*), is of great anthropological and historical interest: in narrating her life from childhood to adolescence, adulthood and maturity, she not only relates her wartime activities, but also provides her own, certainly subjective, but very valuable, vision of social change and intergenerational relations. Thanks to her strong interest in people, in narrating their vicissitudes and changing circumstances, she also probes their motivations, ideas and thoughts in the historical context of the Second World War.

The book's dedication reads: 'To my father / and to my great love, / the wind of Quarnero, the Bora'. Indeed a strong theme – one also present in many other women's accounts of their resistance – is that of the great importance of her relationship with her father. It is of interest that part of Francesca's narrative was included as a chapter in her father's autobiography, *A Patrician Revolutionary* (G. Tonetti 1970, *Un patrizio rivoluzionario*). When she published her own book in 1994, she in turn quoted or paraphrased passages from her father's writings. With a clear division of intellectual labour, Francesca based chapters on Italy's political history on his rather dry journals, while her narrative of her actions and thoughts, based on her own memory as well as old diaries, is far more open, emotional and, in parts, poetic. The way father and daughter's writings are woven together is an example of a then conventional set of gendered oppositions between ideas, political competence and action as male prerogatives, as against sentiment and alleged maternal/feminine motives for women's participation in the Resistance. Like other male/female oppositions, that is now widely critiqued and rejected; it does, however, effectively mirror Francesca's family's lifestyle and circumstances.

Very briefly, Francesca is the daughter of Count Giovanni Tonetti (1888–1969) (from now Giovanni), heir to a Friulan family of ship owners and captains long established in Istria,[3] where they owned vast tracts of land surrounding their castle. Her mother was Lucia Caracciolo-Borsa, a Neapolitan noblewoman of princely descent. She died of tuberculosis aged twenty-eight, when Francesca was only three years old.

The Tonetti family usually divided their time between Venice and Istria, where they mainly spent the summers. Giovanni, who, as we shall see, was a powerful figure in Francesca's life, is affectionately described throughout her narrative. As she writes, referring to his autobiography, the most important turning points in his life took place in 1919, first when he married Lucia, with whom he was deeply in love, and, second, when he read the works of Marx, Engels and Lenin, and decided to dedicate his life to the socialist cause. He abhorred fascism and was continually harassed for his participation in workers' protests and strikes. Because of his political activities, he and Lucia had to spend long periods in exile, leaving Francesca with Giovanni's mother. Francesca recalls that the first words she learnt, while living in Venice with her grandmother, were the cries of gondoliers touting for passengers, and the more threatening '*mandato di arresto*', 'warrant of arrest', of the fascist police. She remembers the days when, still in the arms of her nurse, she watched them while they searched her playroom.

After her mother's death, Francesca with her father and grandmother shared their lives between Istria, Venice and Rome. She was not allowed to attend school, because she was thought to be frail, but during their long stays in Istria, where she enjoyed great freedom, exploring her family's vast estates, and where she was allowed to own all the dogs, horses and pets she desired, she toughened up and developed a deep love of nature that sustained her in difficult times. She also grew very independent and competent, because, still a child, she had to care for her grandmother who suffered from angina. The book's early chapters include lively descriptions of her life in 1930s Rome, with her two aristocratic grandmothers, both forever wearing deep mourning and entertaining high prelates and bishops, because at that time of political uncertainty they turned to the Church, while Giovanni would escape to his rooms and bury himself in reading.

Come September 1943, as soon as they heard of Italy's armistice with the Allies that followed Mussolini's resignation in July, they returned to Venice and Giovanni joined the Resistance as a representative of the Socialist Party. Their palace, Ca' Giustinian, had been requisitioned in earlier years, when he refused to accept membership of the fascist party, and in it were then housed the offices of the Fascist National Guard and Nazi propaganda.

Francesca and her grandmother then had to stay at a hotel near Saint Mark's Square. Crowded with different, and potentially hostile people, thrown together by the absurd circumstances of war, the hotel became an excellent vantage point for Francesca's observation of the confused and rapidly changing life of the city. On the ground and first floor were Francesca's grandmother and a number of old ladies, most of them titled and bejewelled, mainly longstanding clients and friends of the kind hoteliers. There was Countess Fabbro, who was ancient but extremely elegant in a black breitschwanz and ermine suit with diamond and emerald jewellery, a generous and warm-hearted lady from Rome, and then Mrs Miollo, a rich landowner who was secretly in love with Francesca's father and wrote him love letters that caused him terrible embarrassment every time he chanced to meet her.

Mixed with them, especially at mealtimes, were people who had taken refuge from the Allies' bombing of inland cities, and a number of Roman officials transferred to Venice with various fascist ministries. Indeed it was at the hotel that Francesca met and married a young man who offered her and her grandmother solidarity and help – and shared his food rations with them! On the top floor lived and worked an elderly Viennese baron, at that time a colonel, who edited a German-language newspaper, *Adler in Suden*. Thanks to Francesca's grandmother's title, bestowed on the family by none other than Emperor Franz Joseph, the colonel held the lady in great respect and never failed to click his heels as he encountered her in the hotel.[4]

Francesca, just sixteen, was immediately plunged into the war situation. As she writes, 'On the 8th of September, Venice was in chaos. Italian Navy officers, some in uniform, others in their ordinary clothes, stood about in the hotel's lobby, wondering what to do ... They had to rid themselves of their weapons'. She then decided to collect their guns and munitions; she hid them in her room and, childishly, she said,

> I will bring them to papá. Perhaps it is time for the Revolution. Grandmother sees me and she says that I am just like my father and I always want to play with the most absurd and dangerous things. (112–113)

Giovanni, then staying at one of their properties in Piove di Sacco in the neighbouring countryside, sent a local woman to fetch them. As at other moments when she had to face some testing situation, Francesca looked at herself in the mirror; as she recalls, 'I was pleased to see that in my light cotton dress, red with little white flowers, my tidy tresses, and my nose covered in freckles, I looked younger than my age'.

With her grandmother and the woman accompanying them, she left for Mestre, where they had to change to a local train. They found that the Germans had arrived. The station was in total confusion; on the walls were large notices: 'Anyone carrying weapons will be shot on sight'. Francesca's bag was heavy; she needed to get out of there as quickly as she could; she got the country woman with the luggage on the train to Piove di Sacco, then, walking arm in arm with her grandmother, under her other arm the bag full of guns, and over it the chihuahua trembling with fear, she made her way through the armoured cars in the station square. She went straight to the station hotel, she ordered a good meal, and then a taxi that would drive them to join Giovanni in the countryside. Back in Venice, against her father's and grandmother's advice, Francesca joined a Red Cross nursing course.

Some Resistance leaders favoured a steady but low-key opposition to the German and fascist oppressors, but Giovanni was a maximalist: he knew that in Venice's jail there were prisoners waiting to be executed or deported to Germany, and that the archives concerning political prisoners and Resistance fighters were kept in Ca' Giustinian, formerly his family's property, then ruled by the ferocious Zani. With another senior fighter, he planned the destruction of the palace wing in which the Nazis and Fascist Republican Guard (actually ruthless torturers) had established their offices.

When, a few days later Francesca heard a loud bang and was running through St Mark's square to go and see what had happened at Ca' Giustinian, a man caught her by her pigtail and told her that he was a friend of Giovanni's and that she had to go right back to the hotel. Knowing that her father was behind that action, Francesca ran to find him in the home of a woman friend and persuaded him to spend the night elsewhere. As she writes,

> My father is playing the violin. The setting sun lights up the Venetian drawing room and makes his blond hair shine. He is dressed in white and is very handsome. The scene is peaceful, and for a moment I look at him as if he were a painting. Then, breathless, I urge him not to sleep there. And he tells me that a lady must not get agitated and speak so excitedly. (122–123)

And that lesson probably served Francesca well in the following days. Indeed members of the Fascist National Guard did arrive at dawn; they were so disappointed at not finding Giovanni that they stayed on the premises for four days. Then they decided to take Francesca as a hostage. Again, to appreciate the strangeness of those times, and Francesca's fluctuation between her adolescent concern with her body and her overwhelming anxiety over her father's safety, it is probably best to quote her own words:

> At the hotel with my grandmother, at seventeen, I had a grave problem: the device for straightening my teeth and the war. I was half asleep and I was feeling

the heat, even at dawn. Then, loud banging at the door, men with machine guns order me to get up. I was a hostage; I had to go with them. My eyes were closing with sleep.

At the fascist headquarters they lock me up in a cell. The following morning a man in a black shirt opens my cell and takes me downstairs. His name is Gallo and I know all about him: he is bad, bad, the worst ... On the floor below, he orders a soldier to open a door; for a second I only see the pearl grey sky of dawn through the window, then as I look around me: on the floor are men, they are leaning against the wall, almost lying. I look at the man nearest to me: his face is covered in blood that flows from one of his eyes, his ear and his mouth. This is what they call ... torture! (133)

She was shaken by the voice of Gallo, who said 'for the time being I have spared you all this, but, if you don't speak, if you don't tell us where your father is hiding ...' She told them long stories she had made up and rehearsed for hours, but she feared she might contradict herself later, when they ordered her to repeat them shining a dreadful light in her face. But, she writes,

I am not afraid, and I behave very politely, as if I were in boarding school ... This morning they slapped a girl younger than me very hard. I feel I am in the midst of a herd of angry buffaloes. One must not make sudden movements, must keep very calm, and look at them: only that way one can avoid getting torn to pieces. ...They take me down again, to the large hall of Ca' Littoria (the palace next to Ca' d'Oro), the hall of the fascists; they are all dressed in black, with their machine guns and their boots and skulls on their berets. On the walls are mirrors and frescoes. It is an odd vision to see those black brigands armed to the teeth in the drawing room of a Venetian palace. In the mirror, I see myself in my white and blue gingham frock, my white collar and my long tresses. Strange: I look frail, but I feel very strong ... On Venice's walls are posters offering a reward for finding my father. I am in the hands of the enemy. I think of Salgari's adventure books I read at the Castle in Cherso. (133–134)

Francesca was questioned by three ferocious leaders of the Black Brigades, Pepi, Zani and Cafiero.[5]

Cafiero is fat; he speaks in a southern dialect. He begins to shout that if I don't tell him where my father is, he will get me executed. He gets angrier and angrier, and he comes close to me with his fists. Another fascist, Damiano, who has watched me from the day of my arrest, steps forward and looks at Cafiero, in silence. I think, 'Perhaps now they will beat one another up'. And I say, as coldly as I can: 'I do not understand why you can't sentence a lady to death politely'. All around me they laugh, and they take me back to my cell. (134)

Following more interrogations, Francesca was told that she was going to be executed with other hostages the following day. As in many comparable stories, we have a description of the prison sounds in the early morning, the heavy steps, the rattling of keys, more steps, then shots in the courtyard.

After fourteen days Francesca was taken back to the hotel, but kept under house arrest. Her room was searched, her writings destroyed; she lay on her bed in the August heat, looking at the reflections of the canal water like gentle waves on the ceiling. But all she wanted was to get out, to walk out in the streets, to be free! Then, one day, they let her go! She wondered if her release might have been due to the Viennese baron in the hotel, because it was reported to her that when he heard that she had been arrested by the Black Brigades, he had got very angry; 'The Countess and her little granddaughter, with a title conferred by no less than Franz Joseph, Emperor of Austria-Hungary, could not possibly have done anything wrong!' (144).

At last she heard that her father had joined partisans on Mount Grappa.[6] There, in September 1944, during a German round-up, followed by horrendous reprisals against the civilian population; Giovanni too was arrested and sentenced to death.[7] But, while fourteen men were shot and others hanged in the following days, he was transferred to a prison in Verona, actually the cellar of the SS headquarters, and kept for a grand public execution (130–132).

Meanwhile Francesca, who had contacted members of the Action Party, then hidden in the Benedictine Monastery of Santa Giustina in Padua, learnt that the Germans were beginning to negotiate exchanges of American and English or partisan leaders with German prisoners held by the Allies.[8] Braving the dangers of travel, when 'anything that moved' was continually targeted by Allied planes, rail travel was impossible and she had to take lifts mainly on military vehicles, Francesca decided to go straight to Verona to the SS commando. Speaking German, she told General Karl Hass [9] that she was the daughter of an important political prisoner, she had been looking for him for four months. The general gave orders for Giovanni to be brought up. As she recalls,

> Now all my strength has gone. I cannot speak any more. I have found him. (140)

A plan to exchange Giovanni for a nephew of General Karl Wolff never actually took place, because the young German, then in an English prisoner-of-war camp, could not be found, but the negotiations did serve to keep Giovanni alive.[10]

As the war continued, both the Germans and the fascist Black Brigades were becoming increasingly violent. Conditions worsened, but while her father remained in prison, Francesca continued to make her perilous trips to Verona to bring him clean shirts and whatever food she could find, while she suffered the pangs of hunger. At the hotel, her boyfriend looked after her grandmother, while the old lady's friends all shared her anxiety when they heard that Francesca was about to undertake one of her increasingly dangerous night-time journeys to visit her father in Verona's prison.

Countess Floridi di Prato, a good and generous woman who had cried bitterly when Francesca was arrested, was the only one who realized the danger of those journeys; she asked the girl if it was really necessary for her to go, and as Francesca said it was, she brought her a blessed little medal of the Virgin and pinned it onto her dress for protection; Mrs Miollo gave her an image of St Antony, and Countess Fabbro removed her own precious scapular, with its miraculous relic, for Francesca to wear inside her sweater, close to the skin. 'I am so well protected' she writes, 'it is impossible that anything could happen to me!' (150)

But travelling remained painfully hard: she describes the long waits for a lift at the German checkpoints in the cold winter nights. Having got close to the enemy, in a way that would probably not have been possible for a man, she occasionally remarks on their humanity, their tiredness and their longing for home in the general chaos and disruption of the last months of the war. 'A German soldier near me is eating. He offers me an apple and a large slice of dark bread spread with lard. After two days' fast, the food going inside me gives me a wonderful sensation, my hands and my face are getting warm.' And, although she says that she was not at all nostalgic about her rich and pampered childhood, she comments,

> It seems such a long time from the days when the butler in his gold-buttoned white jacket and white gloves used to bow before me saying, 'Little countess, dinner is served'. (140–145)

On approaching Verona, she could hear the Allies' bombs falling and she prayed that they should not hit her father's prison. All she could do, in the grey fog and icy sleet, was to sing quietly a partisan song: 'The wind whistles, the tempest howls, our shoes are broken, and yet we must walk ...' (*fischia il vento, urla la bufera, scarpe rotte eppur ci tocca andar*), to the tune of Russian Katyusha, then she added, 'ah, the wind, my friend ...' (144).

By the end of April, in Venice, as the war was coming to an end, the population had risen in arms, but German soldiers continued hopelessly to shoot from their rafts on the Grand Canal, while boys with red kerchiefs round their necks shot back from the Accademia bridge.

Once every hour, the radio broadcasts: 'We request news of Dr Giovanni Tonetti held in the SS prison in Verona'. No news. For the first time, I cry. I feel so alone, while the whole of Venice is celebrating the arrival of the Allies and the end of the war ... Four days later, father arrives at the hotel. His hair uncut, dressed like a beggar. After nine months in the underground cell ... a long winter of hunger and cold ... his blond hair has turned silvery. (153)

He explained that, on leaving Verona, the Germans had taken him to a concentration camp in Bolzano; that too was dissolved when the war ended, so he had gone to Milan to confer with his comrades. Francesca just asked: 'And me, daddy?' But, she adds, she was 'too happy to have him [there] with us, free and safe, to chide him'.

## The Father as Hero

Francesca's gentle hints of protest against her father, at the end of the war, were in the end always overcome due to her unstinting affection. On the very day of his arrival at the hotel he was surrounded by comrades; the Mayor and other important people had come to confer with him in his room all day. Francesca waited for him sitting on the stairs, her head leaning against the wall, but her father's visitors were important, they had to discuss important things. As Giovanni was nominated High Commissioner for Justice, he spent his days in a vast hall in the Royal Palace in St Mark's Square; if she needed to see him, she always had to wait. She would have liked to join him at some of the sumptuous dinners put on by the Allies; after all, she protested, she had not eaten any good things for a long time, but Giovanni told her firmly that he was not going to have his daughter cosying up to English and American officers. 'I am a woman who has fought a war, but for father, who thinks I cannot even go with him to some officers' dinners, nothing has changed!' (157).

Feeling like a new Cinderella, Francesca then decided to move back to their house in Rome. Life was not altogether easy there, either; she had financial problems, but, after the solitude of the war years, she wanted to be young again. And, as she told herself, she was not going to go back to being the delicate, overprotected little girl of the past. She did not always agree with all of her father's decisions, indeed she was not sure that he was right in not recovering the property of their palace that had been requisitioned by the fascists when, back in the 1930s, he had refused to join their party. But because he was against private property on principle, he left it to the Venice Commune. Both Francesca and her grandmother were worried and disappointed, but 'As he looks at me with his light blue eyes, clear as mine, I understand that I cannot ask of him something so contrary to his principles'.

She admired her father's coherence and dedication to his political ideals, and she recognized their deep-seated affinities of character as well as appearance. Indeed, she took pride in his good looks: 'He is handsome, tall, blond, his eyes are blue-green, but they get as cold as steel when they see injustices, when the weak are oppressed' (20). 'His apparent coldness, his unnatural reserve in expressing emotion concealed a great sensitivity.' She knew that the tragedy of her mother's death was a cause of remorse and sorrow for all his life, because he thought that his ideals of social justice had only caused her anguish and that the hardships she suffered in exile had been the cause of her illness (51).

In Rome, in the years that followed Lucia's death, what with his sorrow and his bitterness at the growing strength of fascism, he lived like a Trappist monk, almost always shut up in his room in the dark, but he did come down to dinner and conversed mainly with Francesca (61–63). He was against his mother's old-fashioned attitudes to education, and when she and Francesca's governess tried to censor her reading, he assured Francesca that she could read all the books she liked, but she had to do so in his room – and she was even allowed to go there with her collie! When he told Francesca how much he loved her, she hugged him and stroked his head in a motherly way. He too, painfully concerned that Francesca had had to grow up without a mother, tried as best he could to make up for that absence; he always advised the girl on her reading, her demeanour, and even her clothes and appearance.

Looking back on her childhood, Francesca wrote that she had grown up and lived in two different worlds: that of her two grandmothers, who led a luxurious and active social life among the old Roman and Neapolitan aristocracy, the high prelates, and a lot of rich people who, satisfied in their wealth, hardly concerned themselves with the country's political and social problems. On the other side, her solitary, handsome father who lived like a monk in his room and his study full of books, only received two old comrades, and always 'spoke about the social injustice of capitalism and of fascism that would have brought Italy to war and to ruin' (63).

> This wonderful father, a dreamer, revolutionary, detached and sentimental, is giving me weapons; we shall look after each other, also when this rich life will not be so any more. We shall be together and that will be our strength. I felt so motherly towards him and at the same time I felt he was such a rebel ... and I wished to be like him. (63)

Having heard almost every day that the only aim in life was that of fighting fascism, that had become part of her nature, and when the black times
arrived – without money because everything had been confiscated – the
times of her father's imprisonment and the death sentence, Francesca was
ready to confront them, without fear and almost without sacrifice, smiling
and putting up with the cold and the hunger, singing revolutionary songs.
The black times, in her memory, had become 'the best years because they
were full of hope and faith in the morrow' (63). After the war, like many
others who had fought for freedom, she found Italian politics disappoint-
ing, but she remained dedicated to her socialist and egalitarian principles.[11]
Although she received a Socialist Party card *honoris causa*, with a beautiful
letter for her 'activity in the Resistance and for saving [her] father's life'
(170), from the point of view of some historians, Francesca would not fully
qualify as a partisan, but she does consider herself one, both in her actions
and in her full dedication to Resistance values and ideology.

Like her father, Francesca sometimes expresses deep pessimism about
human nature; she fluctuates between sadness and hope, but she draws new
vigour from her great love of nature, and from her memories of her free and
happy childhood in Istria with its mountains and rivers, its fjords and its north
wind, the Bora – 'the wind that is everywhere', 'abstract, above life's miseries'.

## Gendered Memories

In the years that followed the Second World War in Italy, the official definition of a partisan, or 'a person who had fought against German invaders
and their allied Italian fascists from September 1943 to May 1945', was 'One
who had carried arms for at least three months, had served in a formation
acknowledged by the *Corpo Volontari della Libertà* (Body of Volunteers for
Freedom) and had taken part in at least three battles or sabotage actions'.
However, women who participated in the Resistance, many of whom did
carry arms and fight, were commonly defined as 'couriers' – a description
that does not adequately account for their contributions, or for the dangers
and hardships they faced, and fails to take account of the fact that being
a courier actually involved a wide range of actions and required great
courage, endurance and intelligence. Women's resistance, as recent historians have remarked, was an 'unspoken Resistance'. Little was written about
the women's participation in the struggle. For Venice and the Veneto some
narrative accounts appeared, mainly in women's magazines and journals
like *La Donna Italiana* of the Union of the Italian Women of the Left (UDI),
the Christian Democratic *Voce della Donna* and *Cronache Veneziane*. Later

some of those narratives were included in an edited volume, published to celebrate the 25th anniversary of the Liberation (Turcato and Zanon Dal Bo 1976). Part of Francesca's narrative was included as a chapter, 'In Search of My Father', in Giovanni's autobiography, *A Revolutionary Patrician* (G. Tonetti 1970).

However, from the end of the war in 1945 to the present day, approaches to history – and especially to women's history – have changed, and the people who fought in the Resistance now view their experiences in new perspectives, obviously due to cultural, as well as personal change in the intervening years. From about 1970, partly in the wake of the 1968 student protests, dissatisfaction with the then current state of knowledge on the Resistance thus began to lead to new research and to a substantial body of publications. As Sega writes, from 1984 a disturbing change in Italy's political life, with the entry of the neo-fascist party (MSI) into government, has added a further very strong reason for recording memories of the Resistance, in order to counter the progress of fascist revisionism and the negation of the principles for which so many people fought – and so many died (Sega 2008: 13).[12]

A Venetian Institute for the History of the Resistance and of Contemporary Society, IVESER, founded in 1992 by the National Association of Italian Partisans (ANPI), is now connected with the university's history faculty, whose students and graduates are currently collecting large numbers of interviews with partisans. As Mario Isnenghi, the president of IVESER and history professor at the University of Venice, explains,

> We move between memories and history: IVESER relies on the presence of two generations ... the old and the young, that is, the partisans and their historians.[13] ... Grandfathers and grandchildren – with some silences and some absences in the generations between them, some of them disappointed after the end of the war.

'Valuing their voices' writes Giulia Albanese, one of the main coordinators of their project, 'seemed to us a first step to start reasoning about the Resistance ... and for rediscovering values [that are] not too remote, but are still alive and actual, also for those who have not lived that period of history almost sixty years after the end of the war' (Albanese and Borghi 2004: 12–15).

Both the informants' answers and the interviewers' questions – especially those with a feminist approach – show that attitudes to the past today are significantly different from the attitudes that immediately followed the end of the war. Also significant are new approaches to historical research methods and writing. Questions are in general well-informed but brief, indeed little more than promptings, while some of the answers are extended autobiographical narratives that offer opportunities for comparison and for some (however cautious) generalizations. Thanks to reflection and to a wealth of knowledge of facts and events, recent research has thus led to new conceptual frameworks, different from those held implicitly in earlier narratives.

An attentive reading of the women's recorded interviews shows that their actions were critical and would certainly support a wider definition than that of 'couriers'. As Tina Merlin writes,

> The women's Resistance took place in many different ways: simple peasants and housewives contributed; couriers carried out information and linking tasks – necessary and no less dangerous than fighting, some did fight in battles but were described as having support functions, comrades but not equal. (Cited in Sega 2008: 15)

Thanks to much reflection, the participation of women in the Resistance is gradually becoming better understood. While in early narratives their actions were generally described (also by the protagonists) as being inspired by 'maternal' feelings, whereby women were instinctively inclined to provide food and offer care, protection and nursing, while men were animated by clear political awareness and conviction, motives now appear far more varied and nuanced. Many women did follow tradition in leaving political and ideological discourses to men, but they were well aware of the political implications of their activities.

As we have seen from Francesca's narrative, and as is mentioned in numerous interviews, a maternal attitude was certainly present, even in very young women, but, as Sega points out (2008: 16), there was also a new reality of comradely and brotherly feelings and of behaviours quite different from those traditionally prescribed as 'feminine'. In a country dominated by centuries-old honour codes and an emphasis on female sexual purity (Sciama 2003), for a woman to take up arms and join her comrades in some remote mountain hideout, to cycle long distances under cover of darkness to deliver messages, weapons and food to the men, or, like Francesca, to take lifts from enemy vehicles, was certainly contrary to dominant ideas about desirable feminine behaviour. Not everyone was prepared to acknowledge the exceptionality of those years, and when the war was over, some women partisans were burdened with a 'bad reputation'. During the trials that followed the end of the war, a fear of being permanently marked as dishonourable made some women recoil from speaking about the rapes and sexual insults they had suffered at the hands of their interrogators. As Sega writes,

> many preferred to remove or not to speak about the memories of the sexual humiliations and violence they suffered when arrested and questioned ... normalization required a return to the old social order. (Sega 2008: 16–20; Caporale 2008: 99–114)

The women's accounts of their activities also show that in some ways they were freer than the men: many of them did not act within the dictates of a political party, and often had to take decisions and devise their own actions and choices. As couriers, they maintained communication between leaders and between groups of partisans spread through the mountains and the countryside. Especially in the cities, while men had to lie low in hiding, it was the women who had to circulate. And it was they who, like Francesca, used all their resources and mobilized their social networks, asking for help from anyone in a key position and using whatever influence and connections they could, to try and get their husbands and sons released from prison, when they were arrested on some suspicion or detained after some random round-up.

On analysing her forty interviews of women throughout the Venetian countryside and foothills, Margaret Frazer points out that the nature of women's wartime activities clearly goes against a private/public opposition, so that an association of women with private and men with public spheres is reversed. She also points out that the witnesses themselves follow the dichotomy between feminine activities and the values of family, neighbourhood and private spheres, as against masculine, rational, public – in fact the old opposition between women-nature and men-culture. Indeed, many women explain their Resistance activities as 'natural, due to family, or humanitarian sense and to disgust with fascist brutalities. But they do see these motivations as woven in with political reasons beyond the personal (2008: 159–161).[14]

Gendered differences, according to Sega, also characterize many narratives: men's memories are generally self-centred and focused on their closest comrades; they emphasize male bonding, and they describe partisan brigades as male groups that tend to marginalize women and exclude them from political discussions – although they sometimes include an affectionate mention of their women. By contrast, women tend to see their lives as part of family and social networks, they are 'embodied in their relationships'. As I found through participating in various gatherings and memorial celebrations, they also see their writing or speaking about the past as an effort to maintain or revive old friendships, to remember others and keep open a dialogue with distant loved ones (Sega 2005: 142–144; 158).

Like Francesca, many women attribute their convictions and their readiness to fight to love of family and, especially, to fathers' influence. Tosca Siviero, the daughter of a socialist artisan tells how, still a child, she used to follow him when he attended political meetings, and once when there developed a scuffle with fascist thugs, she too had tried to provide the men with pieces of asphalt to aim at their rivals, before her father sent her running home. 'It was he who taught me about the workers' struggle, he taught me many things' (Sega 2005: 152–153).

Franca Trentin, the daughter of a very prominent trade union leader and actor in the Resistance since the earliest days of fascism, said that what she did was of no special merit and no real choice of her own, because her family always was antifascist. She totally accepted her father's views, especially after the Spanish Civil War. By contrast, her brother, Bruno, at the interviewer's suggestion that his first contacts with the Resistance may have been due to his family's environment, admits:

> I knew persons who frequented my father's bookshop [during the family's exile in Toulouse] and since the days of the Spanish Civil War I lived in an environment in which there came through all the antifascists from various countries. But my personal choice was distinct from those of my father and brothers, in the sense that I sought to collaborate with a small network of students ... we published a clandestine paper, spread notices, and attacked a Gestapo spy ... we were arrested and tried ... (Albanese and Borghi 137–138)

It is thus of interest that men appear to have been less ready than their sisters to acknowledge the importance of their fathers' role in influencing their actions and political views. Another partisan, Mario Osetta, says that he knew his father was against fascism, but he did not have a political dialogue with him and he acquired his political education while still a teenager from a senior factory worker during his apprenticeship as a mechanic (Albanese and Borghi 2004: 26–27).

## Conclusion

To end: an interesting aspect of Francesca's narrative, as well as those of many other women, is their mixing and weaving together of traditional ideas, deeply rooted in the culture and education of the times. For Francesca such ideas and attitudes go together with a very personal, almost impulsive, and certainly intelligent inclination to act in an emergency.

She prefers to leave systematic 'rational' thinking and writing about politics to her father, and her narrative is in fact characterized by strong emphasis on sentiment, but a conventional separation of sentiment from reason is in fact quite misguided. Good examples are Francesca's decisions, first to get quickly out of Mestre station, just invaded by threatening Germans, with her bag dangerously full of guns, then to confront German generals and propose the prisoners' exchange that saved her father's life.

Indeed, at times of strong tension and danger, emotion and reason can come together quite powerfully, as the most efficient guides to life-saving decisions and actions. As Tim Ingold writes, 'Feeling – as the tactile metaphor implies – is a mode of active and responsive engagement in the world ... thus, far from characterizing mutually exclusive categories of behaviour 'volitional' and 'emotional', intentionality and feeling are two sides of the same coin, that of practical involvement in the dwelt-in world (Ingold 2000: 410–411). That is, I think, particularly true in times of war for men and women alike.

## Notes

1. As a Jewish child escaping from Nazi arrest, from October 1944 to May 1945, I was hidden with my sister in a convent at Venice's periphery, while my father was in a German labour camp and my mother was dangerously hidden in the attic of our own home. With no contact with the outside world, we felt completely cut off and isolated, as bits of confused and fragmentary news only reached us occasionally (Sciama 2008).
2. With the soldiers were also captured about fifteen adolescent apprentices, just because they were wearing sailors' uniforms while learning some technical skills at the Venice arsenal.
3. The Istrian peninsula had been part of the Venetian Republic since 1267, while its far eastern areas belonged to the Holy Roman Empire. Like Venice, in 1797 it was taken over by Napoleon and ruled by the French between 1806 and 1815, then returned to Austria with the 1797 Treaty of Campoformido. While Venice joined Italy in 1866, Istria, like Trieste and Gorizia remained under Austrian control until 1918, and was returned to Italy after the First World War. During the 1920s and 30s, Italian fascists imposed a policy of forced Italianization of Croatians and Slovenes. The Tonetti family settled in Istria after Giovanni Tonetti was appointed Governor of Parenzo, in 1500.

4. Conferred at a time when Istria, like Venice, was part of the Austro-Hungarian Empire.

5. Ernani Cafiero and Waifro Zani were sentenced to death and executed after the war by Venice's Extraordinary Assizes Court (Bonghi & Reberschegg 1999: 108–110).

6. Mount Grappa, at the Alpine foothills, is an important place in historical memory; on it Italians, after their defeat by Austrian armies at Caporetto, made a desperate stand in late 1917. The Grappa, overlooking the main supply routes from Germany, the Valsugana and Val del Brenta, was a good vantage point for sabotage. The Germans surrounded the mountain, they forced women, children and old people to march ahead of them, and they murdered any partisans they met and anyone suspected of sheltering them.

7. Francesca writes that the partisans had been informed that they would be rounded up by two thousand German soldiers in the autumn of 1944. Giovanni would have advised withdrawing to a safer position, but he allowed an English captain who wanted to confront the enemy to take over, and the outcome was a disaster.

8. Ferruccio Parri, later Italy's Prime Minister, was released on 2 January 1944.

9. Karl Hass was SS commander in Rome, then Northern Italy. After the war he spied for the United States against Russia in exchange for immunity. Eventually he was tried in Rome, after attempting to escape from a hotel window. He was condemned to life in 1998, then allowed limited house arrest in Switzerland. He died in 2004.

10. Karl Wolff (1900–1984) was the Supreme SS Police leader in Italy. From February 1945, aware of the futility of continuing the war, he conducted secret negotiations with the Allies to hasten its end. After meeting with U.S. representative Allen Dulles in Switzerland, Wolff negotiated the surrender of all German forces in Italy, ending the war on 2 May 1945, six days before Germany. Taken into custody by the Allies, Wolff escaped trial by testifying against other Nazis at Nuremberg. However, he was sentenced to four years in prison by the West German government after Eichmann revealed that he had organized the deportation of Italian Jews and ordered the murder of innocent people at Rome's Fosse Ardeatine. He was sentenced to fifteen years in prison, of which he only served half.

11. When I last met Francesca, then over eighty, she told me that she still went to schools to talk to the students about the horrors of racism.

12. Berlusconi's political ascendancy and his election victories in 1994, 2001 and 2008 are also significant.

13. As Isnenghi writes, 'They have all read their Halbwachs!' (2004: 14).

14. Such constant references to maternal behaviour, which shows a limited and narrow concept of motherhood, may be more a matter of discursive and narrative habits than of real conviction. Surely, mothers provide their offspring with ideas, as well as food and care!

# Bibliography

Albanese, G. and M. Borghi (eds). 2004. *Nella Resistenza. Vecchi e Giovani a Venezia sessant'anni dopo*. Instituto veneziano per la storia della Resistenza e della società contemporanea. Nuova dimensione.
———. 2005. *Memoria resistente. La lotta partigiana a Venezia e provincial nel ricordo dei protagonisti*. Istituto Veneziano per la storia della Resistenza e della società contemporanea. Nuova dimensione.
Bellina, L. and M.T. Sega (eds). 2004. *Tra la citta di Dio e la città dell'uomo. Donne Cattoliche nella Resistenza Veneta*. A.N.P.I.
Bobbo, G. 2005. *Venezia in tempo di Guerra. 1943–1945*. Padua: il Poligrafo.
Carazzolo, M. 2007. *Più forte della paura. Diario di guerra e dopoguerra (1938–1947)*.San Zeno, Verona: Cierre Edizioni.
Carli Ballola, R. 1957. *Storia della Resistenza*. Venice: A.N.P.I.
Frazer, M. 2008. 'Memoria della Resistenza nei racconti di donne', in M.T. Sega (ed.), *Eravamo fatte di stoffa buona. Donne e Resistenza in Veneto*. Istituto veneziano per la storia della Resistenza e della società contemporanea. Nuova dimensione.
Isnenghi, M. 2004. Preface, in G. Albanese and M. Borghi (eds), *Nella Resistenza. Vecchi e Giovani a Venezia sessant'anni dopo*. Instituto veneziano per la storia della Resistenza e della società contemporanea. Nuova dimensione.
Marinetti, F.T. 1909. *Manifesto del Futurismo*. Gazzetta dell'Emilia 5 February. English translation by Robert Brain et al. 1973. London: Thames & Hudson.
Morris, P. 2008. 'Raccontare la Resistenza al femminile? Giovanna Zangrandi, partigiana veneta', in M.T. Sega, *Eravamo fatte di stoffa buona. Donne e Resistenza in Veneto*. Istituto veneziano per la storia della Resistenza e della società contemporanea. Nuova dimensione.
Sciama, L.D. 2003. *A Venetian Island: Environment, History and Change in Burano*. Oxford and New York: Berghahn Books.
———. 2008. '1943: The Flight from Home', in Esther Herzog (ed.), *Life, Death and Sacrifice: Women and Family in the Holocaust*. Jerusalem, New York: Gefen.
Sega, M.T. (ed.). 2004. *La Partigiana veneta. Arte e memoria della Resistenza*. Nuova dimensione.
———. 2008. *Eravamo fatte di stoffa buona. Donne e Resistenza in Veneto*. Istituto veneziano per la storia della Resistenza e della società contemporanea. Nuova dimensione.
Tonetti, F. 1994. *Il Vento del Quarnero*. Rome: Il Ventaglio.
Tonetti, G. 1970. *Un patrizio rivoluzionario*.Venice.
Turcato, G. and A. Zanon Dal Bo (eds). 1976. *Venezia nella Resistenza. Testimonianze*. Venice: Comune di Venezia.
———. 2005. *Tina Merlin. Partigiana. Giornalista. Scrittrice*. Nuova Dimensione.
———. 2008. *Eravamo fatte di stoffa buona. Donne e Resistenza in Veneto*. Istituto veneziano per la storia della Resistenza e della società contemporanea. Nuova dimensione.
Viganò, Renata. 1949. *Agnese va a morire*. Turin: Einaudi.
———. 1955. *Donne della Resistenza*. Milan: Mursia.

**Lidia Dina Sciama** is former director of Oxford's International Gender Studies Centre, where she is currently a research associate. She has conducted long-term research on women in Italy and England, with a focus on crafts, city life, narrative, memory and relations between anthropology and literature. Among her publications are *A Venetian Island: Environment, History and Change in Burano* (Berghahn Books 2003), and *Humour, Comedy and Laughter* (2016).

# 2

# Ank Faber-Chabot

## A Dutchwoman who Sheltered Jews in the Second World War

### Marieke Faber Clarke

It is the Hunger Winter of 1944–1945. The Netherlands are occupied by Hitler's forces. In the pine forests of the Veluwe, the occupiers' Grüne Polizei (Green Police) hammer on a door. 'Open!' they shout. A tall, calm, elegant chestnut-haired Dutch woman comes out. The Green Police ask if she has accommodation for their personnel. Speaking German, Ank Faber-Chabot smiles, and says, 'We should have liked to help you. But we have a case of whooping cough in our home. Would you mind coming back another time?' Terrified of infection, the Green Police fled.

Ank went back inside her temporary wartime home, a big wooden holiday chalet called '*Ons Hoekje*' ('Our Corner'). For the time being, she had saved her household. At that moment it consisted of her four small flaxen-haired children, her husband, Adriaan (a committed anti-Nazi), and four adults hiding from the Nazis at the back of the house. Two of these four, Lodewijk Prins and Gerda Bloch, were Jewish. The two others were probably Jan Erik and Annelies Romein, children of famous historians. Also in the house at that time, on the dining room table, was a consignment of weapons that Allied Forces had dropped nearby.

Ank Chabot was born on 24 September 1914, the second of four daughters, in an affectionate and prosperous Rotterdam merchant family, which had French Huguenot ancestry.[1] Ank's father, son of a banker, ended his career as director of a family timber business. Ank's mother was known

**Figure 2.1** The Faber household in April 1945 with the house, *Ons Hoekje*, in the background. Back row: Lodewijk Prins, Ank Faber, Gerda Bloch, Adriaan Faber, Annelies Romein, Jan Kronenberg. Front row: Hanna Faber, Edward Faber, Pieter Faber, René Faber.

for her good taste in creating a home. The family, like many of Huguenot descent, were members of the Remonstrant Brotherhood, resembling the Congregational Churches in England and Wales before the formation of the present United Reformed Church. The Remonstrant Church was part of the Liberal Protestant wing of the Netherlands' churches. To be Remonstrant was to be careful, dutiful and self-controlled. Ank's self-control and self-discipline were indeed remarkable, and these qualities no doubt supported her courageous anti-Nazi activities during the Second World War. But the young Chabot daughters were allowed certain pleasures: they played tennis, had music lessons and went to concerts. Ank became a keen Girl Guide and remained one into her adult life.

The people of the Netherlands have long lived by trading: a fluent command of foreign languages has always been an important skill for élite women as well as men. German was the first foreign tongue before the Second World War. German was the language of culture from the Greater Russian marches to the French borders (Hobsbawm 2013: 80). As a schoolgirl, Ank went to Switzerland and heard German spoken during family holidays. After passing her school-leaving examinations, Ank went to England for a few weeks to a Horticultural College at Swanley. She then returned to the Netherlands and did a formal gardening training course. This she much enjoyed, using her knowledge and organizational skills.

It was an added asset for the daughter of a Dutch merchant's family to have a thorough knowledge of French. Ank spent a year on a nursing course in French-speaking Switzerland. The aim of the course at Bon Secours, in Geneva, was to train relatively well-to-do young women in basic nursing skills. The students were taught to work with doctors (overwhelmingly male) as equal partners in the care of the sick. By extension, in marriage, men and women should work together as equals. In the 1930s this was a revolutionary concept. A strong spiritual and ethical element pervaded the Bon Secours training, particularly the injunction to serve. 'None of you lives for herself', the young women were taught. 'Each of you should put at the service of others the gifts you have received'. These were important guidelines for Ank's future life. She returned to the Netherlands in autumn 1936 to marry Adriaan Faber, when she was twenty-two, some months before she might have taken her examinations.

Adriaan (born 19 June 1911) was the fourth child and third son of Douwe Faber, a minister of the Dutch Reformed Church, and his wife Maria van der Wiele.[2] This church has various streams or tendencies: Douwe Faber was on the left wing of the Liberal or Modernist tendency. An intellectual man and fine pastoral worker, Douwe spoke or read eight languages. He was a Unitarian and a pacifist associated with Kerk en Vrede and a teetotaller.[3] (Adriaan did not share all these convictions, but studied for a time at the liberal Manchester College in Oxford.) The Liberal tendency within the Dutch Reformed Church was ideologically close to the Remonstrant Brotherhood. Despite the considerable economic class differences between the Faber parents and the Chabot parents, Adriaan and Ank were united by their ideals.

The young couple had known each other for more than two years, and he adored her. He was offered a post as Dutch Reformed minister in the province of Zeeland. Ank and Adriaan married in February 1937 and moved to Renesse in March. From the start of the marriage, Ank showed great planning, organizational and business acumen. She brought with her a trousseau worth 1,250 guilders, when her husband would be earning about 200 guilders a month. The trousseau ensured that no capital expenditure on linen would be required for decades to come. Ank equipped her household with bed linen, seventy-four towels, table linen and serviettes as well as fifteen different kinds of cloths. So far did she plan ahead that two sheets, purchased in 1937 and in their packaging at Ank's death in 1999, were still used as tablecloths in 2013!

It was desirable in the pre-war Netherlands that a minister's wife be able to run a garden. Adriaan's mother had grown vegetables for her husband and six children from gardens around some of the manses where the family lived. Adriaan's elder brother Heije has described how each day their father would harvest seasonal vegetables from the garden. The gardens that Ank designed with her professional eye were always beautiful as well as productive.

The Netherlands had been neutral for a hundred years: many people in the late 1930s hoped that their country could remain neutral if there were another war. But Adriaan's brother Heije, familiar with conditions in Germany, had in 1937 taken a leading role in Eenheid door Demokratie (Unity through Democracy), informing the Dutch public of the dangers of National Socialism and opposing its ally, the NSB,[4] in the Netherlands.

When Hitler's forces invaded the Netherlands on 10 May 1940, the heart of Rotterdam, Ank's native city and the country's biggest port, was razed to the ground. The whole country was fast brought to its knees. Before the war started, Adriaan felt compelled to volunteer as a chaplain to the Dutch armed forces. After the Netherlands surrendered, and following an absence of two and a half months, Adrian returned to his family. The Netherlands endured a particularly vicious occupation by the Nazis. Seyss-Inquart, Hitler's personally nominated Reichskommissar, in an infamous speech in 1941, threatened that anyone in the Netherlands who helped Jews would be treated like a Jew.

By the autumn of 1941, when Ank and Adriaan moved from Renesse to the bigger and more central parish of Kampen, the pair had two children and a third was expected in February. Kampen was sometimes called 'the Jerusalem of the North' for its wide range of Christian communities. As minister of the Liberal Protestant stream in the Reformed Church, Adriaan was a man with a certain authority. Despite shaky physical health,[5] he built up good contacts with parishioners, who included people living in IJsselmuiden and Kampereiland, the polder to the north of Kampen,[6] as well as in the town itself. At the end of 1941, Ank wrote: 'We are very thankful that we have [this year] always had it so good', and celebrated an enjoyable Christmas. The close relationships with the local farmers and producers ensured that the minister's children had enough nourishing food. It was, Ank wrote, 'a year in which many people had a difficult time, and how will things fare in 1942 with little coal and little food?' But conditions scarcely changed for the Fabers until the autumn of 1943.

## The Bloch Family Seek Refuge in the Netherlands

A Jewish family, with whom the Fabers' lives would soon be closely linked, was having very different experiences. Richard Bloch, born in 1879, an architect with his own bureau, and his wife Ilse Cats (born in 1896), who had received advanced technical training, were in the early 1930s members of the comfortable middle class in Berlin, Germany. In 1925 they had a daughter called Gerda and in 1928, a second daughter, whom they named Doris. Like the Chabots in Rotterdam, the Blochs took part in their city's cultural life. Richard Bloch, who had fought with German forces in the First World War, was active in the synagogue.

The family was not Orthodox: Ilse, of Dutch origin, was interested in Sufism and Freemasonry. But a shadow hung over their lives. Gerda Bloch wrote later, 'In my youth there was anti-Semitism everywhere'. And in late 1938, Richard Bloch was officially informed that, after 31 December, he could no longer work. On the so-called Kristallnacht (also known as the Night of Broken Glass) of 9/10 November, Nazis marched into the Bloch home, which was also Richard's office, and smashed the contents. The Bloch parents knew now that they had to leave Germany. Their only option was to go to the Netherlands, where Marion Hollander-Cats, Ilse's sister, found rooms for them in Zandvoort aan Zee.[7] The family could take no money or possessions with them: only one small suitcase per person was allowed. In April 1939 the family had to move to a converted stable belonging to the Jurriaanse family in Hulshorst, near Harderwijk, in the central Netherlands. The four Bloch family members stayed there until November 1942.

The attitude of many Dutch people to Jewish refugees was, however, not friendly. Many Dutch householders required the refugees to pay for their accommodation. The Blochs were spared that indignity. Gerda and Doris attended the Hulshorst village school and learned Dutch. But, from 1 September 1941, Jews in the occupied Netherlands were excluded from state schools. And, on 29 April 1942, it was announced that all Jews aged over six years must wear a yellow star. As one newspaper put it, 'The inhabitants of this country are through this edict divided into two camps: friend and foe'. For fourteen months, always wearing yellow stars, Gerda and Doris went by train to the Jewish Secondary School at Zwolle. They had to use a travel permit, which, however, expired on 23 November 1942. From that time onwards, if the Bloch girls went into the street, they could be arrested and sent to concentration camps.

It seems that the Bloch daughters had urged their parents to go into hiding. But probably the parents, who for ten years had been giving up their freedom little by little, thought they could wait just a bit longer. Finally Gerda took the initiative. After the war she wrote:

> The violent round-ups became worse and worse so that we were forced to hide, if we did not want to be taken from our temporary homes at night by the Green

Police. So thank God we found an address and Doris and I went underground on 23rd November. Pappi and Mammi had no place to go, but were able to go underground one week later. Monday 23rd November we said goodbye to Pappi and Mammi. It was a difficult moment to leave them behind. That was the last time we saw them.

Years later, Gerda said, 'I wanted to survive'. Pretending she wanted to go for a bicycle ride, Gerda visited a half-Jewish couple whom she knew. They made contact with the Resistance in a town called Epe and after that, things moved fast. In Epe, in the Veluwe pine forests in the central Netherlands, a religiously liberal parish in a fairly orthodox area, was an active Resistance group. This group supported about seventy Jews through the war. The nucleus of the group was formed by Mrs E.J. (Bets) van Lohuizen-van Wielink (wife of the grocer), the postman Jonker and the schoolmaster Hendriks.

Bets van Lohuizen was a member of Kerk en Vrede, the Christian Pacifist organization of which grandfather Douwe Faber was also a member. She regarded the bearing of arms as unchristian and instead exerted spiritual resistance to the occupation. Her Resistance group hired unused summer houses in the forests and hid Jews in them.[8] The group provided food and ration cards; addresses to which Jews could go if they had to go underground; fuel, false identity cards, medical care and sometimes even care in hospital.

Doris wrote after the war:

At a time of terrible round-ups, Gerda and I left for Epe on 23rd November. A few days later, Pappi and Mammi went to Nunspeet. I can still see us that Monday. We two stood on the station. Gerda got tickets and I cried, cried with grief that I had to leave.

The girls tore the yellow stars from their clothes and climbed into the train for Zwolle. They arrived safely and spent the day with Dr and Mrs Spanjaard, with whom they had eaten their lunch when they went to school. That evening, Mrs van Lohuizen-van Wielink from Epe came to fetch them. This was the first time they had met.

On 23 November 1942, Bets van Lohuizen wrote in her diary:[9]

On the way home, in Zwolle, I received two girls who went home with us. During the afternoon, another one had arrived. All nice children. The two sisters came here three years ago from Berlin. We have found a place for the one girl. The two sisters will stay here till we have somewhere for them to go.

After the war, Gerda wrote: 'This woman, with her family and her lovely mother took me in. What this family did for me and for hundreds of other Jews and other fugitives is indescribable.'

A place was found for Gerda in one of seven properties in the woods that were rented to house Jews. Those were difficult months. Gerda, only seventeen years old, experienced Green Police round-ups as well as tensions among the people in hiding. The sisters were separated. Fourteen-year-old Doris went to live with an older couple in Epe. She saw Gerda occasionally, but was anxious and unhappy. Later she also moved into one of the seven houses. 'I went with Gerda to the "Larikshof"', wrote Doris, 'a villa where many Jews were housed. In the wooded garden, the boys built a cellar where we could hide if there was an alarm, and indeed we did have to go there sometimes'.

Sometimes Gerda and Doris appeared in public, so they needed ID cards. Gerda, who had red hair, looked much less Jewish than the dark-haired Doris. Gerda said forty years later in an interview:

I now became Nancy Halman. I had to create a new persona for myself, as well as a new life story, which would make sense to anyone interrogating me at any time. After a while, I was so identified with my new self that I had even forgotten German.

Doris also was given a new name.

After the Bloch daughters disappeared, the parents found an address in Nunspeet with the Alblas family. For about eighteen months, Richard and Ilse hid there in a small building. Meanwhile, news about the annihilation camps in Eastern Europe was beginning to seep through to the occupied Netherlands.

In February 1943, Gerda moved to the house of Mrs van Lohuizen herself, and they became close friends. But in September 1943, there was no place for Doris in Epe. A number of Jews had been seized and Mrs Lohuizen's own son had been arrested on suspicion of helping them. So Doris went to live far away at Lobith with Mr and Mrs Derksen, the farmer parents-in-law of the minister at Epe. Mrs Derksen was half-Jewish, the granddaughter of converted German Jews named Bernstein. Doris stayed with the Derksens for a year and a half. The Bloch sisters did not meet again until after the liberation.

The occupying forces were watching out, not only for Jews, but also for Dutch people of working age. One means of resisting the Nazis was to prevent Dutch labour from being conscripted to work in Germany. Adriaan and Ank Faber helped shelter their brother-in-law William (Wim) Keizer,

the husband of Adriaan's youngest sister Miek. Wim had been sent to work
in Germany shortly after his marriage to Miek in February 1943. On home
leave, he pretended to have a stomach ulcer and thus avoided being sent
back to Germany. When, in October 1943, Ank gave birth to Pieter, her
fourth child and third son, Miek came to help. The Keizers stayed with the
Fabers until March 1944, when Wim found a job in a somewhat safer part
of the Netherlands.

In November 1943, Gerda, too, had to leave Epe, as it had become too
dangerous, with frequent house searches and arrests. Gerda went 'underground' in Amsterdam for some months, but she was not allowed to make
a sound in her room. Mrs van Lohuizen herself was taken into custody, but
released after three weeks. Both her husband and son were for a time locked
up in the concentration camp at Vught. On 25 January 1944, members of
the Resistance sent seventeen-year old Gerda Bloch to Adriaan and Ank's
house in Kampen. Until after the war, the Fabers did not know her real
name, but they would have realised she was Jewish. Although we do not
know how the contact was made, the following is a plausible theory. The
Epe Resistance group probably knew that Gerda needed a safe place to stay,
and may have made contact with Ank through regional gatherings of the
Liberal Reformed Protestant Women.

### Gerda Bloch Goes to Live with the Faber Household

Ank and her five-year-old daughter Hanna met Gerda at Kampen railway
station: gradually Gerda became used to the Faber household. Her role was
to be a household help, which aroused few suspicions. She remarked later:

> The children gave lots of work but were darlings. I had a fairly quiet time as I
> went around as the household help of the Faber family. Nobody knew who I was.
> I was Nancy. So identified was I with my new identity *[sic]* that I had actually
> forgotten much of my past ... Totally isolated, not yourself, no one really knew
> anything about me. I started to get a terrible case of eczema. Unable to go to any
> doctor because of fear that someone may find out about me, and report me and
> endanger this family ... The Faber family is one of the thousands of combatants
> who did everything to save people's lives [and did it] with so much love. Moreover
> there was such a lovely atmosphere in the house that everyone felt comfortable.

Gerda did not go out of doors to do errands, but she did sometimes open
the door to strangers. Having Gerda in their home was a big risk for Adriaan
and Ank to take. Severe penalties were attached to sheltering Jews.

Why did the Fabers do it? Perhaps out of sympathy, or out of revulsion against the measures taken by the occupying forces. Certainly Ank, with three small children and a new baby, was in need of domestic help. Indeed, her activities extended beyond bringing up children and running the minister's home. In early 1944, Adriaan wrote: 'Mummy is now busy with her *twenty-thousand sandwiches* campaign for the big prisoners' camps.[10] Our parish is responsible for three thousand sandwiches'. This at a time when food was hard to come by for one's own family!

The Fabers left nothing on paper about their motivation, nor did they tell their children why they accepted Gerda into their home. Ank and Adriaan's childhood environments and their moral education do suggest that conviction guided their actions. Douwe Faber's Liberal Protestantism calls for tolerance and rejects absolutism. In Ank's parental home, daring and decision making were necessary qualities. All Huguenots, of course, bore with them the folk memory of being driven from France after 1685. And all Netherlanders were accustomed to living in a country where minorities enjoyed full civil rights: most people greatly resented the removal of these liberties by a cruel aggressor. Girl Guiding taught Ank to do her duty, and in her training at Bon Secours in Switzerland, she had learned to care for people in need.

In the second half of her life, Ank assembled a file of cuttings and poems that were important to her. Among these was a small board with the words: 'Shelter the homeless, do not betray the fugitive' (Isaiah 16:3). Clearly this was a Bible passage that was deeply meaningful to Ank, and one on which she acted. Adriaan wrote some years later:

> Like most people, we had for years hidden all sorts of things under the floor ... The wine was in the attic between the ceilings.[11] The hiding places were high cupboards via a trapdoor in the attic. You could just fit in and a cradle would be placed on top. Secret papers were, for example, hidden in the children's play pen or in the dog's basket.

The food situation became worse and worse, but Ank was an excellent organizer and even acquired a licence to go to the fertile North East Polder, known for its high agricultural yields. Parishioners helped the Fabers, probably out of the old conviction that they should sustain their minister. In the baby book that Ank kept for her son Pieter, she wrote:

> We in our family must just thank God for all the privileges that we may remain healthy and happy. For we are not really short of anything, though life is very busy and it is difficult to obtain all sorts of necessary foods and clothes, wooden

shoes.[12] For example, we have exchanged your 12 best nappies at the house of a farmer for the few ounces of tea that we still had. Indeed, with that tea, we can do wonders. Of course we have not ourselves drunk tea for ages.

But thirty years later, Miek Keizer-Faber told Pieter that, when Ank was breastfeeding him, he cried a lot, and probably did not receive enough nourishment. Ank was not the woman to despair, but she did say in April 1944:

We are very privileged that we can regularly obtain a couple of litres of milk. Otherwise there is not a single article of any kind that we can find in the shops, only poor substitutes, everything is rationed or on licences which are very hard to get. The black market flourishes, a single litre of milk costs three guilders in the town and sometimes more. Butter is 33 guilders a pound when a coal merchant earns 15 guilders a day and a bicycle tyre costs between 200 and 300 guilders. Only drinking water is freely available.

That spring, Richard and Ilse Bloch were arrested, though the Faber household did not know. After peace came, Gerda wrote:

Pappi and Mammi were arrested in Nunspeet in May 1944 by the Germans at the home of a certain family Alblas, where they had been hiding. They were collected during the night and then went via Arnhem to Westerbork where they met acquaintances, the Fraenkels and others.[13] Both were in solitary-punishment barracks for people who had been hiding, Barrack S 67 1. Poor things. After that they went to Theresienstadt. How difficult that must have been for them. They would have survived, but the bad luck was that they had to go with one of the last transports to an even worse concentration camp.

This camp was Auschwitz, where they died on 14 October 1944.

On 6 June 1944, the Allied invasion of Europe started. That summer, Adriaan and Ank's household left Kampen for a holiday at Doornspijk in the dense pine forests of Gelderland. The household returned to Kampen when Edward, the eldest child, was due to start school in mid-August. Doris Bloch wrote later:

In the first days of September, the Allies moved very fast through Northern France and the whole of Belgium. There were even the first radio bulletins of the crossing of the Dutch frontier. We were crazy with joy ... On 17th September, Allied air forces landed near Arnhem and Nijmegen. After a long fight, Nijmegen was liberated, but the campaign at Arnhem failed. At Lobith we saw that evening all around us fire ... The failure at Arnhem was a huge disappointment.

The liberation of the country stalled at the great rivers. After the end of September 1944, the entire Faber household left Kampen and returned to Doornspijk. First the two eldest children, Edward and Hanna, went there to live with grandparents Douwe and Marie Faber because there was poliomyelitis in Kampen. Douwe had retired: he had earned so little as a minister that buying a house was impossible, so he and Marie were staying in temporary accommodation.

Then Adriaan himself went underground in Doornspijk: 'The Germans are taking hostages left and right'. The family probably thought they would only be in the forests for a couple of weeks. Gerda wrote forty years later:

> Soon the Nazis marched through this [Kampen] house also. I had nothing to lose, had gained so much already, but still wanted to live! Then the Nazis came again, yelling '*Juden raus!*' [Jews out!] The [occupying forces] were surveying this house and [then] the Faber family decided we needed to [leave] ... The risks that [Adriaan and Ank] took became greater and greater because the Nazis were on their heels. The Green Police searched many houses and made many arrests. But [the Fabers] never asked me to leave. I stayed with them for the next two years. Their courageous behaviour can only be attributed to their strong wish to help people in need.

So in October 1944, Ank and the two younger children, René and Pieter, moved to Doornspijk. The house was called '*Ons Hoekje*' ('Our Corner') and stood opposite to where grandfather and grandmother Faber lived. Ons Hoekje was the summer home of Dr Euwe, former world chess champion. The Faber family could stay, provided that a Jewish chess player, Lodewijk Prins, lived there too.

Doornspijk was safer than Kampen, but also more pleasant to live in. Ank wrote in October 1944:

> It is a great privilege to have been able to be here these last weeks. In Kampen there is often no electricity and hardly any gas. To obtain food is an urgent problem. Sometimes there is no water. The shops shut one after the other. Outside we manage with wood and a bit of oil for the lamp.

Life in Kampen and Doornspijk brought its daily concerns, but these must be understood against the background of the more and more vicious occupation by the Nazi forces. Everywhere Jewish families had disappeared. Rumours about trains leaving for Eastern Europe had spread. Listening to the BBC was a punishable offence. Many intellectuals, artists and opinion leaders had been arrested and put in camps as hostages. Food disappeared to Germany. The pro-Nazi NSB members behaved more and more aggressively towards other Dutch people. Some NSB members, particularly Dutch policemen with Nazi sympathies, earned considerable sums of money by hunting Jews. Nazi police organized round-ups in trains and on the streets: young Dutch men could easily be picked up and sent to German war factories. Arrested Resistance members were often killed on the spot. In Renesse, Adriaan's first parish, on 10 December, the occupying forces publicly hanged ten members of the Resistance. Fifty of their family members and fellow villagers were forced to watch. The corpses were left dangling for twenty-four hours.

The weeks became months and the months dragged on. The war continued through the terrible Hunger Winter, which cost the lives of about 20,000 Netherlanders. Conditions were especially bad in the cities in the west. In desperation, some people ate sugar beet and the bulbs of flowering plants. Many urban people burned their furniture and their internal house doors to provide warmth in what was a very early, cold, dark winter.

Doornspijk lies close to the main road between the important transport node of Amersfoort and Zwolle, with its strategic bridge over the River Yssel. Tens of thousands of desperate people came on foot, with sacks or carts, or bicycles without tyres from the western Netherlands trying to reach that bridge.[14] In the north, beyond the bridge, there was a better chance of finding food. Many of the migrants died of hunger on the road.

The Fabers, for their part, had good contacts with local farmers. Gerda also went to fetch food from them. Ank wrote in the baby book she kept for her daughter Hanna:

> We felt ourselves very privileged to be able to live in a wooden summer house in the forests and to obtain milk and butter from the local farmers. We always had people in hiding and people passing through. On average we had ten people living in our home. Quite an anxiety at that time. But everyone helped, cutting wood or fetching food. [Gerda] our household help was fantastic in the cold and difficulties of that winter.

Ank's great organizational skills kept her extended household fed, warm and safe throughout that terrible time.

One of the extraordinary aspects of this story of great courage and amazing organization is that excellent photographs were taken of the eleven people living or staying at Ons Hoekje between January and May 1945, when the Netherlands was in the grip of the Nazi occupation. In the front row are the Faber children Hanna, Edward, Pieter and René. Behind them, from left to right are: Lodewijk Prins, Ank, Gerda, Adriaan, Jan Erik Romein, Annelies Romein and Jan Kronenberg. Ank wrote in René's baby book:

From January we had as permanent house companions Lodewijk Prins from Amsterdam, a Jew aged 32 with false papers; Jan Erik Romein, student in sociology at Amsterdam, and his sister Annelies Romein, from Hilversum where there was severe hunger; both the Romein youngsters had been in the Resistance. There was also Jan Kronenberg, a boy from Pappie's parish, aged 22, all of them of an age to be attractive to the Krauts for their war industry.

Nobody now living knows how far Ank and Adriaan were involved with the armed struggle against the Nazis. The Faber parents almost never talked about the war to their children. The historian has to piece together the evidence from other sources. Certainly Adriaan's poor physical health would have prevented his taking an active part in military training. Years later, a Faber family member would spend holidays at Doornspijk with Adriaan's sister Miek and Wim Keizer.[15] They showed their visitor a depression in the sand dunes with an isolated oak tree. She was told that this was called 'Adriaan's tree'. The Keizers told their own children that Adriaan and Ank were involved in weapon drops while Wim and Miek looked after the young Fabers. In 1944, a painting was made of this oak, which always hung in Ank and Adriaan's living room. Why? Probably the oak tree was where Allied pilots were ordered to drop the weapons.

That the Fabers were involved in receiving weapons seems all the more likely because Douwe Faber, the lifelong Christian pacifist, did reluctantly agree to store arms in his attic. When Douwe objected, probably saying that, for a Christian pacifist, the ends do not justify the means, Adriaan replied: 'Vader, U bent niet goed wijs' ('Father, you are out of your senses'), and the old man agreed to his son's request.[16] Family tradition has handed down the story told at the start of this piece, that there were weapons on the young Fabers' dining room table when the Green Police were seeking billets for their men. The extreme danger in which Ank and Adriaan's household lived is shown by the fact that the Nazis found a large group of people who were in hiding, only a couple of houses further down the road.

But at last liberation came. 'At the start of April (1945), the Allies re-started their offensive in the Netherlands', wrote Gerda. 'Anxiously we looked at the map three times a day.'

The area in which Doornspijk, Epe and Kampen are situated was liberated in mid-April. Together with the people in hiding, the family celebrated by eating a meal of pancakes (Dutch pancakes are big, and regarded as a very special treat) on the terrace of the house. Gerda wrote:

So happy as I then was, have I seldom been. But Pappi and Mammi were not there and I had not seen Doris for years ... How happy everything was; how extensively and spontaneously the liberation was celebrated everywhere. I can't believe that I can do what I want, can go around freely, sleep peacefully. The war was over.

Ank wrote on 17 April in her daughter Hanna's baby book:

(Today) then at last after many tensions the day of liberation (comes) for us. From now on, we call Nancy by her real name, Gerda Bloch. Her parents were sent to Poland following a round-up of Jews.

On 1 May the Fabers returned to their comfortable house in Kampen. Ank wrote:

The Krauts thoroughly destroyed the Yssel bridge as they were leaving, which also caused a lot of damage in the town, but there was no fighting in Kampen.

On 8 May came the General Surrender and all of the Netherlands was free. Gerda wrote:

We forgot for a few moments all the suffering of these years and, when the Canadian tanks came through the streets, the cup was full. Tears of joy and happiness. We were free. We could not believe it.

## After the War

Gerda travelled with great difficulty to Lobith and found her sister Doris on 19 May. Gerda told her that their parents had been arrested. Both young women then went to Kampen and stayed with the Faber family. They made enquiries about Richard and Ilse Bloch-Cats but had to conclude that they had died. At a certain moment, the news came that Ilse Bloch had been found. But this person turned out not to be Ilse Bloch, their mother. Gerda herself wrote: 'I cannot find any further information about them. We do not expect to see them anymore. I cannot think about that any more'.

Gerda, who turned twenty in October 1945, went to Zwolle to live independently and finish the schooling she had started in 1941. She kept contact with Mrs van Lohuizen until the older woman died in 1947. Doris stayed with the Fabers and attended the secondary school in Kampen. She also joined the Girl Guide group that Ank led. Gerda often went for the weekend to Kampen to stay with the Fabers and see her sister. 'We are both convinced that we have drawn a lottery ticket to be taken up into such a family', wrote

Gerda. 'It's not a home, but ... they understand everything and are loving to us and concerned about us.'

Gerda and Doris set about becoming Dutch citizens. But relatives of their father living in the United States suggested that Gerda and Doris should move there. Gerda emigrated in 1947 and became a psychotherapist. Doris left the Netherlands for America in 1949. On her departure, Adriaan and Ank gave her a letter which read:

> Gerda and you have had to do without many things in your youth and we have often admired you that you have yet remained so strong, and that you as adults and dedicated people will face your work for society in the world. Though all our paths will diverge in the years to come, and the letters will be fewer, we shall always think of you with the best of feelings and memories. May the good God strengthen and bless you. May your youth and the work thereafter make you truly happy and make you into a character that can serve and lead, but also be humble.

In the United States, Doris achieved her doctor's degree in nursing. After working for several years in Africa, she became a top civil servant in Washington at the National Institute of Health in Bethesda, and died in 2003.

Gerda married Albert Mossé and had two children, a son and a daughter. But she and her husband divorced. She later married Ben Kazan, a famous physicist, who died in 2009. Gerda's son died as the result of a robbery at an ATM. At the time of writing, Gerda Mossé-Bloch lives in the United States, not far from her daughter. Gerda and Doris Bloch returned to the Netherlands several times. Ank and Adriaan also visited the Blochs in the States. Ank, a widow since Adriaan died in 1990, travelled alone to see them in 1996 when she was eighty-two. She died in 1999.

The war cost the Netherlands (whose population in 1939 was just under nine million) about 280,000 dead. The Jewish population, of a country where this group had had full civil rights since 1796, suffered losses proportionately far greater than in all other countries of Western Europe.[17] About 140,000 Jews had lived in the Netherlands before the war. Only about 35,000 Dutch Jews survived till 1945.

Ank, besides successfully bringing up four healthy children, who all survived to have their own children, had at the same time also run the household in the pine forests of Doornspijk that saved the lives of the two Jews, Lodewijk Prins and Gerda Bloch, and sheltered various other fugitives from the Nazis. In due course, Gerda and Doris Bloch set in motion a process that led to the award on 24 February 1993 of the Certificate of Honour to

Ank and Adriaan Faber at Yad Vashem in Israel. Yad Vashem, in Jerusalem, established in 1953, is Israel's official memorial to Jewish victims of the Holocaust. Gerda Bloch accompanied Ank to Israel for the ceremony in 1993. Adriaan and Ank Faber were declared 'Righteous among the Nations' and given a medal. On its rim is a sentence from the Talmud:[18] 'Whosoever saves a single life, saves an entire universe'.

By the end of 2002, Yad Vashem had acknowledged 20,000 people as Righteous among the Nations, 5,000 of whom were Dutch. Among them were members of the Resistance group at Epe: Mrs E.J. (Bets) van Lohuizen-van Wielink, the postman Jonker, the schoolmaster Hendriks, his wife and their daughter Els. Els Hendriks and Gerda Bloch met again in 2010. Carl and Helene Derksen-Bernstein in Lobith, with whom Doris Bloch stayed from 1944 to 1945, also received acknowledgement as Righteous among the Nations at Yad Vashem. Gerda Bloch came to the Netherlands in 2010 and spoke to the grandchildren of Ank and Adriaan about their grandparents.

Pieter Faber, who has recorded Ank and Adriaan's history, emphasizes that his parents would have regarded what they did in saving Gerda's life and supporting Doris as perfectly normal and natural. Ank Faber 'would not have wished that even a slight chance existed that a narrative about her could be understood to be boasting'. Nevertheless he believes that it is important to tell stories like these. He likes to mention the deep feeling of connectedness that existed between his parents and the sisters Doris and Gerda Bloch. Many, many times in public speeches and to friends, Gerda has said: 'Imagine the risks they took! What would you have done?'

## Notes

1. The Huguenots were French Protestants who from 1598 could practise their religion in France. This right was withdrawn by King Louis XIV in 1685, through the Revocation of the Edict of Nantes, which led to a migration of Huguenots to countries like the Netherlands, where they could practise their religion freely. The Revocation of the Edict of Nantes reverberates still as an immensely dishonourable and misguided act of state.
2. Douwe and Maria Faber-van der Wiele parented Heije, twins Jan and Hanna, Adriaan, Titia and Miek.
3. Kerk en Vrede: Church and Peace, the International Fellowship of Reconciliation.
4. Nationaal-Socialistische Beweging; counterpart of Oswald Mosley's British Union of Fascists.
5. In 1940 he had such severe stomach problems that he spent months in bed. His work was done by a deputy.
6. A polder is an area of drained land.

7. Marion Hollander-Cats was later arrested and murdered.
8. These summer houses were used by urban dwellers for holidays.
9. Right through the war, Mrs E.J. van Lohuizen-van Wielink kept a diary of several hundred pages. It is now in the Dutch Institute for War Documentation.
10. Present writer's emphasis.
11. One branch of Ank's extended Rotterdam family were wine merchants.
12. It is normal for everyone in the Dutch countryside to wear *klompen* or wooden clogs. These were all the more valuable in wartime when leather shoes could not be replaced.
13 Westerbork was a camp from which Dutch people were sent on to camps further east.
14. When the present writer first visited the Netherlands in the summer of 1946, people were still riding bicycles without tyres.
15. The present writer.
16. Grandfather Douwe Faber to present writer, personal communication.
17. The reasons for this have often been discussed and the consensus now is that the well-organized administration at Town Halls made persecution easy.
18. The Talmud is an extensive Jewish religious work containing interpretation of, and commentary on, the Torah, the primary source from which the rest of Jewish religious law has developed.
19. The biography of the Bloch family at the *Wir Waren Nachbarn* exhibition at the Schoeneberger Rathaus in Berlin, under the name of *Gerda und Doris Bloch*, is based on research by Pieter Faber under the title *Waarom schrijf ik nu in dit boek?* ('Why do I write now in this book?') The title refers to the paragraph in the 'baby book', a kind of child biography, of Gerda Bloch in which, after the war, she takes over writing, in Dutch, from her father. A similar baby book was made by the Bloch parents for their daughter Doris, who also continued the writing after the war. Electronic copies of these baby books are kept in Washington at the U.S. Holocaust Museum and in Berlin. Pieter Faber can be contacted at pieter-faber@hetnet.nl

## Bibliography

Hobsbawm, E. 2013. *Fractured Times: Culture and Society in the Twentieth Century.* London: Little, Brown.

## Primary Resources

*Narratives of the Faber and Faber-Chabot family*

*Leven en Werk van Adriaan Faber en Ank Chabot* ('Life and Work of Adriaan Faber and Ank Chabot'), by their son Pieter Faber.

Other works about the Faber family: *Rekenschap van een zoektocht: een auto-biografie* ('Account of a Quest: An Autobiography'), by Heije Faber. (Baarn: Uitgeverij Ten Have, 1993).
Family letters and albums of Titia Faber, Adriaan's second sister (who married Richard Clarke); conversations between Douwe Faber and Marieke Faber Clarke, Titia's daughter.
Baby books of Edward, Hanna, René and Pieter Faber kept by their mother Ank Faber-Chabot.

*Narratives of the Bloch-Cats family*

The story of the Bloch family can be viewed at the remarkable *Wir Waren Nachbarn* ('We were Neighbours') exhibition in the Rathaus of Berlin-Schoeneberg. There is an English version. An electronic copy in English was sent to the U.S. Holocaust Museum in Washington.[19]

**Marieke Faber Clarke** read modern history at Oxford University, and her research interests are Zimbabwe and India. Publications include *We Are the Original People: The Story of a Development Project in South Gujarat, India* (Ajanta Publications 1991), and with Pathisa Nyathi *Lozikeyi Dlodlo, Queen of the Ndebele: A Very Dangerous and Intriguing Woman* (Amagugu Publications 2010).

# 3

# Hildegard Jaschok's Testimony

## Expulsion and Hope in the Second World War

### Maria Jaschok

The story has two beginnings, on 18 January 1945 and 18 January 1995. My narrative engages, as it must, with both beginnings. On 18 January 1995, a cold wintry day, my mother sat down at the writing table in her sitting room in Deidesheim, a small medieval town in southern Germany. Unbeknown to her large extended family, she had purchased a thick notepad, carefully prepared her favourite fountain pen (she preferred to use blue ink for intimate writing) and then wrote in longhand, in her impeccable, print-like (*wie gestochen*) handwriting the story that could not be written for fifty years. She started writing on 18 January 1995, exactly fifty years after she was forced to leave her home. On that day, she wrote two sentences before coming to a halt. Hildegard told her middle daughter later that she was shaking too much to be able to continue writing. But write she must. In order to find her way through this moment of crisis, she phoned my sister Gabriele to tell her that she had just started writing about the day, fifty years before, when she, her children and her own mother went out into the bitterly cold winter's day and turned their back forever on their *Heimat*, and that, although she felt compelled to write, she was unable to continue. And this is how my sister came to play an active role in the telling of my mother's story, which is the basis, and more so, the inspiration for this chapter.

**Figure 3.1** My brother Wolfram Jaschok's etching 'Der Trek' served as our mother's book cover. © Familie Jaschok.

## Historical Contexts

What my mother was not entirely aware of (but I may do her an injustice) was the fact that others, who had similarly been forced to suffer expulsion and long months of uprooted existence, were opening up about their history in private conversations and in public presentations. At the same time, historians of Germany, and of causes and consequences of the Second

World War, were turning their attention to the Allied policies of ejecting up to fourteen million ethnic Germans from their homeland. Only recently has the intellectual, cultural and political processing begun of what historians of the Second World War and of its aftermath are coming to characterize as the 'Horror of *Vertreibung* [expulsion]'.[1]

Effectively these policies amounted to radical and large-scale ethnic cleansing. Yet this examination of the recent past, always involving self-examination, is painfully sensitive. It is inscribed by searing guilt, carried collectively and individually, over the burden of Nazi atrocities against a background of relentless imperialist expansion, fired by an ideology of the master race. This ideology ultimately legitimized the extinction of peoples, particularly but not exclusively of Jewish people, who were classified as sub-human and thus excluded from protection accorded by basic human rights. Persons with dissenting voices, and those who in some way were regarded as deviating from or perverting the Aryan ideal, were dealt with in a similarly ruthless manner. The Nazi policy of conquest and occupation rewrote the political map of Europe and tore apart in equally brutal fashion community relations and family ties.

But the inhumanity of Nazi racism, and the cruelty and death inflicted on those defined by the state as undesirable, had far-reaching and enduring consequences. Sometimes these uncomfortably complicated the relationship between perpetrator and victim of German inhumanity. With the defeat of the Nazi regime, the victorious Allied Powers drew up new borders and reassigned territories, with the consequence that large populations suddenly found themselves made homeless, foreign and unwelcome in their own country.

Already in 1941, Josef Stalin had issued a decree for the 'Resettlement of Germans from the Wolga-*gebiet*.'[2] On 13 December 1944, a few weeks before my mother was ordered to leave everything for an unknown destination, Winston Churchill addressed the House of Commons. He stated:

> The resettlement of millions [of people] from the East [of Europe] to the West or the North must take place as well as the expulsion of all Germans – this has been proposed: that is, the complete expulsion of Germans – from those territories which Poland shall gain in the West and in the North. The expulsion is, as far as this is possible to ascertain, the most satisfactory and permanent solution.

The Potsdam agreement of 1945 by the Allied Powers then transferred the German-speaking Upper Silesia Province to the Republic of Poland, providing for the expulsion of all German residents and German speakers.

So it happened that, after the war, Poland received most of the German territory east of the Oder-Neisse demarcation, including the industrial regions of Silesia (Schlesien), where my mother's home was located at the time of her flight.

As the historian R.M. Douglas (Douglas 2012) points out in a recent study of the large-scale expulsion of ethnic Germans from their homeland and the consequent suffering inflicted on a dislocated people, it would be naïve to confine descriptions of the arbitrariness of revenge under conditions of lawlessness. The terrible plight of an expelled people was a direct outcome of the deliberate project of the Allied Powers to 'cleanse' Eastern Europe of its German inhabitants. The few voices of warning against such policies were given little hearing.

## Die Stunde Null (Zero Hour)

Although many ethnically German residents chose to remain, or were unable to flee, whether due to illness, age of family members or fear of the unknown, the number of people expelled from the contested borderlands of Germany, as set forth in the agreement reached between the Allied Powers in Potsdam, totalled between about twelve and fourteen million. According to some estimates, between 500,000 and two million people died as a consequence of this forced expulsion, that is, one in six refugees lost her or his life in the course of the flight from advancing Russian troops. Massive tidal waves of population movement took place during late 1944 and 1945, dislocating vast numbers of people from what had been home in the former eastern region of Germany to what became the 'Four Zones', thereby dividing what was left of the German Reich after the return of territory to Czechoslovakia and to France. Thus were created the Russian, French, British and American military zones. In 1949, the Federal Republic of Germany would be created out of the Western zone, while the Soviet zone became the German Democratic Republic, or DDR. Out of the total population of *Vertriebene* (expelled or displaced persons), an estimated eight million arrived in the Western sectors; and about four million *Vertriebene* ended in the sector under Russian military occupation.

When people started fleeing during the winter of 1944/1945, it was one of the coldest winters on record in a region of Europe used to cold winters. Constituting the final chaotic months of war, they became popularly referred to as *Die Stunde Null* (Zero Hour), thus signifying a society in limbo.

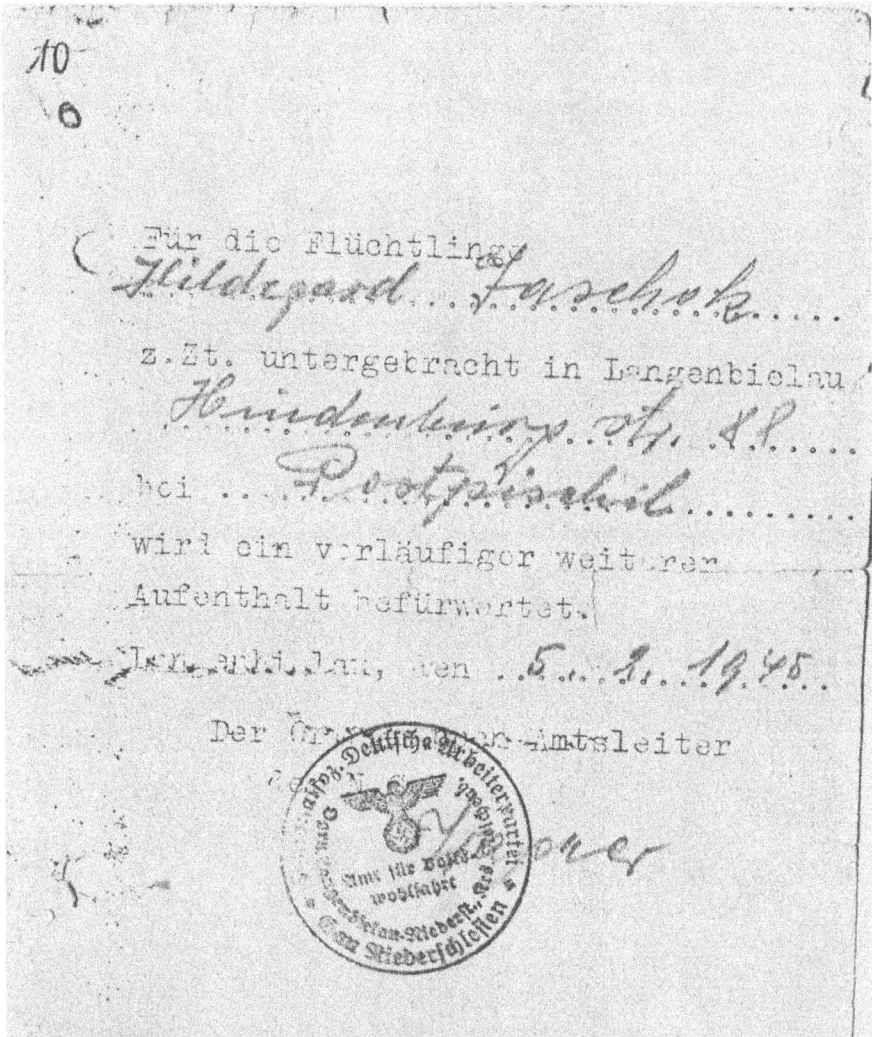

**Figure 3.2** Registration card issued to refugees, dated 5 February 1945, bearing the name of Hildegard Jaschok, allowing her temporary refuge in Langenbielau, Lower Silesia. © Familie Jaschok.

## Nowhere to Go

The millions of German refugees and *Vertriebene* were looking for safety and permanency. Those who had family or friends in the 'West' would in the first instance be aiming to reach them. But as accounts of the months during and after 1945 indicate, most of the refugees seeking as much distance as

**Figure 3.3** My father's sketch of a soldier's boots (1945). Bruno Jaschok wrote, 'Das Marschieren ging Zuende' (The marching came to an end). © Familie Jaschok.

*Ein Kennzeichen der Zeit vor 50 Jahren: Züge mit Flüchtlingen und Hamsterern.*

**Figure 3.4** Illustration from my mother's book, 44, taking trains in immediate post-war Germany (photo reproduced by permission of *Nordwestzeitung*, Oldenburg, 1995). Caption reads, 'Ein Kennzeichen der Zeit vor 50 Jahren: Züge mit Flüchtlingen und Hamsterern' (A feature of the time [as they were] 50 years ago: trains [packed] with refugees and hawkers).

possible from approaching victorious armies, or from reprisals by local inhabitants, had nowhere to go; indeed the majority had little sense of destination or orientation. Rumours and unsubstantiated hearsay furthermore destabilized people on open roads and urban streets aimlessly seeking elusive protection from wanton brutality and random lawlessness. The images transmitted from memory archives on life during 'Zero Hour' are of landscapes of destruction and of desolate public spaces where no protection existed. Vulnerability to ever-present danger to life and possessions interrupted normality and diminished compassion for one another.

The massive waves of refugees rolled and dispersed across a devastated Germany, only to pass through habitations of people in similar dire straits who were barely eking out a living. The refugees, who were already exhausted by months of uncertainty and fear of Allied bombing and of random violence were viewed with distrust and not infrequently were turned away from gates and thresholds. In this Germany of the 'Zero Hour', the flattened ruins of cities, towns and villages offered little with which to sustain life. Resources, such as clean drinking water, food, medicine, living space, clothing, heating and opportunities for paid work, were scarce. For too many, so archival records indicate, the fate was downward social mobility and outsider status, which excluded them from gaining a respected identity or membership of a local society. Many *Vertriebene* were forced to live year after year in transit camps or barracks, waiting for the regeneration of German society with functioning government institutions, private living space and a safe public infrastructure. The dread was that such transit camps were threatening to become permanent institutions.

The trauma of flight and loss of home was exacerbated by social exclusion and the stigma of being the uninvited guest, among strangers with whom one shared the common vicissitude of national downfall and shame, but not of individual fate. The newcomers had to start again with nothing, having left behind (but not forgotten) their houses, gardens, neighbourhoods and land. Whatever possessions they may have taken with them, were for the most part confiscated by occupying forces, valuables having long been sold and pawned to ensure survival. Their lost status counted for little among members of their new neighbourhoods and communities; instead they were resented for intensifying competition for scarce social and economic resources.

## My Mother's Flight at Zero Hour

I know that the historical context and images retrieved from libraries and archives serve to nourish my imagination, and are helping me to write. They do not allow me to make this visual aid a substitution for my mother's terror as she allowed herself, fifty years after her flight, to reawaken memories. Her flight in the icy winter landscape was shrouded in the terror that threads itself through her account. It was the fear that her mother and her small child would die far removed from the reach of her arms. The challenge for me has been to imagine the psychological and material hardships without diminishing her despair, and to understand that I am told a story in which silences, omissions and circumventions evoke as much of her state of mind as do her words, rendered in sparse prose.

What did she see and experience, and how was she changed by the odyssey through war-torn land which took her three hundred days (that is, 7,200 hours) to complete? How did she bear the constant, unsettling dread that her frail elderly mother, who suddenly had to assume sole responsibility for her newborn grandson, Christian, was dependent on the kindness of strangers for survival, separated from and without news of her daughter, my mother, without a destination and yet always desperate for food and warm clothing for the baby. My mother was afraid that her elderly and rather cosseted mother might be taxed beyond endurance in an unstable and hostile environment when she needed the physical and mental strength to bargain daily for continued existence.

My mother's memory map, one of relentless forward movement and enforced stopovers, always obsessively searching for my grandmother and the baby, is hazy, partially visible, with places, events and people embedded in the mist of remembrance of daily terror and corrosion of optimism over the possibility of change for the better; with milestones of hope associated with quickly dashed disappointment; vague references to sightings drawing her onward and into unknowable danger. My mother's map is thus one of blanks and uncertain connections between places and events. I depend on the story 'she could live with' (Winterson 2011) or, perhaps more accurately, the story she felt that her children could live with ... And so the story began in January, precisely, 18 January 1995, fifty years after she and her mother and two children and Marie, her *Kindermädchen* (nursery maid), were forced to abandon home. In that year, she was ready to write her story, more than fifty years later, reframed (but only made partially visible) by her first-born daughter.

## *Vertrieben* (Expulsion)

On a freezing wintry afternoon on 18 January 1945, a German officer knocked loudly at my mother's front door. Unexpected and sudden, his appearance at the house where my mother was living with her two young children signalled the crisis long feared. Along with other families vulnerable to reprisals and internment by the approaching Russian troops, they were given two hours to leave their home.

My young mother left her home with a three-year-old, my brother Wolfram, and a newborn baby, Christian, her widowed mother who happened to be visiting, and her most loyal nursery maid, Marie, who chose not to return to her parents in a remote village in order to stay with my mother. They somehow hoped that this was to be a short absence. She left the keys with the caretaker and handed over care of plants and goats (a source of milk for my baby brother), promising upon their return to reward him for his loyalty. They never returned. The caretaker was shot dead by Russian soldiers and all household possessions including gardening equipment and plants were taken away. Only a precious china tea set had been taken away by a local family, to be kept for their own use – as my mother would discover many years later, on the occasion of a brief return visit to her former homes. The house and its grounds were occupied by members of the Russian command headquarters.

Before my mother locked the doors to the house, she went from room to room, floor to floor, and she remembered with great intensity how much happiness was enclosed in these spaces, which had been her first home as an adult and as a young married woman.

My mother succeeded in the short time available to gather important documents, money and jewellery and sew them into her undergarments and dress. The bitter temperature allowed for the wearing of several layers of clothing, conveniently concealing her valuables. Afraid of losing contact with my absent father, who was then in the army, she concealed a hastily written note to him, informing him of her intended road of travel, in a previously agreed-upon spot under a large oak tree. She also packed one suitcase to provide for the children and two adults, most importantly clothing and toys for the children, nappies, some underwear. A neighbour, the local headmaster's wife, stayed behind to look after her sickly daughter. My mother wrote:

> As I heard later, many people fled into the forest to return after a few days. They were simple people who had little to fear. Yet as I heard, many young men were shot after being herded together in our grounds. Our neighbour, Frau Wollny, staying behind to care for her sick daughter, was brought to the internment camp and kept for the use of men. Her children were with her in the camp. Many years later, [she] paid me a visit [when already settled in West Germany], and when she finally talked, she suddenly became nauseous and choked on her words. They could not be uttered. Hers was the fate intended for me.

## Fear and Revenge

My parents' families reflect in their religious/cultural and geographical backgrounds the extraordinary history of Silesia. During different eras it was conquered and ruled by Bohemia, Austria-Hungary, Prussia, Germany and Poland. This added to the complexity of its heritage, which included Slavic, Catholic, Prussian, Austro-Hungarian and Jewish, and made 'ancestry' an unreliable marker of identity. With a shift in political rule, cultural, religious and ethnic practices would realign, subject to the vagaries of a new regime, granting safety or threatening vulnerability. At the time when the German military commander ordered my mother to leave her home in January 1945 to flee from the approaching Russian army, she lived in the German-speaking western part of Upper Silesia where, so my mother once told me, the community had been riddled with political tension and vocal dissent during the Nazi era, with loyal supporters of Hitler's ideology and government instilling fear in those who were critical of the government. On both sides of the family, vocal dissent and critique of the Nazi regime brought repercussions and punishment. There was an impact on employment prospects, fear of random visits by the dreaded Gestapo secret police and surveillance of family members by secret spies and ordinary members of the local community, which together created an atmosphere of fear and vulnerability in chaotic and lawless times, when revenge was easily exacted.

Many historians maintain that the first wave of refugees was caused by rumours describing in vivid details the brutalities inflicted by SS soldiers (Schutzwaffeln, the Nazi Party's security guards) and soldiers from the Red Army. In Lamsdorf, close to where my mother and her family were staying, a prisoner-of-war camp was turned into an internment camp. Nazi Germany had emerged in large part on the waves of a pan-German appeal, claiming interests in lands where ethnic Germans had been long settled. After the Nazi invasion of the Soviet Union in 1941, and the collapse of the alliance between Stalin and Hitler, the Soviet government denounced Germans who had been forced or who had chosen to stay behind, accusing them of having collaborated with the Nazis. They were transported to a labour camp where many died. Between January 1945 (the time when my mother embarked on her reluctant flight from fear) and autumn of 1946, more than six thousand Germans, among these 623 children, all from surrounding areas, died in this camp. Concentration camps were appropriated by the occupying Russian regime to serve as internment camps. Many adult men were absent, missing in action, killed, or prisoners of war.

## Tracing the Flight

My mother and her family made their way from the district of Rosenberg, just inside the German border, into the terrifying war zone that was Germany. Their enforced departure was in the early afternoon of 18 January 1945. By the time dusk fell and rapid darkness began to obscure the frozen landscape, my mother, her three-year-old – my brother Wolfram – and Marie, sitting together on a light summer carriage that was also carrying their few belongings, were separated by a retreating Germany army from her mother and the baby, Christian, only a few months old. They had been sitting in the more comfortable travelling carriage, protected by a weather-proof roof. It would take my mother about three hundred days of constant travelling across war-torn Europe until she had news that her mother and baby Christian had survived. My grandmother was more fortunate. After fifty days of travel by a horse-driven carriage she arrived in Lower Saxony in northern Germany. There a local landowner provided a safe refuge and unstintingly generous hospitality for an elderly lady and her baby grandson. As soon as she recovered from the hardship of a harsh winter's journey, she would start the search for the daughter and for other members of the extended family.

The caravan of carriages took my mother to Karlsruhe (Carlsruhe), where they arrived late at night. Not that long ago, my mother had been a pupil in the same finishing school where they sought refuge. The same nuns who had been her teachers welcomed a weeping young woman, a very quiet little boy and an anxious nursery maid. My mother describes the consolation of warm words of reassurance from the nuns, the bowls of soup provided for the hungry travellers and the offer of a hot bath. But, before the bath tub was filled with water, all were commanded to leave immediately and return to the road in the pitch darkness of night. No one was allowed to stay behind, and thus the nuns also took leave of their convent. My mother describes how a depressing numbness set in at this point. She could not stop weeping and all fell away from her. She gave herself up to depressing images of dying and hopelessness that she might never see her own mother and the child again. She says that a kind of vacuity set in, a numbing lethargy, in which she ignored everything, even her small child.

They continued on to Breslau and Langenbielau. Just as her carriage crossed the river Oder, Allied bombing was targeting the bridge. They had made it to the shore when she saw the bridge crowded with carriages and people on foot thrown into the river by the force of a massive explosion. The survivors had to carry on as fast as possible. When she turned round a last time to look at the impact of the explosion she saw a group of refugees stranded on the other side of the shore, unable to get across. One old man she had seen at the back of the caravan that same morning threw himself into the river to join the remnants of carriages and bodies of humans and horses carried by the force of the water. The nightmare of the day continued. With Allied military planes having caught sight of the caravan, they returned to renew their bombing. Getting off their carriages as quickly as possible, they crouched in a ditch beside the road. Close to her, her best friend, who formed part of the caravan, and her friend's entire family were hit by a bomb; all died instantly.

Despite the violence she witnessed, my mother remained numbed by grief and desolation over the presumed loss of her small son and her mother. One evening, however, as she lay 'with her face to the wall' in a temporary refuge that sheltered them from bitter cold, she was shocked to overhear a conversation among fellow refugees who had witnessed her decline, who said that they did not expect her 'to make it for much longer'. It was that, she writes, that shook her into awareness over the fate of the child with her. She said that those words made her come to her senses and to an overriding determination to be there for the child as well as to continue with her search for the family.

Newly-found strength brought hearsay that immediately instilled hope. Rumours had reached Langenbielau that carriages carrying refugees from Upper Silesia had been seen driving in the direction of Glaz, near Ullersdorf. Galvanized into action, she succeeded in getting a lift on a military truck for herself, the child and for Marie. Suddenly unafraid, she took control, calmly taking the child into her arms whenever Allied bombers were heard approaching high above them. She had decided that if she were to die it would be together with the child, so as not to leave him behind unprotected, while she steadied Marie with an unruffled voice. This rediscovered vigour was badly needed as, after an exhausting journey, they reached Glaz only to discover that no Silesian refugees had been sighted.

This pattern of hope and disappointment, euphoria and depression, nourished by rumours picked up en route that all too quickly turned out to be without foundation, shaped my mother's experience of her flight. However vague or unreliable the source, she was not able to ignore any news that came to her. Any time there was report of a sighting of a refugee caravan from Silesia she had cause for hope. Frantic search for means of transport would follow when there was little transport to be had, grasping opportunities to move to the next site of hoped-for reunion, my mother put her trust in strangers to keep their word and deliver them safely to their destination. Cold, hungry, unsafe, always listening to noise signalling danger from the skies or closer still, dangers lurking on the dark, lawless roads they were traversing, this became their unending normality. At this point in their journey, my mother decided, reluctantly, to leave Marie with a community of nuns. Marie had established herself quickly in a congenial environment of women, and had made friends with a servant who hailed from her home town. The ever-growing dangers of the journey ahead of them to an uncertain destination made my mother increasingly fearful for the safety of Marie. They wept when they parted, having shared so many crises and supported each other through so many dangerous situations. But it turned out to be a wise decision. Marie eventually made her way safely back home, able to rejoin her overjoyed parents.

And thus it came about that only my mother and my little brother, Wolfram, joined military officers on a train ride to Prague – only to be disappointed by further setback. The family my mother sought out, expecting they would be able to provide information on her mother's whereabouts, was nowhere to be found. And here more insight can be gleaned about her daily life, as it became, from my mother's brief understated references to generous hospitality where least expected and to hostile closing of doors where she had assumed sympathy. Even in normal times it would be a considerable undertaking to receive into your home a strange woman with a small, precocious child; in times of material scarcity and social uncertainty such generosity would entail still greater personal sacrifice. And yet, so my mother writes, they would at times be taken into a home for a night, given a bed where possible, or a mattress if no other space could be found. It is such experiences of generosity extended to strangers that are recalled more often in her account than the hurtful rejections and slamming of doors. Indeed, such moments were experienced during the short time spent in Prague, in a completely destroyed Dresden where they could not find a place to stay, and then in Leipzig, where a dangerous train ride nearly cost their lives.

Bitter experiences in my mother's account are left understated and, with an implicit awareness of her readers' and her family's feelings, conveyed in a conciliatory tone. And yet the reader, her daughter, cannot but imagine her vulnerability, dread and danger. Yet ever palpable is also my mother's stubborn refusal to lose hope.

A small vignette – my mother's desperate clinging to the bag in which she kept the most basic possessions for herself and the child when a stranger, seizing his opportunity on a crowded platform in Leipzig railway station, pushed against them, snatching the precious bag, containing their lifeline, from her grasp. Despair gave her a sudden burst of energy and she was able, with the help of a sympathetic bystander, to pull the bag from the man, just in time to climb onto the crowded train to Halle. She writes that she had been brave throughout the struggle but she broke down and wept when she discovered a tear in her beautiful winter coat! This had proved too much. Throughout the long journey to Halle she could not stop shaking.

At the end of a dangerous train journey, frequently interrupted by stoppages to escape the attention of Allied fire that threatened to blow up the entire train, they arrived to find Halle razed to the ground, the outcome of sustained Allied carpet bombing. My father's extended family had assembled in Halle – fearful of the chaos and lawlessness the imminent defeat of Hitler's troops would bring – to prepare for evacuation to safer areas. They were found in the cellar of the family home, sitting around a large table, all dead. Around this time, my father's sister, Maria, who worked as a nurse, was killed in Leipzig under circumstances that were never clearly established. My mother only heard the news much later, when she would also hear of the death during the war of her beloved cousin, an only son and promising young student, as well as of other family members who died at the front or in Auschwitz concentration camp. I would be given my late Aunt Maria's name.

As they moved from destination to destination, to Querfurt where they found brief respite and the unexpected hospitality of a clean bed in safe surroundings, and to a place near Leipzig where Silesian refugees had sought temporary refuge, news arrived of the utter and comprehensive defeat of Germany, of the imminent arrival of victorious troops, first the U.S. army, in turn followed by the Russian army, which occupied Sachsen (Saxony), the region in which my mother found herself. Here her journey came to a temporary halt, necessitated by the lack of a means of transport and more crucially, by the dangers of what historians call the *Null Stunde* (Zero Hour) of a dismantled, ruined civil society where women were the most vulnerable targets of random acts of barbarity. Yet, unexpectedly, my mother found refuge with an old lady where she and the child were 'in paradise', as she put it, in possession of a tiny, yet safe and private attic room. Here they would spend the next months of occupation under Russian authority. Having sold all her jewellery, my mother was forced to do unaccustomed agricultural work under the harshest conditions to feed them both.

## Women as *Freiwild* (Fair Game)

In this time of social void, women, particularly but not exclusively young and unprotected women, turned, in the words of my mother, into something akin to 'Freiwild' (fair game) for any man. Whether the man encountered in the lanes or market square, in a transit camp or a public building was a Russian officer or a member of the disbanded German army, women had to beware. And yet, they were forced, like my mother, to emerge from behind locked doors to find food, pawn possessions, get news of new arrivals of refugees and to take part in what under Russian occupation became mandatory agricultural labour. In times of war, so the historian of medieval Chinese society, Glen Dudbridge, remarked in his study of a tenth-century war memoir, the dividing line between criminality and warfare, illegal and sanctioned violence, is barely distinguishable.[3] A document created by the Koblenz Federal Archive says in relation to the conduct of the occupying forces in the immediate post-war period: 'The rape of women and girls by Soviet soldiers are not individual occurrences; we must refer to these incidents as mass rape.'

My mother makes only careful references to noisy attempts by soldiers to enter the house where she lived, to her terror when she made her way to the fields every morning to work, and to the daily transgressions that reduced women to the status of fair game for all men. Many women she knew experienced rape; I think, from rereading my mother's account many times, that she escaped outright rape and suffered from daily assaults on her confidence and self-esteem. Maybe my little brother's presence steeled her resolve to overcome all obstacles in her way, maybe it was an innate pride (which she never lost), and maybe she was sustained by her faith.

I need here to fill in omissions in my mother's memoir, omissions that nevertheless haunt her text. The use of rape as a weapon of war, and the rape of German women – in particular, but not exclusively, under Russian occupation – received attention only relatively late. Ethnic Germans were singled out for brutal treatment. Soviet Political Officers encouraged Soviet troops to terrorize the German population, seeking revenge for the German invasion of Russia and the human toll that Nazi expansionism exacted from the Russian population. The estimation is that altogether 1.9 million German women were raped at the end of the war by Red Army soldiers. About one-third of all German women in Berlin were raped – a substantial minority multiple times – by Soviet forces. In Berlin, contemporary hospital records indicate that between 95,000 and 130,000 women were raped. About 10,000 of these women died, mostly by suicide (see also Grossmann 1995; Heineman 1996).

## Dangerous Passage to Hope

My mother fell ill from hard labour, from the interminable waiting and the impasse which her journey had entered. She was cared for by her small son Wolfram, barely four years old, who carried her food and her bedpan. As she experienced the onset of depression (and she called this depression), a postcard reached her that carried the news she had been waiting for. The postcard, which had mysteriously been kept for months following my grandmother's passage through Leipzig, informed her that her mother and baby Christian were known to be on their way to Westfalen (Westphalia in northern Germany, a British occupied zone).

This galvanized my mother to get well and organize as hastily as possible her passage through the Russian zone, as Saxony came to be called, to its border with the zone controlled by American military forces. The approach of winter and worrying news about ever-increasing security at the borders called for urgency.

She succeeded in getting a ticket on an overcrowded train to the terminus station and sought out a man, recommended to her as a reliable guide, to help her reach the border village from which she would attempt the illegal crossing. She found a group ready to cross the border but was let down by the reluctance of their leader, a middle-aged woman, to burden themselves with a small child. At the height of despair, my mother, as she put it, wiped the tears from her face, took her little son with her and looked for the woman from whom she had purchased expensive cigars the previous day, with which to bribe the Russian border guards. On telling the cigar vendor about her rejection by the woman she had trusted to help her, she was informed that another group consisting of two families was ready to make the border crossing that very same night. Nor did they mind adding a small cart, which would carry my brother and their few possessions. Going from despair to euphoria within a short hour, my mother relates the joy with which she made preparations for the dangerous night walk.

On a moonless October night in sub-zero temperatures, she and the child joined a nearly silent group of women and men. Their immediate destination was Wanfried, a transit camp in the American zone. Placing a small cart behind the large horse-drawn carriage, the child and their possessions were pulled and pushed across a barely visible, slippery stretch of land. The need for utter silence had been drilled into my brother, as any sound might have brought the border guards who did not hesitate to shoot anything that moved. Despite the utter darkness and the freezing temperature, despite the breath-taking hasty repair of a broken carriage wheel, they reached the foot of the hill that formed the border:

> We could not see much, we went on instinct. Suddenly a woman came over to me to tell me that the small cart had to be disconnected so as not to burden the main carriage that everyone had to help to push up the hill. The horses would

not manage the weight. Also we had to ensure that the carriage would not turn over. I had no choice but to leave Wolfram alone in his cart and I had to help push the carriage. The carriage was old and the noise added to our terror of discovery. With all our strength and driven by fear the carriage stayed upright and we reached the top of the hill, close to the border-barrier. It was terrifying and I was haunted by anxiety for Wolfram. As soon as the carriage was safe and the horses could take its weight, I was running, or I should say I was sliding down the hill as fast as I could, and thank God Wolfram sat obediently where I left him and waited for me. He was used to trusting my words and was thus perfectly calm.

My mother was helped to pull the small cart up the hill, and after a short but nerve-wracking period of waiting, the Russian border guard appeared to accept their bribe.

Only about ten minutes of waiting, and then the barrier went up. And we drove, God be thanked, into freedom.

This account by my mother of her terrifying border crossing, and the trusting relationship between her and her little son has a special poignancy for me. His being left in the total darkness of a terrifying night, and waiting patiently for her return, were possible for him because in all these many months of flight under the most unsettling and uncertain conditions, he had never needed to doubt the certainty of her words. It was important for my mother to explain this to her readers, the other children of a family marked by dislocation and uncertainty.

Within days of the border crossing, after duly registering with the Military Government of Germany, my mother received the news that her mother and child were alive, that they had found a safe haven with a most generous family and that they had sent out enquiries in all directions to discover my mother's fate.

Nothing kept my mother from taking the first available train, finding herself in the darkness of night in a small railway station in Niedersachsen (Lower Saxony). Within two hours, she recalls, her mother's host family, after receiving a phone call from the stationmaster, had collected them and reunited three generations of grandmother, mother and children.

My grandmother and little Christian, my mother discovered, had found a warm welcome on a large estate. Given a small cottage to turn into a home for herself and her grandchild, my grandmother taught the children in surrounding villages the rudimentary skills of reading and writing. There they would wait another one and a half years for news of my father.

**Figure 3.5** A first home in West Germany (British occupied zone), a sketch by my father; from my mother's memoir, 60. © Familie Jaschok.

## Writing to End War

Memory cannot preserve the past, but is a process of reconstruction, Assmann and Czaplicka (1995) maintain, recovering a semblance of order from what would otherwise remain fragments that threaten the integrity of the self. Such is the functioning of narratives of the past, yielding meaning upon which to build a meaningful identity. In the course of this process, Jens Brockmeier (2002) says, remembering and forgetting become two sides of a process that includes the specific predicaments and challenges, and also the strength, resilience and coping strategies of individuals engaged in the labour of reconstruction.

My mother's writing is a carefully rendered narrative of loss, overwhelming grief, of relentless daily grind, near-death and rape experiences, of the constant horror of unchecked imagination, the imagined deaths of her child and family, all in the quest for survival.

At the end of her account, she explains what drove her (or perhaps encouraged her) to fill the long and deep silence with writing, with a story that her children could live with. She explains in conclusion:

> So, my dear children, I have now done what for so many decades I refused [*verweigert*] to do: bring my flight to paper. I was motivated by the fiftieth anniversary [of the flight] and by my love for you. Perhaps this account has granted you a closer insight into the experiences of those times and perhaps this has contributed to a better understanding of your parents.

As my sister Gabriele said, our mother was greatly relieved when she had recorded her story and thus had *abgegeben* (surrendered) her story to her children. She wanted to rid herself also of the stories left unspoken. She did not know that she had set new narratives and reconstructions in motion, through which her children sought to make sense of the silence as much as of the written stories.

On 18 January 1995 she called upon my sister Gabriele for support, so as to marshal her strength for the painful narration. My sister remembers,[4]

> Writing the first sentence was for her the most painful step, and for this to happen took her fifty years. For the other seventy pages, she merely needed a few more weeks.

My sister surmised, in a letter to me, that it had been a concern to Mutti for quite some time to record her *Fluchtgeschichte* (story of her flight) for the benefit of her children, and in particular for the following generation, as she knew that we had heard only what were at best fragments of her experience. Moreover, she was afraid of our *Vergessen* (forgetting) of the family's past in a distant homeland which some of the children had never visited. Perhaps more importantly, she felt that knowing something of these experiences during and just after the war might help us (that is, the children) to understand more recent family history.

Then came 18 January 1995, and thus the fiftieth anniversary of the day that my mother and her family were driven from home. It was a day, my sister recalls, when our mother became 'unbelievably agitated'. She phoned my sister to share the nightmare that had taken control of her. In her despair, she took a sheet of paper and wrote: 'Today is January 18th, and it is on such a day, exactly fifty years ago that we were forced to leave our home in Silesia'. There she stopped. She was unable to continue writing, such was her inner turmoil. Yet, my sister remembers, she was determined to make an effort even if this meant writing just a few lines every day, taking however long was necessary to finish her task. My sister came to understand that for our mother there were two priorities: to leave us with a record of her flight into a distant and strange part of Europe, and to give herself the best (and perhaps only) means of coping with and processing the maelstrom of long-dormant memories.

## The Process of Unburdening

And thus the labour of writing began, confronting her with haunting images and long-repressed terror. It took many comforting phone calls from her daughter to reassure her and to free her from the pressure of painful memories, to enable her to rest, to be able to summon strength and courage once again. It exhausted her body, and her hands would shake so badly at times that she had to stop. But she did not give up, determined to face her demons so that her children need not be terrorized by an unknown past.

She was so fearful of sharing her frightening experiences with her family that it took my sister much patient listening and reassurance to instil my mother with the confidence to carry on. Offering support with the typing, proofreading and layout of the *Büchlein* (booklet), as my mother's reminiscences came to be called, and helping to engage in some additional research into the historical context of her flight, gave my mother the security she needed to carry on her daily discipline of body and mind. She grew weary, but my sister's support meant that she was not alone when overcome by fears of old.

## Taking Responsibility for Writing

It was important for my mother, so it emerged from conversations with my sister, not to burden her children by unburdening herself. Hence the measured tone in which her narrative was written. But nor did she want to add to the vast volume of 'victim narratives' through which old and new prejudices were sustained. My sister sent her a number of recently published accounts by women refugees to enable her to see her experiences alongside those of other women of her generation and of similar backgrounds, but my mother soon set these aside, unable to muster the strength to carry others' suffering. My sister reflected in a recent conversation:

> How much I would like to talk about their experiences with our mother and our grandmother. In an ever more volatile Europe, their stories, their personal reflections become ever more pertinent to us. We have too few of such testimonials. Is it unthinkable that so many of the fearful scenarios through which they lived could be repeated? They were witnesses, their courage, resilience and faith might have had so much more to teach us about how to withstand and survive such times.

A record of loss, separation, grief and terror in our mother's words also became a legacy of faith and her testimony to hope. The novelist Jeanette Winterson (2011) talks about her own early writing (*Oranges Are Not the Only Fruit*) in relation to the many things that were left unsaid about her mother's rigid control over her family, and her expulsion of her daughter from warmth, support and affirmation.[5] And she says that in looking back she has come to understand how she 'was writing a story she could live with' – this made her invent a loving character, Testifying Elsie, who looked after the lonely child. Elsie never existed: 'I wrote her in because I couldn't bear to leave her out'. The other (lived) story was too painful to be told.

Our mother, I feel, wrote a story that she thought her children could live with. We were after all the readers whom she told about herself. However, it wasn't an invented human character who entered the narrative, but the benign presence of a God – in whose presence she placed her faith, however sorely tried. Alleviating thus her own troubled and long-suppressed memory of pain, loss and inhumanity, I have come to believe that she also sought – ever courageously, yet never naïvely – to alleviate her children's pain and to instil hope.

## Notes

1. Expulsion, or forcible eviction: *Vertriebener*, someone who is forcibly evicted or expelled, is a highly charged term; but among the first generation of German refugees, and even among some of their descendants, this term is still used in preference to the term *Flüchtling*, refugee. Documents from the Dokumentar Archiv suggest that when it comes to *Flüchtlinge* or refugees, they are those 'who in consequence of events in Europe were forced to leave behind their homes in consideration of danger for their life and liberty'. *Vertriebene* or those who were expelled or driven out, are those 'persons who were driven out from their homes by force or other means, regardless whether this was based on a treaty or other agreement or without such a treaty'. A recent scholarly account detailing the suffering and deprivation to which Germans expelled from their homeland were subjected comes from R.M. Douglas (2012). Expulsion of Germans towards the end of the war and during the main part of 1945 was treated by officials in charge of Polish and Czech territories as an opportunity for revenge, exploitation and self-enrichment. Also see Ulrich Merten (2012). The *Bund der Heimatvertriebenen und Entrechteten* (literally the League of People Driven from their Homes and Deprived of their Rights) played an important part in the domestic politics of post-war West Germany.
2. The Volga Germans were ethnic Germans who since the eighteenth century had lived along the River Volga in the region of southern European Russia.
3. Glen Dudbridge, 'Disasters Public and Private in Tenth-century China', 27 January 2012, a seminar presented in the *Ethnicity and Identity* seminar series, ISCA, University of Oxford.
4. When preparing to present my mother's experience at the Women and War workshop (5 February 2012) at IGS at LMH, Oxford, I got in touch with my sister Gabriele. Only then did I discover her crucial part in the accomplishment of our mother's painful project of self-narration. I was not in Europe in January 1995

and thus was ignorant of my sister's role. Without her, my mother would not have had the strength to bring closure to her writing.

5. On the occasion of the publication of Winterson's 2011 novel *Why Be Happy When You Could Be Normal?* see 'Jeanette Winterson: All About My Mother', in *The Guardian* (London), 29 October 2011.

## Bibliography

Assmann, J. and J. Czaplicka. 1995. 'Collective Memory and Cultural Identity', *New German Critique* 65: 125–113.

Brockmeier, J. 2002. 'Remembering and Forgetting: Narrative as Cultural Memory', *Culture & Psychology* 8: 65–78.

Douglas, R.M. 2012. *Orderly and Humane: The Expulsion of the Germans after the Second World War.* New Haven, CT: Yale University Press.

Grossmann, A. 1995. 'A Question of Silence: The Rape of German Women by Occupation Soldiers', in *Berlin 1945: War and Rape 'Liberators Take Liberties'*, October 72: 42–63. MIT Press. Article stable URL: http://www.jstor.org/stable/778926.

Heineman, E. 1996. 'The Hour of the Woman: Memories of Germany's "Crisis Years" and West German National Identity', in *American Historical Review* 101(2): 354–395.

Jaschok, H. 1995. *18. Januar 1945.* Privately published.

Merten, U. 2012. *Forgotten Voices: The Expulsion of the Germans from Eastern Europe after World War II.* Brunswick, NJ: Transaction Publishers.

Winterson, J. 2011. *Why Be Happy When You Could Be Normal?* London: Jonathan Cape.

**Maria Jaschok** is director of the International Gender Studies Centre and a research fellow at Lady Margaret Hall, Oxford and has a PhD in Chinese Social History from SOAS, University of London. Her research interests and publications relate to modern China, including religion, gender and Asian (Chinese) contexts, gendered constructions of memory, feminist ethnographic practice, marginality and identity, and gendered spirituality. Her current three-year collaborative research project in Central China concerns the history and legacy of Islamic chants, part of an age-old oral tradition that was nurtured within the relative cultural autonomy characteristic of Hui Muslim women's mosques.

# 4

# Mau Mau Women

## Sixty Years Later

### Tabitha Kanogo

Many women who have been in the struggle for the creation of a new
social order for us and for the future generations have names, hearts that
ache, eyes that weep and feet that hurt. We must know these women by
name. They stood on the line of duty ... They have names and faces and we
must remember them ... Mekatilili wa Menza, Mary Nyanjiru, Prophetess
Moraa, Ciokaraine, Field Marshal Muthoni, Sara Wambui, Sara Sarai,
Tabitha Ogega ...

(Wanjiku Mukabi Kabira, *Time for Harvest:
Women and Constitution Making in Kenya*)

This chapter explores the contemporary reflections and activities of Kenyan
female ex-combatants in the Mau Mau war of liberation in Kenya in 1952–
1955 in an effort to evaluate their plight, aspirations and general engagement today within Kenyan society and state. In recognizing the muting
of female voices, the chapter addresses the near total elision of female ex-
combatants in scholarship, a situation that begs an appraisal of the production of historical knowledge of Kenya. Female ex-combatants are extremely
disappointed about the nation's disregard for their contribution to the Mau
Mau rebellion. The female veterans question their marginalization in the
nationalist discourse in Kenya.

Importantly, the chapter examines the women's involvement in a recent
last-ditch effort to salvage some dignity and economic redress from Britain,

the former colonial power. Female veterans participated in the recent constitutional review process, where they articulated their hopes and aspirations for post-2012 Kenya. Today all women in Kenya, including ex-combatants, expect full inclusion in all public institutions. The women's movement in Kenya has gained tremendous momentum, culminating in significant change in women's inclusion in public decision-making institutions at local, regional and national levels.

Why are existing narratives predominantly silent on women's roles in the liberation struggle? It has been said that female Mau Mau veterans lacked formal education and were therefore not in a position to write their stories. While most veterans and some scholars are critical of existing nationalist histories, which they deem incorrect, a handful of male ex-combatants have written their memoirs (Itote 1967; Barnett and Njama 1968; Kariuki 1976). Only Wambui Otieno amongst the female ex-combatants has written her memoir (Otieno 2002). Gender disparity in Mau Mau narratives is highly conspicuous.[1] Female veterans' passion for inclusion, gender equity, economic independence and political participation remains strong. Their participation in the recent constitutional review process, especially on matters touching on women's economic independence and involvement in governance reaffirms the veterans' persistence in seeking to realize the full empowerment of women.

Mugo (2004) complains that, despite their gallant participation, female guerrillas have for the most part remained unsung heroes. Although female combatants faced danger and death in support of the liberation movement, initially male combatants resented their entry into the Aberdare and Mount Kenya forests. Determined to be involved, women negotiated, even demanded, to be accepted as equal co-combatants. They succeeded, and as armed combatants, support staff in the forest and civilian networks providing material supplies or logistical information, female civilians and combatants constituted an indispensable lifeline for the freedom fighters.[2] Coming from a cultural background that traditionally did not allow women to participate in warfare or in major decision-making processes, nevertheless valiant women like Field Marshal Muthoni did rise to positions of leadership. But first we must look briefly at the run up to these events.

## Colonial Background

The Mau Mau war was a nationalist struggle born of agrarian, social and political frustrations among African peasants, the urban unemployed and proletarian Africans in Kenya (Rosberg and Nottingham 1966: 234–319).

The establishment of a white settler plantation economy at the beginning of the twentieth century necessitated the alienation of seven million acres of land – equivalent to twenty per cent of the most fertile land or fifty per cent of all the usable land. Infrastructure, capital, agricultural and veterinary services were concentrated in the settler sector and financial and political pressure was put on Africans to force them to provide cheap and abundant labour for the settler plantations (Brett 1973). In a virulently racist society, with some exceptions, Africans were not allowed to grow high cash value crops lest they become financially independent and withdraw their labour from settler plantations. Faced with land shortages, deprived of political participation for half a century, and relegated to fourth-class citizenship after whites, Indians and Arabs, Africans in colonial Kenya experienced gross oppression.

Efforts by regional political parties to remedy specific grievances under the colonial rule between 1920 and 1946 were unsuccessful. The Mau Mau liberation war of 1952–1955 was a major attempt to uproot the colonial government. The guerrillas, who referred to themselves as the Land and Freedom Army, hoped to dislodge the colonial system, free and redistribute land in the White Highlands and establish a democratic government.

## Mau Mau Women

The civilian wing of the struggle supplied logistical information about the movements of enemy troops, provided food, medical supplies, clothing, shoes, arms and ammunition, administered oaths and recruited new combatants. They offered safe houses for endangered compatriots, and raised cash for the multiple needs of a liberation movement that lacked external support. The civil wing, which included thousands of women, was the lifeline of the liberation movement. This was a most creative, secretive, resilient, highly motivated and very efficient network of volunteers, a group that operated right under the noses of colonial forces and their retainers, thus attracting vicious reprisals upon suspicion of or apprehension for Mau Mau-related activities. Without them the forest guerrillas would not have lasted as long as they did in their uphill fight against a well-equipped colonial army with bomber jets and fusilier troops. In short, women's participation in the liberation struggle in Kenya was indispensable. Children were also used as messengers.

Some women even rose to hold military ranks in the guerrilla troops. Field Marshall Muthoni wa Kirima, known as Nyina wa Thonjo (Mother of

Beaver Birds) attained the highest military office possible. For all practical purposes, Field Marshal Muthoni became the second in command in the forest combat once the previous deputy, General Mathenge, mysteriously disappeared. Muthoni, who entered the forest early in the struggle, was among the last combatants to leave it on 16 December 1963, after attending the independence celebration on 12 December 1963. Guerrilla leader Field Marshal Dedan Kimathi Wachiuri was captured on 20 October 1956 and executed on 18 February 1957 (Kanogo 2011: 78–79). Muthoni, a much respected leader, close ally of Dedan Kimathi and known for her bravery, ingenuity and dedication to the struggle remained in leadership standing shoulder to shoulder with surviving Mau Mau icons such as Field Marshall Musa Mwariama and General Baimungi.

A renowned and fearless markswoman, Muthoni graduated from handling Mau Mau funds to making and sourcing guns for the guerrillas, reconnoitring, providing political education for new recruits and motivating combatants when the going got tough in the forest. A resolute, hard core but even-handed guerrilla who never looked back, Muthoni was known to run lone errands to bail out fellow guerrillas, including searching for food under dangerous circumstances (Mugo 2004: 17–18). That Muthoni's legendary valour and commitment to the struggle, along with that of other female combatants, has not received its rightful recognition in scholarship and in the national narratives of Kenya's political history, reveals the persistence of gender imbalance informed by patriarchal and class considerations. It is a process of othering that Micere Mugo has explored in her treatise on Field Marshal Muthoni (see also Karani 2005; and Njagi 1991). In recognition of Field Marshal Muthoni's achievements, Kabira says:

> Field Marshal Muthoni has defied political, social and economic upheavals. There are many stories and experiences of our women which still have to find their way into public domain. They have to be part of public knowledge. (Kabira 2012:169)

In the forest, Mau Mau women demanded and achieved a measure of respectability and equality.[3] They were recognized as fellow combatants, not only with some of the women attaining positions of military distinction, as in the case of Field Marshall Muthoni, but with others being incorporated into the administrative and decision-making machinery of the forest combat. Even then, the recognition was not in proportion to the broad spectrum of contributions that the women made to the struggle. More importantly, however, is the fact that these gains in gender equality seem to have been lost after the attainment of independence. Muthoni, not unlike other female guerrillas, suffered double abandonment: first as an ex-combatant and then as a woman. Returning from the forest to an ambivalent independent state that lacked programmes to rehabilitate or provide economic and social safety nets for ex-combatants, Muthoni and her Mau Mau veteran husband Mutungi fell on hard times and at some stage became homeless in the capital city Nairobi. Subsequently abandoned by her husband for another woman, Muthoni has had to rebuild her life, alone. Independence has proved a disillusionment.

Coming from a place of political marginalization, personal impoverishment and the double disinheritance that this entailed (once by the colonial government, and subsequently by independent Kenya), ex-freedom fighters have continued to demand national recognition for their contribution to the decolonization process in Kenya; they also seek acknowledgement for the personal sacrifices that they made during their participation in the liberation struggle, including material losses, psychological, sexual and physical violation, and untold hardships and deprivation in the forests where the liberation war was waged. Many others suffered wrongful imprisonment, detention, internment in colonial villages, harrowing interrogation, public humiliation and many other indignities. As unsung heroes, former freedom fighters have become more relentless in their quest to articulate, legitimate and memorialize their role in the nationalist history of Kenya. In this respect, they expect both state and societal recognition of their roles as patriotic freedom fighters whose blood and sweat wrested independence from colonial oppressors.

## Unfinished Business: Suing the British

In a historic move in June 2009, the Mau Mau Veterans Association sued Britain for brutal abuse and torture suffered during the liberation struggle in the 1950s. The veterans demanded acknowledgement from Britain of the torture that the colonial government inflicted on the freedom fighters, and sought an apology for the indignities and humiliations suffered during the Mau Mau period. Lastly, the veterans demanded reparations for economic losses suffered as a result of incarceration, dispossession, or both. In 2012, seventy-three-year-old Jane Muthoni Mara was one of four veterans who travelled to Britain to give evidence against Britain and sue for damages for abuses they suffered in the 1950s. She was part of an initial party of six veterans enjoined in the lawsuit against Britain. While one of the claimants dropped out, a second, Susan Ciang'ombe Ngondi, seventy-one, died before the party could travel to London. Jane Muthoni was accompanied by Paulo

Muoka Nzili, Wambuga Nyingi and Naomi Nziula Kimweli (*The Guardian*, 5 October 2012; Gander 2013). Naomi Nziula was not a veteran. Veteran Jane Muthoni was very clear about her mission to Britain:

> I want the British government to compensate me for the suffering I have been caused as a result of the abuse I was subjected to in the camps. The abuse has affected my whole life and I relive the events I lived through on a regular basis ... I do not understand why I was treated with such brutality for simply having provided food to the Mau Mau. I killed no one, I harmed no one, all I wanted to do was to help those who were fighting for the dignity and freedom of our people. (*The Guardian*, 17 July 2012)

Jane Muthoni was indeed a food provider for freedom fighters. She was part of what has been referred to as the civil wing of Mau Mau, people not involved in forest combat but who provided material, logistic and moral support to the liberation movement. Her older brother was a freedom fighter in the forest.[4] Jane Muthoni was betrayed by a fellow Mau Mau supporter who, upon being tortured, was quick to reveal that Muthoni was also a supporter. Once arrested, due process did not always follow. Admission into interrogation camps was followed by immediate brutalization; torture and intimidation were liberally applied in an effort to elicit confessions of Mau Mau complicity. For thousands of men and women put in detention camps and prisons, violence became the order of the day.

Caroline Elkins's Pulitzer prize-winning book has revealed the excesses of abuse meted out during the Mau Mau struggle. Abuse including hard labour and flogging, food and sleep deprivation were common in detention camps, prisons and at interrogation sessions as colonial officials and African loyalists tried to force confessions from Kikuyu, Embu, Meru and Kamba people, the four main ethnic groups involved in Mau Mau. Some men were castrated and others maimed. Elkins exposes the extensive nature of sexual violence suffered by Kenyan women. Beyond rampant rape, she unearthed the harrowing sexual abuse of women with all manner of items, including bottles and sticks (Elkins 2005; Anderson 2005). The use of sex as a weapon of war in other parts of Africa is well documented (Baaz and Stern 2013).

Sexual violation was combined with other forms of assault: 'The women that were taken there were violated because bottles were put in their private parts. They would heat a spade, and this would be put on our backs. We were burnt such that one could not even stand. We were not taken to the hospital. It was left to God to heal us.' Jane Muthoni is one of those who suffered a horrendous sexual assault:

On the second day, during questioning about her brother and the Mau Mau, she was held down while a glass bottle containing very hot water was pushed into her vagina. [She was] completely and utterly violated and was forced to watch the same sexual torture, using larger bottles, inflicted on three older women, who had borne children. These women died shortly after their release. (*The Guardian*, 17 July 2012)

For some of the victims of loyalists, gendered assault was fatal and could not be linked to any known Mau Mau activities. Naomi Nziula Kimweli, who accompanied Jane Muthoni to London to give evidence was neither a freedom fighter nor a Mau Mau supporter. In 1952 a chance encounter with the authorities as she and her family travelled from Nairobi to their country home in Kamba territory resulted in the detention of her whole family, including her husband and three children. That Naomi, who was carrying a full-term pregnancy, was not spared a brutal sexual assault underscores the inhumanity of colonial officials. Naomi remembers:

My hands were tied over my head, my eyes blindfolded, legs tied together. Then a bottle was inserted into my vagina. I could hear the children screaming. He just said that we were part of Mau Mau, and when he was inserting the bottle he demanded to know how many oaths I'd taken. We were forced to admit that we were part of the Mau Mau. After [he inserted] the bottle into me I passed out unconscious. When I regained consciousness I realized I was at Kenyatta, King George Hospital [in Nairobi]. I was told that my unborn baby had been fully grown and was a boy. His head and neck had been crushed. He was fully grown. He was a baby boy. All the time I was in hospital I didn't see the [other] children. I assumed they were with my husband. (Kimwele, in *The Last Battle* 2012)

Naomi Nziula lost the baby in a most traumatizing manner, both for the child and the mother. After hospitalization for four months, she went home to a castrated husband. Her three children are still missing to date. It was not unusual for the colonial government to inflict violence on loyal Africans. The sexual abuse of women, a most gendered assault, was juxtaposed with the castration of men suspected of supporting Mau Mau.[5] Sandgren (2012) has captured the trauma of childhood during Mau Mau. Naomi and her husband were robbed of the joy of motherhood and fatherhood respectively. Her husband could not father more children. In her interview Naomi emphasized time and again that the child who was murdered in her womb was a boy. If that was the only boy in the family, the perpetuation of her castrated husband's household was in jeopardy.

The psychological wounds for such violated women are enormous (de Brouwer and Ka Hon Chu 2009). In Naomi Nziula's case, the torture and loss of her unborn child and of her other children resulted in great psychological trauma. 'I used to feel so bad. I felt disturbed and sometimes I would cry.' (Kimwele, in *The Last Battle* 2012). Time might have taken the edge off some of the bitterness, but it has not erased the memories.

Britain has recently acknowledged culpability for the former regime's torture of freedom fighters, and has apologized for the abuses. In May 2013 Britain began to negotiate reparations with veterans. This epic lawsuit could have far-reaching repercussions, should other victims of British colonial brutality throughout the British Empire decide to seek justice. This might extend as far as peninsular Malaysia – formerly Malaya – Cyprus and Aden to mention but a few ex-colonies (*The Guardian*, 5 October 2012). The participation of women in providing evidence against Britain gave voice on a world stage to a group that has remained silenced both at home and abroad for two generations (Clough 2003: 251–267; Ogude 2003: 268–283).

In 2013, Britain finally agreed to pay out about twenty million British pounds to slightly over five thousand Mau Mau veterans. The compensation, which averages about £2,650 per veteran, is a grossly inadequate amount. There are plans to contest the amount of compensation offered. Other Mau Mau veterans, male and female, not included in the original lawsuit are preparing their own litigation against the British government.[6] There are also plans to demand compensation from the Kenyan state.

Six decades later, the emerging details of the assaults inflicted on Mau Mau veterans expose a cadre of demented colonial functionaries whose darkest instincts came to the fore as they abused thousands of women and men suspected of supporting Mau Mau. A heinous and indiscriminate application of sexual assault aimed at shocking the victims into confessing to Mau Mau activities. Experiencing or witnessing such events traumatized the victims and their families, leaving indelible psychological damage. Men, too, were also subjected to sexual assault. Paulo Muoka Nzili, who gave evidence against the British in London, was castrated during Mau Mau (Al Jazeera, 7 June 2013). He was not alone. Many men were castrated in the course of interrogation. Wambuga Nyingi, the third plaintiff in the lawsuit was brutally beaten (Al Jazeera, 7 June 2013).

In bringing their cases to London, these Mau Mau survivors have put a face to the victims of British colonial exploits, and exposed the underbelly of British colonialism to the whole world. Where previously the women had remained silenced and their voices muffled by the din of competing claims in the nationalist struggle, their recent and extremely courageous last strike at their former detractors is unprecedented. Although the United Nations has comprehensive statutes identifying gender-based violence as an abuse of women's human rights, this is not the path that Mau Mau veterans are pursuing.[7] Some female combatants suffered sexual exploitation while in the forest. Unsolicited sexual assaults by male veterans, some of them in positions of power, constituted some of the most aggravating experiences that female guerrillas underwent. Some of the women were turned into sex slaves, or partners in unequal liaisons (Barnett and Njama 1966: 242). Male loyalists who supported the British administration and African male ex-combatants have not been brought to court for their sexual abuse of women or other abuses during the Mau Mau war. A gendered introspection among Mau Mau veterans of both sexes is long overdue. Existing explanations of the sexual exploitation of female veterans as a service to the liberation struggle in the forest are no longer acceptable (Barnett and Njama 1966: 243).

## Mau Mau Women and Land

For most veterans, a dignified livelihood entails, among other things, the ownership of land.[8] Mau Mau detainees lost their land under the Swynnerton Plan, which sought to consolidate Kikuyu land holdings from 1954 onwards (Sorrenson 1967). This entailed the amalgamation of scattered pieces of family land into single contiguous farms deemed to be more economically viable. Consolidation resulted in the individualization and male-based ownership of land (Davison 1988: 165). Female veterans, especially those who were widowed during the liberation struggle, were particularly vulnerable. Some of them remained in the 'concentration' villages at the end of Mau Mau, as other families returned to their newly consolidated farms. In subsequent years, landless women like Jane Muthoni found themselves living in 'poor quarters'.

The Kenyan government's willing-buyer willing-seller arrangement, under which the bulk of the White Highlands were sold to Africans, excluded veterans whose financial standing had been completely compromised during their forest, detention, or imprisonment stints. Veterans consider it a great injustice that loyalists ended up with huge tracts of land (Kanogo 1987a: 162–178; Leo 1984). Women were traditionally excluded from ownership of land. Since the early 1980s, however, legal provisions have been made to enable women to inherit traditional land. What was lacking was the cultural, legal and political will to educate women and girls about their new-found rights. In the last fifteen years or so, gender sensitization advocacy and legal intervention have ensured that an increasing number of women are aware of, and are demanding, their property rights. The recent constitution review process has recognized gender equity in matters of access to, and inheritance of, traditional and family property. Interviewed before this process was completed, Field Marshal Muthoni said:

> There isn't a place I have owned in terms of land that I can show you or anyone as having been allocated to me because of all the effort I put in[to] fighting for my nation and my people ... up to this day. Now what [we live with] are troubles, hardships, poverty, oppression, struggling and wrangling. (Mugo 2004: 23)

Jane Muthoni characterizes her home as 'the poor people's place, those with no property. We do not have farms, we work for others [doing farm work] so that one can get cash to buy flour' (*The Last Battle* 2012). Mau Mau veterans expected to receive land grants from the independent Kenyan government. While Field Marshal Muthoni has managed to buy herself a piece of land, Jane Muthoni continues to live in poverty. Referring to themselves as the Kenya Land and Freedom Army during the liberation struggle, for veterans, the acquisition of land was critical. However, this has proved elusive for most of them. Where land has been made available to Mau Mau veterans, there is an obvious gender disparity with more men benefitting. A few women, like Wa Njuki, were lucky:

> I tried all means possible. I said to myself, when Kenyatta [Kenya's first president] is giving out the first land, Wa Njuki will be there. And now here my land is plot 209. I thank God because my youth did not get wasted. And I am still here. (Kabira 2012: 173)

Wa Njuki had achieved one of the two key ideals of the liberation movement: land. Inequity in land holdings is a major concern (Kabira 2012: 178). This is made more complicated by the enormous variety of soils in Kenya.

## Memorializing Mau Mau Women: The Dilemma in the Academic and Public Mind

Female veterans strongly advocate some kind of memorialization as a sign of respect for the veterans and as a way of correctly chronicling a significant aspect of Kenya's history. Lamenting the lack of instruction about Mau Mau in schools, Anna Wamuyu Kabubi wondered:

> How can that be taught when it is not preserved? The history of Mau Mau should be properly kept and relevant materials should be published. Only then will people appreciate what Mau Mau did for Kenya. (Shamsul Alam 2007: 98)

Diverse sections of the population are keen to have Mau Mau publicly recognized. In August 2013, some secondary school and college students participating in the annual national music festival focused their compositions on its uncelebrated, neglected, unsung heroes. In the songs they urged the government to 'reward those who liberated the country from British colonial rule' (*Daily Nation*, 12 August 2013). Once dubbed terrorists, rebels, retrogressive and barbaric, veterans feel somewhat vindicated. Wambuga Nyingi, who testified against Britain, observed:

> The most important thing for me is that they [The British government] have acknowledged that we were not rebels – we were freedom fighters. That's what matters ... Britain's decision to compensate thousands of Kenyans who were tortured during an anti-colonial uprising in the 1950s is important because it re-writes the history books. (Al Jazeera, 7 June 2013)

The recent constitutional review process provided a space for conversation about Mau Mau veterans. Fearful of Mau Mau's erasure from national memory, Grace Wanjiku Njuki observed:

> Let us step back into the past. There are those who fought for the independence of this country ... that is why we constantly remember them in prayers. Sometimes I look back and wonder whether people ask themselves about where our country came from. Those people who helped us get here were called Mau Mau. Those are the people who are finished today. Those who live in abject poverty. Others are spirits [dead] ... others are only known by their children. I want the new constitution to remember the Mau Mau who brought us where we are. (Kabira 2012: 173)

On the dire plight of freedom fighters and the marginalized masses, Field Marshal Muthoni expressed her disappointment thus: 'Dear Lord, is this what we fought for and went naked for? Went without food! We used to crawl like hunted animals because we couldn't walk. Yes! And this freedom is being played with' (quoted in Mugo 2004: 22).

While the Kenyan public agonizes and contests the nature of nationalism in colonial Kenya, academics are nowhere near agreement on how to read and interpret Mau Mau, and its relationship to nationalism. Described as a multipronged process that resulted from the confluence of disparate players including the Kikuyu, Embu, Meru freedom fighters, the elite, earlier prenationalist ethnic political operatives and the nebulous all-inclusive category embracing the whole colonized population, nationalism remains a troubled category in Kenya's postcolonial history (Atieno-Odhiambo and Lonsdale 2003). Atieno-Odhiambo expressed the dilemma in defining nationalism in

Kenya by concluding that decisions had yet to be made, 'whether we want to maintain the idea of nationalism, rework it, revolutionize it, or cast it aside'. Only then, according to Atieno-Odhiambo, would it be possible to 'write the appropriate history of the state and of the nation' (Atieno-Odhiambo 2003: 45). At the centre of the controversy is the role that Mau Mau played in the attainment of independence, and how to apportion credit between an increasingly widening circle of players in the nationalist and decolonizing process, including Mau Mau veterans.

## What of the Loyalists?

The continuing dominance of loyalists in the political, economic and social domains is a constant thorn in the flesh of veterans. Loyalists perpetuated the trauma of Mau Mau, yet they continue to lead prosperous and successful public lives, they and their well-educated and wealthy offspring (Branch 2009: 148–207). They are seen to reap where they did not sow, while veterans who risked and lost everything in the struggle languish in poverty. In this regard, independent Kenya is held guilty. As one female ex-combatant recently observed regarding Kenya's failure to implement Mau Mau ideals, especially with regard to the redistribution of land: 'I was very disappointed. It was like a football game where after the victory the players are not rewarded. It was the spectators who got the rewards and the benefits' (Shamsul Alam 2007: 97; see also Kinyatti 2009). In 2012 Jane Muthoni said:

> The white man must have contracted someone to beat us. That man now lives along [near] the path we walked along today. He is written about somewhere, where people read [about?] him. What would I say to him after he tortured us like that? We were ordered to lie down or pile up on top of each other, at least five people. Then he would pass through our legs where they would do bad things. They would whip us from the first to the last and then back again ... and other things that are not good.

Living in close proximity to their aggressors, veterans relive their traumatic past daily. Some loyalists were themselves victims of Mau Mau attacks. Mau Mau fighters waged brutal attacks on fellow Kikuyu known for or suspected of opposition to Mau Mau. Chiefs, Christians, home-guards and their loyalist wives were obvious targets. In addition, whites, especially settler families on isolated farms, were also targeted and killed. A truth and reconciliation commission might ease the tension and facilitate the production of a more balanced history of the period. In participating in the lawsuit against the British government, Jane Muthoni was in the early stages of getting her story heard and chronicled. Unlike her loyalist detractor whose story was etched in history in some text, magazine or newspaper, she had been muted for many decades by various forces.

## Mau Mau Women and Feminism

The need for a feminist theoretical framework for analysis of female veterans' history has been raised (Mugo 2004: 9). In many parts of Africa, women who participated in liberation struggles were fighting two colonialisms, a foreign power and local patriarchy (Urdang 1979). Mau Mau women were aware of gender-specific grievances against the colonial government on the one hand, and local patriarchy on the other. Their participation in the struggle called for a drastic redefinition of their relationship with their male guerrilla compatriots. Refusing to be relegated to the domestic sphere in civil society, women in the forest demanded to be included in all organs of the movement, including decision-making processes. The women pushed the men to reform the rules guiding recruitment and promotion in the liberation army. Acting as judges, participating in dual-sex decision-making councils exclusive to the Mau Mau period, and engaging in military combat alongside men were all unprecedented and had to be negotiated from a reluctant patriarchy whose cultural practices and social construction of women reduced women to subordinate status devoid of public power or authority.[9] The current struggle against gender-specific grievances and the call for equality was preceded by the actions of an earlier generation of women. Mau Mau women took the leviathan by the horns. Unfortunately, in Kenya, as in other liberation struggles in Africa, any holes punched in the patriarchal system were short-lived (Mugo 2004: 26–27).

While Mau Mau women received little or no ideological training, they had lived the colonial experience and knew the jarring tensions, conflicts and exploitation that colonialism generated. Colonialism was highly gendered; this was clearly evident in women's activism in the 1920s, 30s and 40s in colonial Kenya. In the 1920s, women who were forced into working on settler plantations were victims of rape as they travelled long distances to and from work. The 1922 Harry Thuku-Mary Nyanjiru protest was partly exacerbated by women's determination to free Thuku, a young politician who among other things was an ardent spokesman for women. In the 1940s, women confronted the colonial government as a result of unpopular and obligatory soil conservation tasks which imposed much-detested communal chores on women, increasing their workload and detracting them from their regular productive and reproductive responsibilities. The resultant protests preceded women's participation in the liberation war beginning in 1952 (Kanogo 1987b: 81–85).

Thus, Mau Mau women drew from a long tradition of female resistance in Kenya. Mekatilili wa Menza, Mary Nyanjiru, Prophetess Moraa, Ciokaraine, among others, represent women of great valour (Njau and Maluki 1984, vol. 1), as do women who took different sides in the clitoridectomy controversy (Kanogo 2005: 73–103; Njoroge 2000; Thomas 2003: 79–102).

## Mau Mau Women and other Kenyan Women

Likewise, for the modern woman, the 2010 constitutional review was the culmination of a long process of female resistance: demonstrations, petitions, civic education and public and personal struggles, all of which fell on deaf legislative, executive and legal ears. Stifling patriarchal and undemocratic processes marginalized women in the colonial and postcolonial periods. Increasingly, the modern Kenyan woman acknowledges the trailblazing role of female Mau Mau combatants who paved the way for challenging the status quo. Not satisfied with the results of their anticolonial struggle, veteran septuagenarians, octogenarians and nonagenarians continue their struggle for change.

Kenyan women have taken great strides in seeking and gaining some access to legislative and administrative offices. As well as forty-seven female parliamentarians representing women in the forty-seven counties, the constitution provides for sixteen female party nominees. The constitution also states that public elective and appointed positions should not include more than two thirds of either gender. These provisions promise greater equity for women. The small successes that Mau Mau women achieved in the forest have been multiplied many times over. There does seem to be a greater appreciation now of female veterans for their earlier efforts at weakening, if not dismantling the patriarchal mantle.

This recent victory is the culmination of a vigorous civic campaign that began in the late 1980s, but it can also be linked to earlier anticolonial and immediate postcolonial women's movements that strove for social, economic and political change and equity (Nzomo 1997a, 1997b and 1992; Kabira and Nzioki 1993). Concerned with good governance and a comprehensive overhaul of institutional bad practices, the struggle began with the basic call for the mainstreaming of women into the political and policy decision-making machinery. The call for women's inclusion and participation in the political process was only rivalled by the need for economic self-sufficiency. These are concerns that have remained important to female ex-combatants. Female ownership and inheritance of property (especially land), the elimination of gender-based violence, the securing of children's rights, access to credit, the inception of youth programmes, provision of adequate educational facilities, honouring freedom fighters (including female ex-combatants) and the memorialization of ex-combatants, were all articulated by women during the constitutional review process (Kabira 2012).

Female ex-combatants have been part of this great debate that has sought to advance the empowerment of the Kenyan woman. In participating in the constitutional review process, they underscored their unfinished agenda and the need to persist in the struggle. These women anticipated and continue to expect an equitable, democratic and dignified livelihood in postcolonial Kenya.

## Conclusion

The Mau Mau movement was proscribed in 1950. Although Kenya gained independence in 1963, the movement remained banned till 2003 when President Mwai Kibaki allowed it to register as a lawful society. Though fazed by the negative, contested, and at times ambiguous imagery of Mau Mau, its veterans and supporters remain committed to its original objectives. Asked whether Mau Mau was a failure, Anna Wamuyu Kabubi says:

> No, it was not a failure. It accomplished what it aimed for; to kick the colonialists out, and it did that. Unfortunately all the [other] ideals on which Mau was fought for did not materialize ... [T]he government posts [sh]ould have been filled by the patriots who fought for independence, not by loyalists who collaborated with the British. (Shamsul Alam 2007: 97)

At independence, the reins of power were passed on to a new crop of African elites who espoused a moderate constitutionalist approach to the politics of the day. Veterans, the bulk of whom were either semi-literate or illiterate, were left out of the bureaucratic and political set-up.

Asking the postcolonial governments to recognize the veterans, Anna Wamuyu also pleads for:

> [A] Mau Mau museum and monuments for a movement that 'paved the way to independence and created the condition of freedom that all Kenyans enjoy today'. (Shamsul Alam 2007: 97)

Wamuyu, along with other veterans, is calling for a rewriting of Kenya's history. As to the future, it is too early to determine whether the large cohort of women who have become involved in national and local decision-making machinery will be instrumental in meaningful changes in the lives of all women, including those of female veterans.[10] Female veterans constitute a rapidly disappearing group. Their days for social action are very limited. Those remaining are hopeful for a more equitable nation.

## Notes

1. Children of veterans are beginning to write their parents' stories. See for example, Berewa Jommo, 'Sarai: Pioneer Nurse and Freedom Fighter'. *Daily Nation*, 14 August 2013. This is a newspaper serialization of a forthcoming book.
2. For a discussion of women in the Mau Mau liberation war, see Likimani 1985; Kanogo 1987b; and Presley 1992.
3. Total equality, as claimed by Field Marshal Muthoni, is questionable. Mugo proposes the possibility of self-silencing on the part of female veterans due to loyalty to the movement's oaths, which makes it difficult for the women to criticize the movement (Mugo 2004: 24). See also Ardener 2005: 50–54.
4. *The Last Battle* (www.youtube.com/watch?v=xEwOICbKXcw). Victims of colonial torture during Mau Mau recall their ordeals in this recent documentary.
5. Paulo Nzili and Ndiku Mutua narrated their castration ordeal to Gemma Gander, the film maker of *The Last Battle* (Al Jazeera, 23 May 2013).
6. 'Scramble for Mau Mau Billions', in *The Nairobi Law Monthly 4(5), June 2013.*
7. Declaration on the Elimination of Violence against Women, Article 1, 1993: A/RES/48/104 Convention on the Elimination of All Forms of Discrimination Against Women (CEDAW)
8. The late veteran Wanjiru Nyamarutu mobilized women in Nakuru to buy land through the Nyakinyua women's group. Personal communication, 1984.
9. For a discussion on the legal status of women in colonial Kenya, see Kanogo 2005: 15–41.
10. The diversity of Kenyan women was especially evident in earlier stages of the constitutional review process. See Mutua 2006.

## Bibliography

Al Jazeera. 2013. 'Kenyans Celebrate Mau Mau Compensation Win', 7 June.

Anderson, D. 2005. *Histories of the Hanged: The Dirty War in Kenya and the End of Empire.* W.W. Norton.

Ardener, S. 2005. Ardener's '"Muted Groups": The Genesis of an Idea and its Praxis' in *Women and Language* 28(2): 50–54.

Atieno-Odhiambo, E.S. and J. Lonsdale (eds). 2003. *Mau Mau and Nationhood: Arms, Authority, and Narration.* Oxford: James Currey; Nairobi: EAEP; Athens: Ohio University Press.

Atieno-Odhiambo, E.S. 'Matunda ya Uhuru, Fruits of Independence', in E.S. Atieno-Odhiambo and J. Lonsdale (eds). 2003. *Mau Mau and Nationhood: Arms, Authority, and Narration.* Oxford: James Currey; Nairobi: EAEP; Athens: Ohio University Press.

Baaz, M.E. and M. Stern (eds.) 2013. *Sexual Violence as a Weapon of War? Perceptions, Prescriptions, Problems in the Congo and Beyond.* London: Zed Books.

Barnett, D. and K. Njama. 1966. *Mau Mau from Within: An Analysis of Kenya's Peasant Revolt.* Macgibbon & Kee.

Branch, D. 2009. *Defeating Mau Mau, Creating Kenya: Counterinsurgency, Civil War, and Decolonization.* Cambridge: Cambridge University Press.

Brett, E.A. 1973. *The Politics of Economic Change, 1919–1939.* London: Heinemann.

Clough, M.S. 2003. 'Mau Mau & the Contest of Memory' in E.S. Atieno-Odhiambo and J. Lonsdale (eds), *Mau Mau and Nationhood: Arms, Authority, and Narration.* Athens: Ohio University Press.

*Daily Nation.* 2013. 'Ex-freedom Fighters' Plight Dominates Fete', 12 August.

Davison, J. 1988. 'Who Owns What' in J. Davison (ed.), *Agriculture, Women and Land: The African Experience.* Boulder, CO: Westview.

de Brouwer, A.-M. and S. Ka Hon Chu (eds). 2009. *The Men Who Killed Me: Rwandan Survivors of Sexual Violence.* Vancouver: Douglas & McIntyre.

Elkins, C. 2005. *Imperial Reckoning: The Untold Story of Britain's Gulag in Kenya.* Owl Books.

Gander, J. 2013. 'Film Maker's View', Al Jazeera, 23 May.

Itote, W. 1967. *Mau Mau General.* Nairobi: East Africa Publishing House.

Kabira, W.M. and E.A. Nzioki. 1993. *Celebrating Women's Resistance: A Case Study of Women's Groups Movement in Kenya.* African Women's Perspective.

Kabira, W.M. 2012. *Time for Harvest: Women and Constitution Making in Kenya.* Nairobi: University of Nairobi Press.

Kanogo, T. 1987a. *Squatters and the Roots of Mau Mau: 1905–1963.* Athens: Ohio University Press.

——. 1987b. 'Kikuyu Women and the Politics of Protest: Mau Mau', in S. Macdonald, P. Holden and S. Ardener, *Images of Women in Peace & War: Cross-Cultural & Historical Perspectives.* London: Macmillan.

——. 2005. *African Womanhood in Colonial Kenya, 1900–1950.* Oxford: James Currey; Nairobi: EAEP; Athens: Ohio University Press.

——. 2011. *Field Marshal Dedan Kimathi Wachiuri.* Nairobi: East African Educational Publishers.

Karani, R.W. 2005. *Field Marshall Muthoni: Mau Mau Heroine.* Nairobi: Sasa Sema Publications.

Kariuki, J.M. 1976. *Mau Mau Detainee.* Oxford: Oxford University Press.

Kinyatti, M.W. 2009. *Mau Mau: A Revolution Betrayed.* BookSurge.

Leo, C. 1984. *Land and Class in Kenya.* Toronto; Buffalo: Toronto University Press.

Likimani, M. 1985. *Passbok Number F.47927: Women and Mau Mau in Kenya*. London: Macmillan Publishers Ltd.

Mugo, M.G. 2004. *Muthoni wa Kirima, Mau Mau Woman Field Marshal: Interrogation of Silencing, Erasure and Manipulation of Female Combatants' Texts*. Harare: Sapes Books.

Mutua, A.D. 2006. 'Gender Equality and Women's Solidarity across Religious, Ethnic and Class Differences in the Kenyan Constitutional Review Process.' *William and Mary Journal of Women and the Law* 13(1): 1–106.

Njagi, D. 1991. *The Last Mau Mau Field Marshals: (Kenya's Freedom War 1952–1963 and Beyond): Their Own Story*. Meru, Kenya: Ngwataniro Self Help Group.

Njau, R. and G. Maluki. 1984. *Kenya Women Heroes and Their Mystical Power*, vol. 1. Nairobi: Risk Publications.

Njoroge, N.J. 2000. *Kiama Kia Ngo. An African Christian Feminist Ethic of Resistance and Transformation*. Legon, Ghana: Legon Theological Studies Series Project.

Nzomo, M. 1992. 'Beyond Structural Adjustment Program: Gender Equity and Development in Africa, With Special Reference to Kenya' in J. Nyangoro and T. Shaw (eds), *Beyond Structural Adjustment in Africa: The Political Economy of Sustainable and Democratic Development*, pp. 99–117. New York: Praeger.

———. 1997a. *The Gender Dimension of Electoral Politics in Kenya: Capacity Building of Women Candidates for 1997 and Beyond*. Nairobi: Friedrich Ebert Stiftung.

———. 1997b. 'Kenyan Women in Politics and Public Decision Making,' in G. Mikell, *African Feminism*. Philadelphia: University of Pennsylvania Press.

Ogude, J. 2003. 'The Nation & Narration: The Truths of the Nation and the Changing Image of Mau Mau in Kenyan Literature' in E.S. Atieno-Odhiambo and J. Lonsdale (eds), *Mau Mau and Nationhood: Arms, Authority, and Narration*. Oxford; Nairobi; Athens: James Currey.

Otieno, W.W. 2002. *Mau Mau's Daughter: A Life History*. Boulder, CO: Lynne Rienner.

Presley, C.A. 1992. *Kikuyu Women, the Mau Mau Rebellion, and Social Change in Kenya*. Boulder, CO: Westview.

Rosberg, C. and J. Nottingham. 1966. *The Myth of Mau Mau: Nationalism in Kenya*. New York: Praeger.

Sandgren, D.P. 2012. *Mau Mau's Children: The Making of Kenya's Postcolonial Elite*. Madison, WI: University of Wisconsin Press.

Shamsul Alam, S.M. 2007. *Rethinking the Mau Mau in Colonial Kenya*. Palgrave.

Sorrenson, M.P.K. 1967. *Land Reform in Kikuyu Country*. Oxford: Oxford University Press.

*The Guardian*. 2012. 'Mau Mau Veterans Win Right to Sue British Government', 5 October.

*The Guardian*. 2012. 'Kenyan Torture Victims Give Evidence in High Court Compensation Case', 17 July.

*The Last Battle*: www.youtube.com/watch?v=xEwOICbKXcw.

Thomas, L. 2003. *Politics of the Womb: Women, Reproduction, and the State in Kenya*. Berkeley: University of California Press.

Urdang, S. 1979. *Fighting Two Colonialisms: Women in Guinea-Bissau*. Monthly Review Press.

**Tabitha Kanogo** is a professor of African history at the University of California, Berkeley. She is the author of *Squatters and the Roots of Mau Mau 1905–1963*, *African Womanhood in Colonial Kenya 1900–1950*, and *Makers of Kenya's History: Field Marshall Dedan Kimathi Wachiuri*.

# 5

# Women and Conflict in Burma's Borderlands

## Mandy Sadan

## Women and the Burmese State

Since 2012, there has been a renewed focus on Burma (Myanmar) in the international media. The release of Daw Aung San Suu Kyi from house arrest and her subsequent entry into the newly convened national parliament along with other members of her party, the National League for Democracy (NLD), suggested that considerable progress had been made in the political transformation of the country. This follows decades of oppressive military rule following General Ne Win's takeover of power in 1962 (Steinberg 2013; Smith 1999). These recent changes have been remarkable for their relative speed, and have had a marked effect upon the willingness of Western governments to consider new engagements with the formerly pariah-like country. For those who have supported Daw Suu Kyi's activities over the years, seeing her become Burma's first woman president would be an appropriate outcome for this particular political drama. Yet Burma still faces considerable internal difficulties and the direction of travel for the country's political system is not yet clear. Key concerns, such as the role of the military in Burma's political life and the relationship of the Burman-majority heartland to its multiple peripheries, are still contested. Both issues have the power to destabilize fragile developments that have yet to acquire deep roots.

The same uncertainty might also be said to apply to transformations in the status of women in Burma's public life. The ubiquity of Daw Aung San Suu Kyi as a symbol for apparently substantive political change might suggest that gender equality is relatively well developed in Burma, perhaps being further supported and strengthened by recent events. However, this would be a misconception. Daw Suu Kyi's family history facilitated the public recognition she received when she decided to enter the political maelstrom enveloping the country in 1988 and it continues to enhance her status (Popham 2012). She is the daughter of the country's nationalist hero General Aung San, who is credited with paving the way for the independence of Burma before his assassination in 1947 (see Figure 5.1). While Burma has ratified the international convention on the elimination of all forms of discrimination against women (CEDAW), the entrenched militarization of the political system, which the current constitution also reinforces, ensures that gender issues are generally not held in high regard in public discourse. Indeed, the well-known human rights activist Ma Thida has recently commented that women remain largely invisible despite their important contributions, particularly to political and social activism. Furthermore, she sees women as being poorly represented in public bodies and suffering from discrimination arising from the dominance of Theravada Buddhist beliefs, which construct a cosmological order that assigns women a lower social place than it does for men.[1]

Beyond the central heartland of Burma, the roles of women in the social, economic and political life of the country are also 'invisible'. Indeed, these so-called 'ethnic minority' women may be considered doubly distanced from the national conscience. While Burmese women are sidelined by the dominant patriarchy of military rule and Theravada cultural attitudes, they are nonetheless recognized in the prevailing nationalist discourse as mothers, as homemakers and as a source of moral strength and piety (Harriden 2011; Ikeya 2011; Than 2011, 2013). They are assigned a supporting yet recognizable role in the narration of nationalist Burma's history.[2] Those women who identify themselves as being of non-Burman descent, and who may adhere to faiths other than Buddhism, are scarcely acknowledged as contributors to 'the nation' at all. Indeed, they are ascribed a role rather as victims, not least of the politically naïve and violence-prone male elites from within their own communities who founded a plethora of oppositional armed groups seeking to overturn the national government, as will be shown.

The best way to envisage the ideological construction of the male authority of the Burmese state as protector, and its relationship to non-Burmese women in particular, is by considering an iconic photograph of

General Aung San with a group of ethnic minority Kachin women taken in December 1946 (see Figure 5.1). This image was taken when discussions were underway between Aung San's nationalist party, which was hoping to become the national government of independent Burma, and local Kachin political elites, over whether an autonomous Kachin State could be created as part of the new nation. This was negotiated as a tool for achieving speedy independence from the British, which was obtained in 1948 (Walton 2008; Yawnghwe and Sakhong 2002; Smith 1999). The Kachin political elites (all male) with whom Aung San was negotiating were nonetheless wary in 1946 of the longer-term political ambitions of the Burmese nationalist movement. They were concerned that a much more powerful Burmese neighbour with a strong army would inevitably dominate the new union to their disadvantage and would subsume them following independence. Their fears proved justified. By the 1960s, armed rebellion consumed all the border states, including that of the Kachin region (Smith 1999; Sadan 2013a).

However, this image has attained an important status in the iconography of Burmese nationalist history subsequently; one almost never sees photographs of Aung San with ethnic minority male politicians, while this image carries the burden of expressing the ideological orientations of the Burmese state to its 'minorities' and is endlessly reproduced. The Burmese state is here visualized as the central, protective, patriarchal father figure, alone capable of bringing unity to the divided nation, while its peripheral regions are feminized as dependent and subordinate. On a further level, ethnic minority women themselves are protected by the virile maleness of the militarized Burmese state, while their own men are removed from the visual record. These male sub-national elites have long been presented as being inherently lacking in political skills and bereft of political insight. They are accused of failing to appreciate that their place was within a strong state with a centralized Burmese core (Silverstein 1956). The notion of ethnic minority women as victims, not of a Burmese state but of the misguided violence of male militarization in their own societies, has become part of the complex ideological contest that has been played out over several decades between Burmese nationalism and a host of sub-national armed movements.[3] The outcome has been that ethnic minority women, even more than Burmese women, when visible, are deemed to have had a passive or victim-like role in the history of conflict in the post-independence state, not even making a moral or nurturing contribution to nationhood within the wider nationalist narrative due to their multiple experiences of marginalization.

**Figure 5.1** General Aung San with Kachin women in 1946. This has become an iconic image, often used to represent visually the ideological conception of supposedly harmonious ethnic relations to which Burmese nationalists claim to aspire.

## Histories of Conflict

Yet the societies in which ethnic minority women live have been equally subjected to dominant patriarchal narratives directed towards opposing the nationalism of the Burmese state. The narrative of how some of those conflicts emerged is broadly as follows: immediately after independence from the British in 1948, a quasi-federal constitution was instituted, which gave some autonomy to key regions at the peripheries of the new Burmese nation. Previously some of these regions had been administered as Excluded and Scheduled Areas by the British administration, reflecting their historical autonomy from the old Burmese kingships. However, the agreements that led to the federalized union in 1948, and the constitution that implemented their vision, were hastily put together and, as noted, mainly had the intention of bringing about independence for the whole of the country more quickly than if the various peripheral regions had sought separate, alternative arrangements with the fading colonial power, such as Dominion Status.

Following independence, therefore, some areas, previously felt historically distinct and autonomous, became incorporated within the territorial boundaries of the Union of Burma. These non-Burmese constituencies, guided by their local political elites, took it in good faith that the new federal underpinnings of the nation would prevent their distinctive languages, cultures and histories from being overwhelmed by assertive Burmese expansionism. It was also hoped that variations in economic development would be flattened while the regions would retain a good deal of internal political control over their own affairs. All of the peripheral regions of the country shared similar hopes and expectations for what independence might bring in this respect.

Yet these aspirations could not override the weaknesses of the new Burmese state, itself wracked by internal political divisions at its centre, by economic crisis and by the increasingly violent eruptions of communist expansion and Kuomintang incursions across its lengthy borders to the east. Against this chaotic internal and external background, the aspiration for democracy and the hope that federalism would protect regional autonomies was soon crushed. An aggressively territorializing militarized Burmese state was ushered in following military coups in the early 1960s.

It is against this background that violence commenced in the Kachin State in 1961, when the Kachin Independence Army (KIA) was founded. Although the KIA started as a relatively small group of fewer than a hundred individuals, it expanded rapidly through voluntary and forced recruitment to become one of the largest, best organized and well-armed of Burma's multiple 'insurgent' armies, also having a relatively high degree of popular support for its actions. Furthermore, it also had from the outset a parallel civil wing, the Kachin Independence Organization (KIO). Together, the KIA and KIO established a system of alternative governance in areas that came under their control during decades of conflict. Although directed towards armed revolt and not development, these local structures of militarism and governance coupled with a strong social belief in the region's historical and cultural distinctiveness made the Kachin region a difficult one for the Burmese state to incorporate.

The Kachin conflict has not been static in its goals, being transformed by local experiences over the longer term as well as by changing geopolitical influences within the wider region as a whole. However, the constant thread connecting the various phases of violence has been the demand of ethno-nationalist elites in this region for greater autonomy and more equitable patterns of economic development. As a resource-rich but infrastructure-poor area, the Kachin State has been subject to peripheralization by mainstream political and economic developments in Burma from the colonial period onwards. The gains made by extraction companies of a variety of national origins are a potent symbol of both ongoing economic disparities and the lack of political means to correct the imbalance (Woods 2010, 2011a, 2011b).

Violence continued until 1994 when a ceasefire was signed with the Burma Army, although the inherent fragility of this agreement was demonstrated in 2011 when it collapsed. It collapsed in part because of the steady erosion of local belief in the idea that the national government was sincere in its claims that the ceasefire was truly a means of bringing real political change, which might restore greater autonomy to the region. When the Burma Army launched an attack on KIA positions in June 2011, the balance of suspicion tipped too far and hostilities resumed. At the time of writing, the situation remains one of occasional negotiations peppered by active hostility, with frequent firefights between KIA and *Tatmadaw* or Burma Army troops. Ongoing attempts to negotiate another ceasefire are taking place, not least because China has also expressed concern about the instability that is spilling across the border. The perceived lack of willingness by the Burmese government to put concrete political proposals on the table as part of the negotiation process convinces Kachin politicians that merely signing another agreement will not bring about the substantive political changes in the governance of this region for which many have fought and sacrificed for such a long time. The resulting return to violence has seen tens of thousands of local people being displaced to hastily-erected refugee camps along the politically charged borderline with China. It is a poignant reminder that, when one extends the range of vision to include areas beyond the national urban centres of political life, the situation remains fragmented, brittle and volatile.

## Women, Conflict and Frameworks of Representation

For many years when international access to the country was tightly regulated and movement into and out of the country was restricted, representations of conflict in Burma's ethnic nationality states tended to interact with those created by democracy activist groups and NGOs of both foreign and Burmese origin. Some of the most important of these groups, until recent changes permitted NGOs to move into Burma, were based across the border in Thailand. These Thai-based groups were typically established to service, support and monitor the often vast refugee camps and settlements that the Thai authorities permitted to contain the flow of forced migration from the war-torn eastern states of her troubled neighbour.[4] The reports and documentation produced by these groups have not been oblivious to the burdens that women have endured as manifold conflicts have extended across decades and generations. Women's groups have also been active, vocal and visible in these cross-border areas in recent years, especially in

Thailand. External funding bodies often influence this outcome, having political agendas that frequently impose demands for the recognition of 'women's rights' as a condition of grant making. Nonetheless, the resulting representations of women in conflict zones in Burma have almost invariably been focused towards making generalized demands for political change in the national system.[5] As such, they have perhaps inadvertently tended to emphasize the passive role of women and their victimhood, homogenizing the experience of 'ethnic minority' women. While there are some thought-provoking and insightful reports about women's experiences, the main focus has been upon their sexual victimization, emphasizing a lack of control or agency in the intricate political and economic entanglements of conflict. Horrific instances of rape and sexual mutilation that have occurred in some areas by poorly disciplined soldiers in the Burma Army, for example, have acquired international attention through the careful yet overtly politicized advocacy work of international activist organizations.[6] The intention of this emphasis is to hold up a mirror to the oppressive force of a hostile national political regime. Rarely do these reports address wider questions of gender relations. In recent years, few if any groups have made claims for changes in gender relations as a prerequisite for political transformations within the state. The violence-prone centre-periphery dynamics define the frames of reference.

In the area in which I research, the Kachin region, the ethno-nationalist movement also pays no real attention to the internal dynamics of 'Kachin' gender relations. There is scant if any discussion of how these relations may have been affected by years of militarized violence more generally. There are complex social codes of sexual conduct within 'Kachin' society, yet the occurrence of sexual violence against women within their own communities is an issue that is relatively ignored. This seems partly to be a result of the dominant, overarching discourse of unifying communities against an 'external' threat. This constrains such discussions in the public domain because of the fear that it may lead to fissures within their own communities. In addition, how militarized ethno-nationalist organizations manage sexual discipline within mixed-sex ranks is just one area of discussion that is deemed not for public scrutiny. In short, aside from ascribing sexual violence as a mode of conduct by the Burma Army in the rhetoric (and sadly often the experience) of ethno-nationalist resistance, gender issues remain a problematic domain of internal debate. When discussing the wider social aims and agendas of armed movements, 'the gender turn' is most definitely an absent paradigm.[7]

In fact, women have played a long and important role in multiple conflicts spanning many decades. Not least, women were incorporated into the armed ethno-nationalist movement from its earliest days. For example, the early KIA included female members, such as Na Hpaw Kaw Mai, the wife of one of the early leaders of the KIO, Maran Brang Seng. Women in the ranks of the KIA/KIO did not carry arms but provided logistical functions, made uniforms, worked as cipher operators, medical staff and so on. Recruitment was similar for men and women. The Kachin Women's Association (KWA) would enlist women and provide training, at the end of which an oath of loyalty would be taken, as would happen with male soldiers in the KIA and recruits to the KIO. The oaths would bind the oath-taker to a lifelong commitment to the Kachin ethno-nationalist movement. From the earliest days of resistance to the Burmese regime, therefore, women identifying as 'Kachin' could be recruited into the movement, as could men. Indeed, the main unit of recruitment was the family, and each household was expected to provide at least one son or daughter to fight for the cause (Sadan 2010, 2013a). Women were clearly far more involved in the conflicts as actors than has previously been acknowledged.

In recent years, the role of women within the wider society has become a focus of concern and interest, although as noted it does not penetrate deeply into the social conscience of the nationalist movement as yet. This pressure has started to emanate especially from well-organized women's civil society organizations associated with church groups and the like. The international recognition given to the remarkable civil role played by Lahpai Seng Raw, winner of the 2013 Ramon Magsaysay Award,[8] has also shone an effective light upon this disparity between women's formal and informal roles, and the gendered disparity within the political and military structures of Kachin resistance. For example, there has only been one woman member of the Central Committee of the Kachin Independence Organisation (KIO), Na Hpaw Kaw Mai, and there is an apparent reluctance to address this as a matter of real concern among the KIO's core elite to this day.[9] Instead, the Kachin Women's Association is assigned a distinct but subordinate status, running parallel to the central committee structure but not integrated into it. Yet there are increasing requests for greater representation of Kachin women in the formal structures of the KIO among some groups of young, urban Kachin women. Their demands also seem to reflect that the KWO is seen as a social organization of relevance to the wider society, often being called upon to adjudicate in disputes over land and other issues in local areas. Nonetheless, there is an apparent resistance even among many young, educated Kachin men to think through in serious ways the construction of gendered politics in their own society, some even accusing foreign funders of forcing this agenda upon them in recent years.

My own observation of attitudes within urban Kachin society to the recent resumption of violence has been that women have been vital as supporters of renewed KIO military and political endeavours. This engagement crosses generations and follows a period when there was a pronounced tendency among the urban Kachin populace in particular to express their disillusionment with the policy of the KIA/KIO.[10] This recent support may seem surprising, given that the escalation of violence now is against a Burma Army that is in fact much stronger than that with which a ceasefire was signed in 1994. However, that women of all generations are actively involved in the social support structures of the renewed conflict is obvious to any observer. In addition, mobilizing responses to the plight of thousands of internally displaced people has relied in very public ways on the active willingness of young Kachin women, as well as those of older generations, both politically and socially to provide logistical support for the refugee camps.

The return to violence has also seen young Kachin women becoming more visible internationally in their advocacy work.[11] In many respects, this reflects the greater social and educational mobility of young, urban Kachin women since the liberalization of Burma's economy from the late 1980s and the ceasefire period that followed. Young women have been able to re-enter the national higher education system, or access educational and work opportunities abroad. Locally, some have become more mobile through greater access to personal transportation, such as motorbikes for example, which have transformed the capacity of women and girls even of a young age to move around urban and peri-urban areas for work, education and social life in a more independent way. However, understanding how women across generations are repositioning this longer-term experience in relation to current violence becomes explicable only if we can understand the deeper and broader roles that women have played in this region during decades of war (Sadan 2014). The desire to fill this particular lacuna of knowledge is confronted by the difficulties of how one might possibly hope to do so in a setting that has experienced such traumatic upheaval over so many years. The rest of this chapter shall consider some of the prospects and challenges that such an undertaking might address.

## Understanding Gendered Histories of Conflict in the Kachin Region

There are some threads of a herstory that can be teased out straightforwardly in this setting. Despite the lack of a coherent historical record,[12] it seems that a common gendered narrative around women's roles may be unfolding. For example, when asking questions about the impact of conflict on women's roles historically, the reactivation of the colonial era Unlawful Associations Act is often cited as a historical marker of general significance. This act was used to criminalize Kachin men as a group, and local women state that 'The act made it more difficult for women who now had to take on many more activities outside the home'.[13] This act stated that:

> 17. (1) Whoever is a member of an unlawful association, or takes part in meetings of any such association, or contributes or receives or solicits any contribution for the purpose of any such association or in any way assists the operations of any such association, shall be punished with imprisonment for a term [which shall not be less than two years and more than three years and shall also be liable to fine [sic]].
>
> (2) Whoever manages or assists in the management of an unlawful association, or promotes or assists in promoting a meeting of any such association, or of any members thereof as such members, shall be punished with imprisonment for a term [which shall not be less than three years and more than five years and shall also be liable to fine [sic]].

The militarized government of areas under the control of the Burma Army interpreted this to mean that every Kachin man was potentially actively involved in an unlawful association, not least because recruitment into the KIA was primarily focused towards the family as the provider of recruits. From the perspective of the ethno-nationalist movement this ensured that commitment to the cause was distributed widely through Kachin society. However, it also meant that everyone potentially had a brother or cousin or uncle in the movement and it was widely believed that this act was used to harass all young men by stating that they were by association potentially contributing, receiving or soliciting the unlawful association of the KIA. Kachin women now seem to perceive this act as responsible for creating a new gendered dynamic to the conflict, which affected their lives negatively: 'We had to do everything because if our men tried to travel or to work, they could be arrested.'[14] Due to the Unlawful Associations Act Kachin men, it is claimed, had their economic lives disturbed. They and their families feared that if they travelled between urban centres to conduct their business they could be imprisoned or tortured under the provisions of this law.[15] Consequently, women perceive that they had to take responsibility for running businesses and occupying social and economic spaces that had previously been occupied by men in urban life and in cross-regional trade. The more visible role that women now found themselves playing, especially economically, led many to suffer mistreatment, including sexual violence, by soldiers in the Burma Army. These kinds of concerns established a framework in which women in this region began to interpret their status as political, social and economic actors. For some it resulted in a distrust of the law, the general sentiment being that the law was there not to protect the people, but to oppress them, leading to a distrust of legal processes.

Other narratives that aim to make sense of what has been a chaotic and traumatic period of extended social change have started to take shape. Many of these also reinforce the notion that change experienced even during years of tentative ceasefire has been negative, increasing the burden on women in the region. It became ever more their responsibility to initiate the action that would hold a deteriorating social situation together. At present, the interpretation of the ceasefire is that it seemed only to perpetuate the ongoing unequal political and economic development of the country: Kachin people were subjected to forced manual labour by the Burmese state as porters,[16] youths turned to drugs, women were trafficked into the sex industry and HIV/AIDS became rampant in the region. This is often given as the reason why Christian churches have become, especially for many groups of elderly Kachin women who have lived through many decades of conflict, the main safe places to discuss politics, economics and their general day-to-day experiences. All of these brief narratives suggest the depth and complexity of the ways in which women's lives have been affected by conflict in recent years. Some of these reference points could be used to begin constructing a Kachin herstory of conflict.

However, beyond these representations, we lack detail of the impact of decades of armed conflict on the lives of women. We do not yet understand the social, political, cultural and economic mechanisms by which transformations in gender relations may have occurred. Understanding this over the longer term, and taking into account the great diversity of communities that comprise the general ethnic category 'Kachin', is an enormous challenge. The lack of locally-produced documentation by which one can begin to study how the family unit might have changed within the Kachin region during years of conflict is one problem. Yet without such a descriptive base, it is quite difficult to mark with confidence the parameters from which change and stability, transformation and consolidation can be understood quantitatively. Churches and other organizations have baptismal, marriage and death records, but these are often in a deteriorated condition or are fragmented. However, in terms of providing data about particular kinds of population groups, this might prove to be one way forward in the future. Nonetheless, if one wants to consider the impact of recruitment into ethnonationalist armed forces upon domestic life, it is very difficult to establish a preliminary descriptive base from which one can then develop research questions and test them.

Yet there may be ways to develop our understanding of these issues in the future. Some locally-produced documentation already exists that suggests ways in which this might be achieved. For example, understanding the military heritage of the Kachin region has been a focus of interest by local historians and independent researchers in recent years. Their interests were also encouraged by the reconnections between former soldiers in the Karen and Kachin regions with the Royal Commonwealth Ex-Services League and other veterans' organizations that were made possible following the easing of travel restrictions to the county from the mid-1990s onwards.[17]

Myitkyina was well known to many foreign ex-servicemen, as the town was a vital part of Allied strategy over 'The Hump' between India and China. There are many narratives about these events, of which that by Ian Fellowes-Gordon (1971) is perhaps the most incisive. Following the partial opening-up of Burma to tourist travel in the mid to late 1990s, some former British and American soldiers returned to the town for the first time since the war. They became aware that former volunteers with the Allied forces were still alive, although often impoverished and in need of medical and other support. Some of the U.S. and British servicemen felt they owed a debt of gratitude to these wartime colleagues, who had no entitlement to a pension or financial support from any government. Similar discourses have of course been played out in the UK in relation to Gurkha entitlements of various kinds, which have attracted a lot of publicity in recent years.[18]

In the UK, it was decided to found an organization called the Burma Forces Welfare Association (BFWA), which would raise money to distribute small stipends to those who could demonstrate that they had fought with British forces. This would typically be in the region of £30 to 300, usually as a once-only payment, although further requests for support could be made in cases of severe hardship. As the numbers of those identified as eligible to receive support increased, inevitably this put pressure on BWFA funds, and most grants were towards the lower end of this range. American servicemen established other local development projects, too. In order to facilitate these linkages and control the distribution of stipends, a local research group was formed in Myitkyina, called the Kachin Veterans Committee. The committee was responsible for identifying individuals active with British forces and verifying their claims. The outcome of significance for this chapter, however, is that it resulted in the production of a dataset, which has been used elsewhere to delineate the changing male demographics (by age) of recruits into different military systems crossing the colonial and the early postcolonial periods (Sadan 2013b).

Collecting biographical data to assess the validity of claims for a stipend had two outcomes in relation to bringing women into this otherwise very male-dominated discourse. One outcome was that some local women were identified who had worked as nurses and auxiliaries, who were eligible for stipends in their own right. However, less obviously, the data collection also came to rely upon women's engagement with the research more broadly. Unsurprisingly, many former soldiers and volunteers had long since passed away, but the BFWA was prepared to pay stipends to the surviving widows or widowers, in the case of the living spouses of women nursing auxiliaries and others.[19] The concept of spousal entitlement meant validating spousal relationships. This resulted in detailed data being collected about the age of the spouse, the date at which the husband or wife died, the number of children and their dates of birth. All of this data was included on the forms. Indeed, the number of widows eligible for grants was very large relative to the group as a whole: 66.58 per cent of those providing information and obtaining stipends were widows. The information they provided extended the range of data about the target population significantly. The oldest widow (whose husband first enlisted in the Burma Rifles in 1925) was 104 years old, and the youngest was 38. However, the trimmed mean age of the widows when they applied for the grants was 73.28 years old.[20] In many respects, therefore, we could consider this a women's project, as it was largely the women of the region who were responsible for passing on these histories.

Elsewhere I have used this data to explore connections between different military systems crossing the independence and post-independence period in Burma (Sadan 2013b). This is an important issue because many assumptions about the emergence of militarized resistance to the Burmese state have tended to assume quite linear connections between colonial armies and the emergence of ethno-nationalist armies in the independent state. Yet, for a social historian of conflict, this data raises questions about the form and content of the recruitment data created by groups such as the KIA, and whether it, too, may one day be deployed for such research. When shifting the focus more clearly to the mode by which this data was created, specifically the role of women in mediating knowledge through it about the family unit, it becomes apparent that it may be possible to use similar recruitment data to explore the impact of conflict on families over an extended period, too, not least because KIA documentation reflects the fact that the family is the unit of recruitment. Similar information to that collated by the BWFA and the Veteran's Committee is contained in the recruitment data of modern armed groups. This kind of material has been collated with some care over extended periods in some of the more disciplined and well-organized armed movements. It too, therefore, could prove useful for developing more socially-orientated secondary research in which quantitative social histories about family size, for example, might be considered. Most importantly, it suggests, too, a way of developing descriptive, quantitative research into the period of postcolonial conflict in ways that seem otherwise impervious to study from within the communities who have suffered because of conflict over the years. It is to be hoped that in the future such records may be used to develop a deeper understanding of the social impact of the extended conflict in this region. They may be one means of revealing some of the ways in which recruitment into armed movements has shaped family units, giving us new insights from which we may be able to develop the most appropriate questions about how military structures have affected the roles and lives of different groups of Kachin women. Only then can these important histories be developed from a secure basis of knowledge in which the lives of individuals can be mapped against a broader understanding of historical change connected through multiple cycles of conflict. In this way, the presently unknown histories of women in this region may gradually be revealed. Significantly, too, using the documentation produced by armed groups themselves to address issues of the gendered experience of conflict within families, and particularly how the roles of women have been affected by these histories, may in itself provide the impetus to initiate internal social debates on these issues. Developing understanding of the experiences of conflict beyond a male-dominated perspective must be forthcoming if women are to be given further agency to influence, improve and deepen the engagement with gender politics as the country's constitutional development unfolds.

## Notes

1. http://www.ipsnews.net/2012/05/women-invisible-in-myanmar/ (accessed 1 March 2014).
2. There was also a lively debate within the Burmese nationalist movement from its earliest days, and especially as it reflected upon the status of women in Burma compared to that of India following the introduction of diarchy as a result of the Government of India Act of 1919.
3. The notion that conflict at a general level causes suffering for women, without engaging with the political beliefs and values of women affected was expressed also by Daw Aung San Suu Kyi, who pledged to assist Kachin women in the recent conflict (see http://www.rfa.org/english/news/myanmar/kachin-01222013181938.html/ accessed 2 March 2014). However, this was criticized by Kachin pressure groups and by some Kachin women who felt that she was not engaging with the truly political nature of their experiences. Statements such as "'The responsibility of mothers is to teach their children to love and value peace. This is practical and long-term work,' the Nobel laureate said in her message to the Kachin women" were considered patronizing. See earlier

comments by http://www.huffingtonpost.co.uk/nang-seng/i-feel-betrayed-by-aung-s_b_1924918.html and http://www.kachinnews.com/news/2458-aung-san-suu-kyi-urges-kachin-refugee-women-to-endure-avoids-criticizing-army.html (both accessed 2 March 2014).

4. See for example the important documentation compiled by the Karen Human Rights Group (http://www.khrg.org/ accessed 1 March 2014).

5. Kachin Women's Association of Thailand http://www.opensocietyfoundations. org/voices/women-violence-and-burma-reporting-frontlines-kachin-state (accessed 1 March 2014).

6. The most well known of these in recent years was 'License to Rape: The Burmese Military Regime's Use of Sexual Violence in the Ongoing War in Shan State' published in May 2002 by the Shan Human Rights Foundation (SHRF) and the Shan Women's Action Network (SWAN). It is readily available online, for example at http://www.burmacampaign.org.uk/reports/License_to_rape.pdf (accessed 2 March 2014).

7. My thanks to Dr Maria Jaschok for her engagements with these issues, not least for gathering together a panel to address the lack of a 'gender turn' in Burmese studies generally, that was held at the Southeast Asia Symposium at Keble College on 23 March 2014.

8. See http://www.rmaf.org.ph/newrmaf/main/awardees/awardee/profile/347 (accessed 1 March 2014).

9. My thanks to Na Hpaw Kaw Mai and her family for their generosity in sharing their memories with me, especially in Yingchang in China in 2008.

10. See Kachin Ceasefire Seminar Report at http://soasceasefireseminar.weebly. com/seminar-reportsummary.html

11. Organizations like the Kachin National Organization (KNO) are often very reliant upon the skills of young women to widen their audience and to engage with politicians and lobbyists, such as Kai Htang Lashi in the UK.

12. Interviews with Zau Bug Than, chair of the KIO History Committee in Laiza, April 2008.

13. Kachin woman living in the UK. See also SOAS seminar 'Ceasefire: Reflections on Community, Politics and Social Change in the Kachin Region of Burma (Myanmar), 1994 to the Present', 12 October 2013.

14. Kachin woman living in the UK.

15. http://soasceasefireseminar.weebly.com/seminar-reportsummary.html

16. Armed ethno-nationalist groups would also insist upon forced labour by many communities in areas under their control.

17. Sally Steen is credited with doing much to initiate this new awareness through her activities in the Karen region and in alerting the Royal Commonwealth Ex-Services League, out of which the Burma Forces Welfare Association was established. Subsequently she has set up the charity Hope 4 Forgotten Allies. On the U.S. side, there have been parallel efforts to make reconnections with former volunteers in U.S. organizations.

18. See http://www.gurkhajustice.org.uk/

19. The movie *Burma Victory* shows footage of the field hospital in Myitkyina with local nurses. Produced originally by the British Army Film Unit and Directed by Roy Boulting, it has recently been republished as *Burma Victory: The Forgotten War*, Imperial War Museum Official Collection, London: Imperial War Museum, 2005.
20. All those 48–94 years old = 99.73 per cent of the total for whom there is age data.

## Bibliography

Fellowes-Gordon, I. 1971. *The Battle for Naw Seng's Kingdom: General Stilwell's North Burma Campaign and its Aftermath*. London: Cooper.

Harriden, J. 2011. *The Authority of Influence: Women and Power in Burmese History*. Copenhagen: NIAS Press.

Ikeya, C. 2011. *Refiguring Women, Colonialism, and Modernity in Burma*. Honolulu: University of Hawai'i Press.

Popham, P. 2012. *The Lady and the Peacock: The Life of Aung San Suu Kyi*. London: Rider.

Sadan, M. 2010. 'Syphilis and the Kachin Regeneration Campaign, 1937–38', *Journal of Burma Studies* 14: 115–149

———. 2013a. *Being and Becoming Kachin: Histories beyond the State in the Borderworlds of Burma*. Oxford: The British Academy and Oxford University Press.

———. 2013b. 'Ethnic Armies and Ethnic Conflict in Burma – Reconsidering the History of Colonial Militarisation in the Kachin Region of Burma, 1918–1948', *South East Asia Research* 21(4): 601–626.

———. 2014. 'The Extraordinariness of Ordinary Lives', in W.-C. Chang and E. Tagliacozzo (eds), *Burmese Lives: Ordinary Life Stories under the Burmese Regime*. Oxford and New York: Oxford University Press, pp. 25–52.

Silverstein, J. 1956. 'Politics, Parties and National Elections in Burma', *Far Eastern Survey* 25(12): 177–184.

Smith, M.T. 1999. *Burma: Insurgency and the Politics of Ethnicity*. London: Zed Books.

Steinberg, D. 2013. *Burma/Myanmar: What Everyone Needs to Know*. Oxford and New York: Oxford University Press.

Than, T. 2011. 'Understanding Prostitutes and Prostitution in Democratic Burma, 1942–1962: State Jewels or Victims of Modernity?', *South East Asia Research* 19(3): 537–566.

———. 2013. *Women in Modern Burma*. New York: Routledge.

Walton, M. 2008. 'Ethnicity, Conflict and History in Burma: The Myths of Panglong', *Asian Survey* 48(6): 889–910.

Woods, K. 2010. 'Community Forestry in Cease-Fire Zones in Kachin State, Northern Burma: Formalizing Collective Property in Contested Ethnic Areas', paper presented at the CAPRi Workshop on Collective Action, Property Rights and Conflict in Natural Resources Management, Siem Reap, Cambodia.

———. 2011a. 'Ceasefire Capitalism: Military-Private Partnerships, Resource Concessions and Military State Building in the Burma-China Borderlands', *Journal of Peasant Studies* 38(4): 747–770.

——. 2011b. 'Conflict Timber along the China-Burma Border: Connecting the Global Timber Consumer with Violent Extraction Sites', in E. Tagliacozzo and W.-C. Chang (eds), *Chinese Circulations: Capital, Commodities, and Networks in Southeast Asia*. Durham: Duke University Press.

Yawnghwe, C.-T. and L.H. Sakhong. 2002. *The New Panglong Initiative: Rebuilding the Union of Burma, Peaceful Co-Existence: Towards Federal Union of Burma [Series No.7]*. Chiangmai, Thailand: UNLD Press.

**Mandy Sadan** is a reader in the history of South East Asia and associate dean (research) in the Faculty of Arts and Humanities at SOAS, University of London. She has written widely on ethnic conflict in Burma. Her most recent book is *Being and Becoming Kachin: Histories beyond the State in the Borderlands of Burma*, published by the British Academy and Oxford University Press (2013).

# 6

# Rebuilding Family, Body and Soul

## New Life on the Cambodian Border

### Janette Davies

Between 1975 and 1978 at least two million Cambodians died from starvation, overwork, torture or execution under the regime of Pol Pot in areas of the country now often described as the killing fields. Pol Pot led the left-wing faction Khmer Rouge, 'Red Khmers', which gained control of the country in 1975. Year Zero was declared in that year, when an idealised communist agrarian society was created, while institutions such as banks and religions were crushed. Cities were emptied of their people, who were pushed out to the country for the agrarian reform. Intellectuals and others were executed as they were seen to stand in the way of the agrarian reform. Spectacles were banned as a sign of educated intellectuals. Those who continued to wear them out of necessity were shot on sight or when they were betrayed by informers. The Khmer Rouge was toppled by a Vietnamese invasion in 1978–1979.

In order to put this in the context of the early 1980s and the ongoing occupation of Cambodia by Vietnam that ended in 1989, I will briefly record why I went to the Thai/Cambodian border and will retrace a few steps prior to my work with the Cambodians. Before that I lived and worked as a nurse/midwife for three years in a shanty town (now a suburb) in Cochabamba, Bolivia, named Huayra Khassa, Quechua for 'Windy Crevice'. The Salvation Army, funded by Swedish Aid (SIDA), appointed me to commence a 'Posta Sanitaria' and oversee the successful building of a fully operational maternal child hospital to be run by that International Non-Governmental Organisation (INGO). I was on homeland leave from Bolivia with my mother and family in January 1981 in London, when I was asked in a phone call from the International Medical Adviser to the Salvation Army, Commissioner (Dr) Paul du Plessis, if I could be in Bangkok within twenty-four hours. There I was to be met and taken to Aranyaprathet, a border town in northeast Thailand in the Sa Kaeo province, which is the busiest land crossing into Cambodia and the most convenient for onward travel to Siem Reap and Angkor Wat.

Sa Kaeo I camp was the first organized refugee relief camp established on the border by the Royal Thai Government with support from international relief agencies under the umbrella of the United Nations High Commissioner for Refugees (UNHCR) and subsequently a specially appointed United Nations Border Relief Operations (UNBRO), built in a short period of time under the direction of UNHCR Director Mark Malloch-Brown (now Lord Malloch-Brown). According to Malloch-Brown the prime minister of Thailand, General Kriangsak, was hesitant about admitting refugees to his country for fear they would become permanent settlers (Malloch-Brown 2011). General Kriangsak wanted a UN demilitarized zone so as to prevent armed conflict between Thai and Vietnamese soldiers. Malloch-Brown points out that although there was no UN zone, the humanitarian nature of the refugee camps emerging along the border became 'the de facto neutral space' (Malloch-Brown 2011). In late 1979 Malloch-Brown and other agencies built camps, often taking only twenty-four hours to get them ready for the thousands of Cambodian refugees who fled over the border. These became Kriangsak's buffer zone as the presence of the camps and many humanitarian workers from around the world somehow kept a fragile peace and prevented atrocities in the immediate post-conflict era. By the time I arrived in January 1981, a purpose-built camp named Sa Kaeo II was operating with a noted air of permanence and identity. Mark Malloch-Brown and I have briefly discussed those early days and the phenomenon of new life in Sa Kaeo II after the experience of the indescribable atrocities on family life that I will refer to in this chapter (Figure 6.1).

I had no doubts that I was fairly well equipped to deal with the rigours of life on a refugee camp, though of course I realised it would be different culturally and that the working conditions would be diverse. This was mainly because I had been one of two expatriate women living in the Bolivia shanty town of 36,000 Quechua and Aymara people, whereas there were approximately fifty aid agencies made up of expatriate personnel on the Sa Kaeo II UNBRO/UNHCR camp. There was no formal census at this stage in the camp but estimates reckoned about 34,000 men, women and children.

**Figure 6.1** Sa Kaeo II UNBRO/UNHCR Military Holding Camp, 1981. Author's photograph.

My mandate was to join a team of eleven other humanitarian workers, and to cover the obstetric services along with two other nurses/ midwives. Out of 34,000 people on the camp 1,200 women were expecting babies due within the next four months. International Non-Government Organisations (INGOs) with teams there included World Relief Committee, World Medical Missions, CAMA Services, World Vision, Food for the Hungry, Thailand Baptist Mission, Catholic Relief Services, Oxfam, the International Rescue Committee and the Salvation Army, but ours was the only team offering midwifery services apart from a Japanese surgical team running an operating theatre for surgical/obstetric emergencies away from the camp.

There was hardly time to keep a journal, so for this chapter I have referred to letters written to my mother, often written on the minibus to and from the camp to the village where we lived on the Thai side of the border. Sa Kaeo II was a military holding camp whose authorities were beginning to note infiltration by the Khmer Rouge, so we lived in the village and travelled daily or by night to the camp. All teams lived off the camp in this way in typical Thai houses – on stilts with domestic needs such as laundry and cooking attended to by household staff who were also willing to help us with the language. I note:

The living conditions are lovely. We have open, airy rooms, fans, no piped water but bathrooms that have tubs with a good supply of water in receptacles. There are squat toilets just like ours was in Singapore, Mum. Breakfast is made for us at 6.30 a.m., often cooked eggs, porridge, toast, pancakes, etc. (not all at once!). Salad lunch prepared by the house staff is taken to the camp to have during a break. Then dinner is taken all sitting down together, that is those not on night duty, at 6.30 p.m. with very good food served in the house. Canned soft drinks and filtered water is always in the fridge for us. (Extract from letter home)

The camp was a well set-out township of 34,000 Cambodians, with each family located to a 'house' on stilts consisting of one room and a veranda, with twelve dwellings forming a quadrangle. The Sa Kaeo II camp was opened in August 1980 when refugees were transferred from Sa Kaeo I, where the conditions were very poor, especially after the rain, as the houses were made of bamboo and the ground of clay, resulting in quagmire. Sa Kaeo II was well built by Thai workers and was eventually to be used as a military camp for the Thais when the refugees went back to their country or a Western country:

The camp hospital is great, each ward is run by a different medical team, such as Save the Children fund which has one, Red Cross another, World Vision another (many different organisations are here). Our team consists of World Relief, Tear Fund, Christian and Missionary Alliance (CAMA), Zoa (which is Tear Fund for South East Asia based in Holland), World Concern and the Salvation Army. Our medical team, therefore, consists of 3 midwives for the obstetric ward, one is Finnish, and she's lovely; one is [from] New Zealand who met me in Bangkok on arrival, and she and I share a room. Another is from the UK, who I have only met once and will be working with tomorrow. She's loaned to our team by another organisation. Apparently they could not take sufficient off-duty since January until I came, so I'm really needed. There is an emphasis on off-duty time so as to prevent exhaustion and sickness. (Extract from letter home)

## Origins of the Crisis

The region had an unsettled history with the build-up of U.S. forces in Vietnam from the 1960s to the mid-1970s. The Vietnam War was a lengthy conflict between nationalist forces who pushed for unification of the country under a communist government, and the United States along with the South Vietnamese, struggling to prevent the spread of communism. Nixon and Kissinger, who lost the American public's backing for the Vietnam

War, which many believed could not be won, negotiated the withdrawal of American forces by 1973. Up until then the United States had also bombed Cambodia in their efforts against the Viet Cong and Khmer Rouge (Shawcross 1984). The Khmer Rouge had been Vietnam's former allies and although the invasion by the victorious communist Vietnamese forces was not what the West had planned or wanted, it revealed to the outside world the horrors inflicted on the Cambodian people and society during the regime of Pol Pot and the Khmer Rouge. Following the fall of Saigon, Vietnamese forces invaded Cambodia, only departing in 1989.

In December 1978 and early 1979 thousands of Cambodians had crossed the Thai-Cambodian border seeking refuge, security and food. By May 1979 many refugees had set up makeshift camps at Kampot, Mairut, Lumpuk, Khao Larn and Ban Thai Samart – all near Aranyaprathet. In October that year, 60,000 Khmer Rouge soldiers and civilians under their control arrived at Khlong Wa, all in advanced stages of exhaustion and malnutrition. The need for some sort of organized living provisions was blatantly apparent. Many of these 60,000 people were eventually transferred to Sa Kaeo I.

The Thai Supreme Command telephoned UNHCR to inform them that the Thai military would transport Cambodians at the border from areas south of Aranyaprathet to a location outside of the Thai town of Sa Kaeo, about forty kilometres from the border. UNHCR was requested to establish a Holding Centre (Sa Kaeo I) there that would house up to 90,000 refugees. As mentioned earlier, Mark Malloch-Brown, together with his Thai assistant Kadisis Rochanakorn, inspected the place, which was then an uninhabited area for rice cultivation, basically a paddy field. The Thai government request to UNHCR was for speedy emergency arrangements for the Cambodians. Land was bulldozed to make roads, and latrines were dug. NGOs such as CAMA donated water tanks, bamboo and thatch to build a hospital and, with many Thai workers, a warehouse was built to store plastic rope, straw mats and baby bottles donated by Catholic Relief Services. All of this was achieved with less than a day's warning, so that a basic camp infrastructure could be in place for the arrival of thousands of severely malnourished Cambodians, including several hundred unaccompanied children.

There was no potable water on-site so the Thai military had to truck water in from Aranyaprathet. Drainage in the campsite was such that shortly after the refugees arrived it flooded, and a few refugees, too weak to lift their heads, drowned as they lay under tents made of plastic sheets.

Various authors (such as Shawcross 1984; Ponchaud 1978; Ashe 1988) give eyewitness accounts of the atrocities that were inflicted upon the Cambodians during the Pol Pot Khmer Rouge era. Questions regarding why these horrors occurred are addressed in later decades such as Gray 2012 and Hinton 2004, in his essay entitled, 'Why Did you Kill? The Cambodian Genocide and the Dark Side of Face and Honour'. Although I wished to address some of these questions, especially when we realised that Khmer Rouge cadre were in the camp, I was in the position of a humanitarian nurse, not an ethnographer, and especially felt that these questions would be enquired into at the later stage of international tribunals. Little did we realise that, in the case of Cambodia, tribunals would take years to set up and many of the perpetrators of violence would have died from old age and natural causes.

## Camp Services

By the end of November 1979 some fifteen Thai and international relief agencies were providing services at Sa Kaeo, including the Thai Red Cross, International Committee of the Red Cross, Médecins Sans Frontières, Christian and Missionary Alliance, World Vision and the Israeli Defense Force. Catholic and Buddhist institutions provided additional volunteers as did several embassies.

Together with many civilian refugees in the camp, some of the Cambodians in Sa Kaeo were Khmer Rouge soldiers who escaped with them to the border. The Khmer Rouge were keen to move some of their cadres into the protected areas of the Thai border, where food and medical attention were provided and where the soldiers could recuperate and return to fight the Vietnamese. Thai official policy endeavoured to maintain separate camps for those Cambodians under Khmer Rouge control, as accepting the provision of aid for these individuals could be politically damaging. It was rumoured that within a short space of time the Khmer Rouge had swiftly reinstated their power base and that they wielded almost total control over camp residents.

In order to demonstrate the United States' support for the Thai humanitarian response, in November 1979 the American first lady Rosalynn Carter visited Sa Kaeo Camp I with some members of the U.S. Congress and many journalists. This official visit was well publicized and televised for all major TV channels in the United States. Mrs Carter was said to have picked up a baby who later died, and with this kind of embarrassing publicity the Thai government along with the UNHCR was able to build more suitable camps at Khao-I-Dang and Sa Kaeo II.

With the stark images of dying refugees at Sa Kaeo being broadcast worldwide, international aid poured into Thailand to assist the refugees, as the images created the impression that Cambodia in general was suffering from famine. The international community's continued response was to deliver large amounts of food aid to Cambodians via the 'Land Bridge' at Nong Chan Refugee Camp. This Land Bridge was set up by Robert Ashe, a humanitarian aid worker with much experience in the region.

This is where an autobiographical note resonates as to the push/pull factor in becoming a humanitarian aid worker. In the late 1960s and early 1970s my family helped with the mailing of letters to donors and prospective donors for the small charity Project Vietnam Orphans (PVO). PVO had been set up in the Leamington Vicarage, where Reverend Pat Ashe, Marion Ashe and their family lived. Marion Ashe had watched Julian Petiffer's TV account straight from Vietnam and asked the meeting of church elders in the vicarage what could be done to help. Out of this was born the Project Vietnam Orphans. It was one of Pat and Marion's sons, Robert, who had been at work in Vietnam and then along the Thai/Cambodian border and who set up the Land Bridge. Robert and I have recently been in touch to clarify ideas and details from that era and here I quote the Ashe family website:

> From 1979 to 1980 Robert was seconded to the International Committee of the Red Cross. He was responsible for planning a cross-border operation, known as the 'Land Bridge' taking food and agricultural tools into Cambodia. In mid-1980, Robert was awarded the MBE (Member of the Most Excellent Order of the British Empire) for his work among refugees.
>
> Shortly after news of Robert's award was announced, he was captured by Vietnamese troops who had invaded Cambodia. He was marched about 25 km inside Cambodia through torrential rain and with no shelter at night. After three days he was freed, and allowed to walk over the Aranyaprathet border bridge back into Thailand.

## Narratives of Family Trauma

But what of the family memories of violence that have since become part of my own biography? They centre on stories narrated to me, often by the fathers-to-be, waiting for their babies to be born, as they and their new wives or partners sweated in labour, awaiting birth in the camp hospital in a land where they were classed as aliens or refugees.

One narrative is etched on my memory. I asked a father-to-be what the deep indented scar on his ankle was from and he answered with a deep, drawn-out sigh and a phrase I would hear often, 'Oh Pol Pot'. In a whisper he recounted his not-oft-told narrative of how he and his family escaped the Khmer Rouge many miles away from their own province; they had worked in fields along the way trying not to be noticed by the Khmer Rouge. A meeting was called by the Khmer Rouge to find out who was 'stealing the rice'. My narrator's son and two other young men 'owned up' to save the rest of the village. The anguish of the punishment he observed was written on his face as he told of the horror of watching his son and two other young men being roughly handled: plastic bags were forced over their heads by the Khmer Rouge and they were hung from a tree at the edge of the village. It was a long death and the father told me that he was rooted to the spot until well after the Khmer Rouge had moved on. This father had already got an open sore on his ankle and while standing watching these atrocious deaths he did not realise that he was standing in a bed of termites gnawing away quietly while he stood there. His quick answer – 'Oh Pol Pot' – to my question was one we began to hear often, in that family narratives were identified by them as being pre-Pol Pot or post-Pol Pot. When he eventually got to the Thai border, he had lost his wife and other family members to illness, probably typhoid or dengue fever. Thousands of people like him began to rebuild new lives by getting married and producing new families, thus showing the unquenchable spirit of the human being.

Pol Pot and his desire to rid the country of Western influence resulted in many pairs of glasses being stored in the camp by the international NGOs. Our team leader was an optometrist from the UK, who was ex-military, serving in the Saudi Royal Air Force before becoming ordained as a Salvation Army Officer. He had requested opticians in the UK to collect and send unwanted spectacles. Why so many spectacles? As mentioned earlier, Pol Pot's edict declared that people were not allowed to wear glasses as it was a sign of being an intellectual, which resulted in anyone seen wearing spectacles being shot or bayoneted without question. The appointment of an optometrist to our medical team was a brilliant move.

Within the first week I performed a procedure known as evacuation of the uterus on a woman who had given birth on the camp and had parts of an adhered placenta left *in utero*. With a Khmer woman paramedic attending we successfully performed this procedure and I could not help recalling how the medical college in Bolivia had made such a palaver about me doing the work of a doctor. As obstetric nurses/midwives we were in complete control of the ward on the camp, including the writing-up and prescribing of medication, and attending to gynaecological and obstetric complications. One day, assisted as always by a Khmer trainee midwife, I performed a vacuum extraction as the second stage of labour had not progressed; but the great result was that mother and newborn baby did well in spite of the difficult procedure. Many babies were born at night, and it was during these night shifts that many of the men, expectant fathers-to-be, would quietly recount the horrors of losing family members. These were the husbands and partners of the 1,200 pregnant women on the camp who were expected to deliver between January and April 1981.

One letter home describes a particularly hectic working day:

> At the 7.30 start, after nearly half an hour's ride to work, we found that we were one Khmer midwife short, so just had one Khmer midwife/translator. In addition we had two student nurses and one cleaner, all Cambodian. So we did the ward round to take over from the night staff, and then non-stop except 10 minutes for lunch at 1 p.m. until 6 p.m. I diagnosed with sepsis one sick newborn babe of four days old, whom I had delivered by vacuum, which was probably introduced before delivery as the mother only told us afterwards that [her] waters were broken for a long time before she came to us for the birth. Then I sat for at least an hour with a mother and babe watching babe slowly die as we could do nothing to save it. Then I did an evacuation of the uterus on a lady who had delivered in the night with a breech, and got rid of [the] placental tissue. Besides that, we have two sets of tiny twins who need constant supervision and of course, explaining all the time to Khmer midwives/nurses what to do. All the time there was the contrast between new birth, which always started off narratives of atrocities suffered by patients and birth attendants, as well as the contributions from the men lounging nearby. (Extract from letter home)

## Trauma of the Soul

How do these narratives affect the humanitarian worker? Also how do the appalling physical wounds seen and the horrendous stories told by the refugees psychologically affect the humanitarian worker? In the UK and the United States at present, counselling is on-hand in the immediate aftermath of a tragedy such as killings in a school or a train crash. But in the 1970s and 1980s counselling was not available to workers, either on the scene or on arrival back in the UK. A letter that is too personal to share, which was written at the end of the trip, is completely different in tone from the excitement of the early letters home. We the aid workers had not been informed that the camp was infiltrated with many Khmer Rouge – though we had our suspicions, and especially when treating them and their families. Only in later years was that knowledge confirmed. Back in the UK I used to feel uneasy if I saw someone walking up a London street in black trousers tied at the ankle or in army fatigues, or upon hearing a helicopter overhead. Some counselling was on offer for the Khmers but as there were few trained counsellors available, as aid workers ourselves we endeavoured to listen to the accounts of devastating family loss, as well as loss of home and possessions, a whole way of life. These stories, most often told during the hours of waiting for babies to be born, seemed to be more intense when told during those dark nights and early mornings with few people about. Narratives such as these take their toll on the listening humanitarian worker.

When the holding camps were set up by the Thai government it was stressed by the Thai authorities that no aid agencies should proselytise. This was respected by all agencies but small events, such as a Khmer woman training to be a midwife praying over the safe birth of a child were tolerated, even ignored, if known by the authorities. Daily devotions were also held each morning on the ward. All parents, whether Buddhist or Christian, knew of this, performed by the Khmer women in the obstetric team, and parents often requested prayers for their newborn. There was a specially-built temple or *Wat* (Khmer) on the camp, where burial prayers were said and where parents could go to have Buddhist priests perform ceremonial rites. Our team had a Khmer pastor as a team member. Dara Pen and his wife had escaped Cambodia during the genocide and managed to flee to the United States. When Sa Kaeo II camp was built he offered to work there in his pastoral role as he was so glad to have survived the events of the Pol Pot regime. Some of the most structured and yet sympathetic counselling given to the displaced Khmers was undertaken by this pastor and his team of Khmer workers. Most workers recognised that his counselling was suitable for all creeds and beliefs in that he did not evangelise, but sought to counsel and help those affected by the atrocities they had seen and felt (he proudly gave me his soft leather Khmer language Bible which I received with humility upon my departure from Thailand).

## Rebuilding the Body

Many refugees from Cambodia were eventually able to migrate to countries such as Australia, the United States and the UK. There were strict criteria about who would be accepted by these 'third countries'. Refugees with academic or professional backgrounds were often successful, while it was those who had no formal qualifications who were unable to migrate. Many of the people on Sa Kaeo II camp had been shopkeepers, and in particular owners of jeweller's shops. The team's mandate was to train women in the art of safe childbirth; many of those women who had previously been jewellers were willing to learn new skills. Moreover, it was these women who also acted as interpreters for the aid workers. The mandate was aimed at a steady return of people to Cambodia, taking with them the skills needed to build up the infrastructure of society again. In a practical way safe birthing was seen to be part of this. Our team had produced a midwifery manual in Khmer and English that these women could take with them on their return home. Every procedure possible was listed, with much use of diagrams. One of the amazing observations made during our time was that many sets of twins were delivered. On talking to parents about the high incidence of twins, many of the men said that they believed it 'was nature's way of making up for the killings and losses'. This was a reawakening – a rebuilding – a renewal of family life (Figure 6.2).

In e-mail correspondence (2013) with Major Dorothy Nisbet, my New Zealander friend and midwife, her recollection of the time is equally memorable. She writes:

> Chandra is another very poignant memory who as a young pregnant woman came to the ward with her husband. She was in advanced labour with her first baby so we monitored her for some hours. Caesarean section was not done at the drop of a hat and in fact, was for 'disproportion' only. Time came when we had to decide to arrange for a C-section as there was no way her baby could be born vaginally. We gave her and her husband full explanation of the implications of having and not having the surgery. We took them to the Japanese hospital on our way home in the evening and next morning called in on our way to work to see how they were doing. How shocked we were to find that despite the delivery of a live, apparently healthy baby boy, the little one had died a

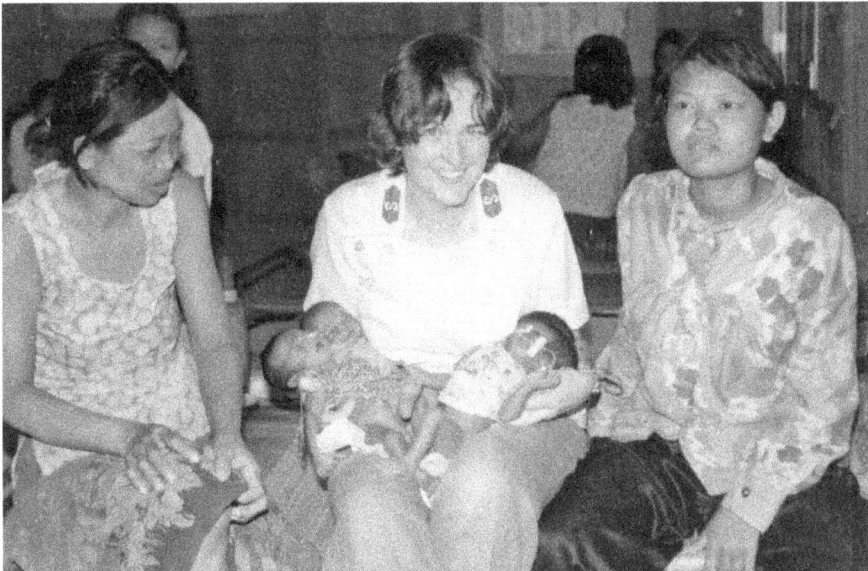

**Figure 6.2** Two sets of newly born twins at Sa Kaeo II Military Holding Camp on the Thai/Cambodian border. Author's photograph.

few hours later. We had no way to find out why things had gone wrong nor [of explaining] to this lovely young couple.

Dorothy continues

The thing that got me the most was that they were so full of gratitude to us for all that had been done for them. It really choked me up that they were thankful despite just having lost this baby but also the opportunity of further pregnancies in the future. A tubal ligation had been performed on the mother due to complications in that pregnancy. Such were the heartaches of working within these situations.

A further memory Dorothy shared by e-mail follows:

Another time a baby was born with anencephaly [the absence of a large part of the brain and the skull]. It is instantly recognizable and almost all babies born with anencephaly will die shortly after birth. We knew this condition is not compatible with life, so we had to make the hard decision to withhold fluid from the wee one. Such was her determination to survive that it was 48 hours before she succumbed. It was so difficult to go through that time together.

As noted already, one of the ways in which our team planned for the future return of Khmer refugees to Cambodia was by transforming all the midwifery classes and procedures used during deliveries into a *Handbook for Khmer Midwives*. This was an incredible challenge that came into being with staff and Khmers combining their numerous skills. All the notes from various tutors, that is, all of the midwives and also the doctors, were collated. These were then translated by the American Chuck Keller, who had previously been under assignment with the World Relief partnership, to conduct a bibliography of the Khmer-language publications that had been produced in the various refugee camps. So it was Chuck Keller who returned to Sa Kaeo II camp under the same auspices to translate and check the Khmer-language edition of the midwifery manual prepared by our team working there. What resulted was not literally a 'handbook' but rather a foolscap-sized tome about two centimetres thick, containing all the lectures given on pregnancy, labour, delivery, neo-natal care – normal and abnormal – and much more besides. There were diagrams and parallel pages of Khmer and English-language procedures. Each of the graduated midwives – nearly seventy people in the two-year period – was given a copy of the publication, which had actually been printed in the camp. They were also given a bag with the basic essentials for conducting a normal delivery. There was a wonderful sense of achievement by the team who considered that their pooled efforts and skills would continue to be useful in the future for those who eventually returned to their country.

## Gender and the Aid Workers

Not only on our team, but also on many others, such as Save the Children Fund and Oxfam, many of the aid workers were women. We could see this in terms of caring being women's work, but it is more than that: it is the predominance of women in certain professions such as teaching and nursing. Even non-nursing positions in some agencies were held by nurses who were prepared to do other tasks and to learn on the spot, such as school homework programmes and non-specialised feeding programmes. Our team had an interesting make-up. There were two male Dutch doctors, one male British optometrist (Salvation Army Officer), one male New Zealander carpenter (Salvation Army Officer), two female children's nurses, two female midwives (Salvation Army Officers), plus the wife of a doctor and the Khmer wife of the Khmer pastor, who helped with anything, especially the logistics of feeding and housing us. The carpenter, a young, blonde and enthusiastic member of the team, and the team leader, older, dark and moodily Welsh, had special roles that were never considered to be anything other than male. Even if they were sick and it was suggested that a strong woman could do it, they protested. Their role involved quietly taking bags of rice to what was known as a 'Land Bridge', to the Cambodian side of the border for impoverished Cambodians still in hiding from the Khmer Rouge. It involved crawling for a mile or so through undergrowth to a prearranged spot over the border and delivering the produce. One of the team volunteered me on the night that one of the men was ill, but they said I would be seen! This seemed a daft protest seeing as the team leader was 6'4" (193 cm) compared to my 5'5" (165 cm) and I was quieter than him generally. But to no avail: the gender bias of a tough job being done by tough men won over (much to my relief). But what did the women do when both men were out working the Land Bridge? Some were on night duty but others sat up in the quiet hours of the night until the men returned.

## Illness amongst the Aid Workers

The team kept surprisingly good health until near the end of my stay when the team leader went down with a bad attack of dengue fever. As we were all living in the same house it seemed likely that others amongst us would also succumb via the dreaded mosquito bite. Three women including myself contracted typhoid and dengue fever at the same time, and we were very poorly. The rest of the team then went down with the fever, by which time it was deemed necessary to get some of us to Bangkok and evacuated home as 'walking wounded'. Only much later did we realise that we were part of the 1981 dengue fever pandemic of Southeast Asia that resulted in many fatalities. Meanwhile the process of getting replacement aid workers out to the border was ongoing; so the life of humanitarian agencies goes on. Organisations such as the Salvation Army will always be able to draw on the pool of idealism and skills found within young women and men, ready to respond at a moment's notice to the tragedies of man's inhumanity to man. This inhumanity is poignantly expressed in a poem on a wall in the Tuol Sleng Genocide Museum, which is located within the former prison grounds of the Khmer Rouge regime in Phnom Penh, Cambodia. Written by former Cambodian prison guard Sarith Peou describing what life was like under the Khmer, it is entitled 'The New Regime' (Peou 2007):

> *No radio. No TV.*
> *No drawing. No painting. No pets. No pictures. No electricity. No lamp oil.*
> *No clocks. No watches.*
> *No hope. No life.*
> *A third of the people didn't survive.*
> *The regime died.*

As each team member applied his or her own skills and expertise to the rebuilding of family life on the Thai/Cambodian border, we reminded ourselves that the atrocities beginning to be spoken of amongst the refugees and later bluntly described in the above poem, all related to the modern era, namely the decade of the 1970s and not a previous historical era.

One of the early humanitarian workers to give medical aid as a physician to refugees was Barry Levy on Khao-I-Dang camp who wrote of his experiences (Levy 1981: 1,440):

> my overwhelming sense there was not of death but of life; not of the Cambodians' ability merely to survive, but of their vitality; not of their grief for the past but their hope for the future; not of our superficial differences but of our shared humanity; and not of the hopelessness of the situation, but of the difference we and they were making.

The same desire to help that compelled Marion Ashe to ask the question as to what could be done, which resulted in the formation of

Project Vietnam Orphans (now subsumed under the Leamington-based charity CORD – Christian Outreach Relief and Development) is what motivates humanitarian workers with professional skills and expertise to address the needs of people in distress. That these professionals often go to the crisis spot, the 'dangerous sanctuary', and observe situations that are morally dubious, such as the misuse of humanitarian aid, does not deter the new batch of recruits ready to serve, especially under the rubric of UNHCR. It is often these individual NGOs on the ground, as it were, who can recognize and accurately analyse these crises situations. Many of the humanitarian crisis situations since Cambodia have been militarised and in some cases the refugee situation has sparked off a political crisis. The aid worker brings a political and moral stance to the response, which cannot always be avoided. The fact that our team was able to respond to the needs of the population, both Cambodian civilians and Khmer Rouge, shows the dilemma of conscience within any ethical framework – civil wars can cross borders with refugee displacement, a dilemma that Thailand and subsequently Western governments had to address due to the magnitude of the humanitarian crisis.

## Acknowledgements

Bridget Miles, CORD, Leamington Spa, England
Major Dorothy Nisbet, New Zealand
Robert Ashe MBE, Indonesia
The Rt Hon. the Lord Malloch-Brown KCMG
Commissioner (Dr) Paul du Plessis, Medical Adviser to The Salvation Army: he made the phone-call requesting me to be ready to leave for the Thai-Cambodian Border in twenty-four hours

## Bibliography

Ashe Family website, http://ashefamily.info/
Ashe, V.H. 1988. *From Phnom Penh to Paradise: Escape from Cambodia*. London: Hodder and Stoughton.
Boehnlein, J.K. 1987. 'Clinical Relevance of Grief and Mourning among Cambodian Refugees', *Social Science and Medicine* 25(7): 765–772.
Curtis, G. 1998. *Cambodia Reborn? The Transition to Democracy and Development*. Washington: Brookings Institution Press and Geneva: United Nations Research Institute for Social Development.
Davidson, R.J. 1974. *Children of the Ashes*. Cambridge: Lutterworth Press.
Gray, T. 2012. *Justice and the Khmer Rouge: Concepts of a Just Response to the Crimes of the Democratic Kampuchean Regime in Buddhism and the Extraordinary Chambers in the*

*Courts of Cambodia at the Time of the Khmer Rouge Tribunal.* Lund University: Centre for East and South-East Asian Studies.

Hinton, A.L. 2004. 'Why Did You Kill? The Cambodian Genocide and the Dark Side of Face and Honour', in N. Scheper-Hughes and P. Bourgois (eds), *Violence in War and Peace.* Oxford: Blackwell Publishing.

Levy, B.S. 1981. 'Working in a Camp for Refugees', *The New England Journal of Medicine*, 4 June 1981, p. 1,440.

Malloch-Brown, M. 2011. *The Unfinished Global Revolution: The Limits of Nations and the Pursuit of Politics.* London: Allen Lane.

Mollica, R.F., K. Donelan, S. Tor, J. Lavelle, C. Elias, M. Frankel and R.J. Blendon. 1993. 'The Effect of Trauma and Confinement on Functional Health and Mental Health Status of Cambodians Living in Thailand-Cambodia Border Camps', *JAMA*, 4 August 1993, 270(5): 581–586.

Peou, Sarith. 2007. 'The New Regime in Corpse Watching'. Tinfish Press. Available at: http://finnovation.tumblr.com/post/467578517/working-in-a-country-with-a-history-of-genocide

Ponchaud, F. 1978.*Cambodia Year Zero.* Translated from the French by Nancy Amphoux. London: Allen Lane.

Shawcross, W. 1984. *The Quality of Mercy: Cambodia, Holocaust and Modern Conscience.* London: Andre Deutsch.

**Janette Davies** has a PhD in social anthropology, having previously been a humanitarian nurse/midwife in Bolivia, Thailand and Bangladesh. She is now a social/medical anthropologist at International Gender Studies Centre, Lady Margaret Hall, University of Oxford. She works on gender and rural water supplies in Zimbabwe and Malawi, and on elders in Tbilisi, Georgia.

# 7

# Rwandan Women at War

## Fighting for the Rwandan Patriotic Front (1990–1994)

### Hannah Spens-Black

## Introduction

This account explores the experiences of a group of exceptional women who participated on the side of the RPF in the war against the Rwandan government from 1990 to 1994. In recent years, Rwanda has featured in the news for having the greatest proportion of female parliamentarians in the world.[1] On the surface, this may appear surprising given certain conservative societal expectations surrounding Rwandan women. However, in fact, the current ruling party – the Rwandan Patriotic Front (RPF) – had espoused gender equality since before the war that it waged against the Rwandan government led by President Habyarimana between 1990 and 1994.[2] The war was remarkable in that it was initiated by a movement of refugees living outside the country who had been exiled for thirty years in which women played integral roles from the beginning. However, little is written about the thousands of women who joined the ranks of the RPF as soldiers, nurses, political *cadres*,[3] secretaries or fundraisers.[4] Literature about Rwandan women has tended to focus on the significant social, economic and political roles they have played in the aftermath of war and genocide. The RPF's belief that women could contribute to the war as equals was unusual amongst contemporary guerrilla movements and merits more attention.

During various stays in Rwanda between 2008 and 2012, I often heard
mention of two war heroines, Aloisea Inyumba and Rose Kabuye, both of
whom became prominent public figures after the war. I soon realized that
it was common knowledge that women had widely participated in the RPF
during the war, yet, in a way, their participation was taken for granted. I was
inspired to hear their stories to discover, not only how they had experienced
war, but also the social stereotypes they had to contend with in order to
participate. In 2013, I visited Rwanda to conduct a series of interviews with
women (and some men) about their wartime experiences in the RPF.[5] In
the pages that follow, their stories weave together with the historical and
political context. I provide a chronological account of women's participation
in different stages of the war, starting with a brief historical background of
women's precolonial lives and the events that led to the exile of hundreds
of thousands of Rwandans (mostly Tutsi). I consider why and how women
joined the RPF, and the often dangerous roles women assumed, both
behind the lines and in the war zone, in spite of strict contemporary societal
conventions governing Rwandan women's behaviour. Finally, I examine
how women perceived their wartime experiences and their subsequent
readjustment to civilian life. I argue that attitudes to women joining the RPF
were complex: women often had to struggle to join and perform the roles
they desired, but once they seized their opportunity, women were highly
respected for their contribution. Historically, Rwandan society accepted
that women could play important public roles, but this was mostly under
exceptional circumstances, and there was often the expectation that women
would resume their previous roles once the conflict ended. This account
considers wartime women's participation in light of these historical trends.

## Women's Lives in Precolonial Rwanda (pre-1884)

Rwanda is often portrayed as a patriarchal society of dominant men and
submissive women (GoR 2010: 8).[6] However, the status of women in precolonial Rwanda is nuanced. Through the centuries, the Kingdom of Rwanda,
which consisted of three broad groupings of people, Tutsi cattle herders,
Hutu agriculturalists and Twa artisans, had been jointly ruled by a king and
queen mother. The queen mother was the king's principal adviser, holding
great power and influence (Maquet 1961: 126); during the king's absence or
periods of transition she ruled in his name. Although there were some female
chiefs in Rwanda's history,[7] there are few documented cases of other women
acting in public roles. In general, there were strong public/private divisions,
with men assuming public personae, representing the family in public and

attending the royal court, whilst the women managed the household, land and cattle. It was unusual for women to speak at or even attend public gatherings. Women's behaviour was governed by strict cultural expectations and taboos; for example, mature women were forbidden from milking cows (Vansina 2004: 27) or climbing ladders. Men from a young age were imbued with a strong sense of duty to protect women.

In precolonial and colonial times, women did not participate in war. The killing of women and children was considered 'taboo and extreme reck- lessness' (Rusagara 2009: 16). Women were not integrated into the Rwandan army; rather their role was to perform rituals and offer prayers to protect their men (op. cit.: xv). The legend of Ndabaga, a girl who joined the eigh- teenth-century army in secret, illustrates the society's gendered perceptions of soldiers. In order to allow her aging father to retire from court, Ndabaga disguised herself as a boy so she could replace him. Ndabaga excelled in battle, but eventually her disguise was discovered. The tale reveals how unusual it was for a woman to fight. Interestingly, once she was discovered, Ndabaga was not killed, as legend suggests she had feared; instead, she was richly rewarded by the king with cows and land for her heroism. This sug- gests that society accepted women acting outside their typical roles in times of exceptional circumstances. Echoes of this legend can be seen in women's participation in the RPF, namely, the secrecy surrounding their leaving home and the acceptance of their going to war in a time of great need.

## The Path to Exile (1884–1973)

When Rwanda was colonized firstly by the Germans in 1884 and then the Belgians in 1916, new laws swept away the customary rights and powers of women (Longman 2006: 134). The Belgians influenced society by designating and fixing ethnicity by use of identity cards and by supporting first the Tutsi monarchy, but in the late 1950s suddenly switching support to the Hutu majority. This is said to have sparked the 1959 revolution that is widely recognized as the starting point for large-scale conflict in Rwanda. The *umwami* (king) was deposed and widespread violence (mainly targeting elite Tutsi men) caused hundreds of thousands of Tutsi (and a small number of Hutu) to flee to neighbouring countries including Burundi, Tanzania, Uganda and Zaire.[8]

When independence was finally granted to Rwanda in 1962, the Hutu majority took power under President Kayibanda. The new regime was anti- pathetic towards the Tutsi who had fled, making it unsafe to return. As a result, one group exiled to Burundi launched a small-scale rebellion against the new government. The rebels, called *inyenzi* (cockroaches),[9] led incursions into Rwanda between 1962 and 1968 (it is said that there were no female *inyenzi* fighters). But they were unsuccessful; instead their actions provoked reprisal massacres of civilian Tutsi still living in Rwanda. The massacres reached their pinnacle in 1963, with an estimated ten thousand to fourteen thousand deaths (Melvern 2000: 21) causing another wave of (mostly Tutsi) refugees to flee. For the first time, the word 'genocide' was applied to Rwanda (ibid.). There was further organized violence against the Tutsi in 1973, with women said to have perpetrated violence for the first time in Rwanda's history (African Rights Organization 1995: 8). Juvenal Habyarimana, a Hutu army general from northern Rwanda, seized the presidency in a coup later the same year. His initial promises of reconciliation were soon replaced by virulent anti-Tutsi discourses (Mamdani 2002b: 190). President Habyarimana constantly refused to allow refugees to return to Rwanda (Reed 1996: 483), thereby concentrating opposition to his regime amongst the exiled who shared a common cause: namely, to return home to Rwanda.

## Life as a Refugee: The Appeal of the RPF (1959–1990)

Life for the three generations of refugees living outside Rwanda was for the most part characterized by injustice and persecution. Some suffered more than others, depending upon the country of exile and the politics of the period. The situation in Uganda is said by many to have been particularly bad, exemplified by President Obote's persecution of both Tutsi and Hutu refugees (Kamukama 1993: 37–40). One woman I interviewed, Liliane,[10] who grew up as a refugee in Uganda, had to change her name to disguise her Rwandan identity and so assumed a Ugandan name.[11] She explained that one day at her youth club she was ordered to participate in a Ugandan campaign forcing Rwandans to relocate to refugee camps. Shocked, she realized that she would never truly belong in Uganda and became determined to return to Rwanda.

Other refugees, living in Zaire, were victimized by civil wars in the Lake Kivu area; those in Burundi were disadvantaged by exclusion from education and employment. Clarisse, born and raised in Zaire, who later became a political *cadre*, described her frustration at the time:

> I had friends from Burundi who were very intelligent but had difficulties getting access to university because they were Rwandan ... you needed to get over 80%, but your [Burundian] colleague got 55% [so she] passed and went to university before you ... it was an injustice.[12]

Almost all refugees expressed feelings of exclusion from their country of exile. At the same time, the story of an idyllic Rwanda, 'filled with milk and honey' (Prunier 1995: 67) was passed down from mother to child, creating a strong desire to return to their 'Garden of Eden' (Prunier 1993: 123).

As a response to the suffering faced by many Rwandans, the forerunner to the RPF, the Rwandan Association of National Unity (RANU) was established in 1979 as a clandestine socio-political organization of several hundred intellectuals, predominantly male, based in Kenya (Prunier 1993: 124). In 1987, this was transformed into the RPF, a politico-military organization now based in Uganda that developed a strong ideology and specifically aimed to repatriate Rwandan refugees (Rusagara 2009: 173–74). The RPF purposely targeted a broader cross-section of society than its predecessor: from peasants to students to businessmen (RPF 1994: 8). It was the first movement to actively reach out to women. Tutsi refugees, many of whom had lived in exile for up to thirty years, were most receptive to the RPF's message, but the movement by no means excluded Hutus, with some taking key positions in leadership (Kamukama 1993: 48).[13]

In the past, given the traditional gender roles, it was rare for women to join political organizations. That they joined this movement can be attributed to the fact that the RPF specifically targeted women, and also to the fact that the RPF emerged at a time of particular hardship and of little hope of change for refugees. The women I interviewed all explained that their underlying reason for joining the RPF was to return to Rwanda, the country of their parents. Clarisse told me she feared that her refugee status would limit her opportunities in Zaire after university:

> For me, the first goal was that with the RPF I would have my country ... I saw the opening of the horizons of my life in Rwanda.

Each exiled woman I spoke with was convinced that by fighting to go 'home' to Rwanda the situation would improve, even if she had never actually set foot in the country.

For those women who remained in Rwanda before the 1990–1994 war, it was often a more difficult decision to join. Their movements were restricted by travel regulations; leaving the country risked putting their family members in danger. Nonetheless, a small number of women did leave Rwanda for the warfront, although more participated as part-time members in Rwanda. One woman I interviewed, Speciose, fled persecution in Rwanda and joined the medical wing of the RPF in exile when she was just fourteen. She had been studying nursing at a school in Gisenyi in Rwanda when, one day in 1990, the anti-Tutsi militia came into the school and started killing pupils. She escaped across the border to the Zairian town of Goma from where she later travelled to join the RPF on the front line as a junior nurse for the duration of the war. For many women like Speciose, the RPF offered the only solution to persecution.

## Becoming a Member of the RPF (1987–1994)

Although each woman I interviewed recounted a different path to becoming a member of the RPF, notably they all joined voluntarily, this was in stark contrast to many contemporary African civil wars where women were often forcibly recruited (Turshen and Twagiramariya 1998); this had implications for the roles women played and how they were treated. Many women were recruited by RPF political *cadres*. One woman who became a part-time member whilst studying at university in Burundi, Sandra, explained that she was recruited by her classmates in 1989:

> When I was at university ... young people would come to see me during recreation. They wanted to see if I was positive towards the movement ... [also] they would come home to visit me. Later someone invited me to go to a secondary school ... We found ourselves in a classroom. We had conversations with someone ... about the history of Rwanda. The next time, we talked about the geography of the country. They only mentioned the RPF afterwards.

Other women were not approached and had to make great efforts to join. Bernadette remembered how as a young graduate in Kenya she had been determined to become a soldier for the RPF. To her dismay, she found that at the time they were not approaching women, only men. Frustrated, she returned to Uganda, but even there she met obstacles before she could achieve her wish to become a soldier. It appears to have been more of a challenge for women to join the movement when it first launched, but those who persevered were able to demonstrate that women were a vital resource for the RPF; they thus paved the way for more widespread recruitment of women.

The RPF movement was highly clandestine. Like Clarisse, many girls concealed their involvement from everyone, including their immediate families:

> Maybe there were people who would want to stop us. But we hid everything ... from our parents, brothers and sisters. My sister would be contacted on her side, and me contacted on my side. We weren't the same age, so we weren't in the same group. It was totally secret; I would return home and say nothing.

Wives even hid their activities from their husbands and vice versa, although it could cause problems. Sandra admitted she had been suspicious of her husband's secretive behaviour:

> I saw his movements during our engagement; I didn't understand. It used to annoy me how he would leave without saying anything. Also, the company he kept. I saw young people from Uganda visiting him. I wasn't happy.

Later, when she became a member herself, his behaviour became clearer. The silence surrounding the RPF's activities certainly facilitated women participating as they could do so without having to explain their actions or ask permission.

## Preparing for War (1987–1990)

From its inception in 1987, the RPF set to mobilizing individuals via a network of cells throughout the region, and even as far afield as South Africa, Canada and Belgium. Each cell was modelled on a central system of commissions including mobilization, fundraising, finance, logistics, youth and women. Members initially joined part-time, attending meetings and donating funds or materials. Others gave up their jobs or education to dedicate themselves to the movement full-time. A plethora of women supported the cause as part-time members behind the lines. They organized cultural events and parties to raise funds, set up small businesses (for example, selling samosas or doughnuts), donated clothes, food, money,[14] or housed political *cadres*.

Separate groups for women were created in many cells, as it was found that female members tended not to speak at meetings with men, or even to turn up regularly. RPF leader, Espérence, explained the problem they had involving women in the early days:

> Traditionally women don't speak when their husbands are there. So we said, if they have their own kind of organization, they will practise ... they will build their confidence, they will analyse this issue which is also being analysed in the main structure, and by the time they come for these other meetings, they are stronger than just coming [for the] first time, [when they are] not sure what to say ... It was a kind of incubation arrangement ... it gave them that confidence.

Thus women attended both their women's groups and the mixed group meetings: twice the number of meetings attended by most of their male colleagues. Women's groups, with names like *Urugo* (Home), provided valuable space for women to express their thoughts and ideas and discuss issues facing their sisters on the front line. Specifically, they were able to fundraise for knickers and sanitary wear that were more difficult to prioritize in mixed groups. The groups also provided support for female political *cadres* travelling the regions alone.

As participation was unpaid, those women who were able to join the movement full-time were mostly in their late teens or early twenties without families of their own. The most prevalent role they were given was that of political cadre. This was a challenging job that required leaving home on one- or two-month deployments to visit Rwandan communities across the region. Initially, each *cadre* attended political school to learn the ideology of the movement and receive practical training. Upon arrival in a community, the *cadres* would lead group meetings (mixed, women and/or youth) to teach the background and ideology of the RPF's cause and other subjects such as philosophy, political science or the history of Rwanda. It was often difficult for them to overcome stereotypes of 'simple, young, African girls' who should not speak in public; they had to fight to gain respect by speaking confidently and knowledgeably.

Josiane, who joined as a political *cadre* in Zaire when she was eighteen, explained how she worked hard to fit in with the communities she visited. She adopted different customs, sometimes wearing traditional *pagnes* (Zairian dresses), sometimes trousers (to the shock of her mother). She tried to stay with the families of many girls in order to blend in and become the 'little cousin from Burundi'. Josiane recounted that in addition to her full workload leading group meetings in the villages, she also had to help with domestic tasks like fetching water, cooking or farming. In such a way, she was able to use stereotypes about women to disguise her political activities.

Although not front line soldiers, female political *cadres* faced their fair share of dangers. In the era before landlines or mobile telephones, *cadres* had to move around with directions and maps drawn on scraps of paper; they had to rely on personal introductions from strangers and to stay for days, weeks or months with families they did not know, some of whom did not speak Kinyarwanda, Rwanda's native language.[15] One political *cadre* explained that she was often scared when travelling around, especially during the first night in a new house. Another, Espérance, remembered the challenges:

> You are doing things that you've not done before and you know you have to do it anyway. You don't have resources; people have to hike ... distances they

have never walked before. I can't forget my time in Tanzania – there were no vehicles, and you walk, and you're not sure, and there is no food, and there is no nothing, but you are walking and making fun of it anyway ... We were even arrested several times because we were doing wrong things ... You don't go to do political mobilization in another country! Our visas expired and ... then they ask 'what's this person doing in this country'?

The network of political *cadres* and part-time members was essential for ensuring that the front line forces had adequate financial and material support for the invasion. Many political *cadres* continued their pre-war work for the duration of the war; others embarked on dangerous journeys to the war zone.

## Invasion of Rwanda: Women Leaving Home to Fight (1990)

On 1 October 1990, the RPF invaded the northeasterly point of Rwanda from Uganda. The RPF's stated aim was to fight for the right of refugees to return to Rwanda; the failure of peaceful negotiations had shown that force was the only alternative. Estimates suggest that the invading rebel army was between four thousand and ten thousand strong: mostly Rwandan refugees who had grown up in Uganda (Reed 1996: 488). The fighters were well prepared; for several years, RPF leaders had been encouraging Rwandans to join Museveni's National Resistance Army (NRA) in Uganda with the expressed intention of preparing for one day leading their own fight for Rwanda.[16] The women I interviewed estimated that a handful of female officers and several dozen female soldiers had formed part of the initial invasion. They had fought for the NRA in Uganda; it was rare for women living in other countries to have military experience as they were not permitted to join national armies.

The invasion was not the success that the RPF had anticipated. The RPF's army was heavily outnumbered,[17] and the Rwandan national army had superior materiel and financial support from France, Belgium and Zaire (Kamukama 1993: 48), whereas the RPF affirm that they received no external backing.[18] The RPF suffered heavy defeats in the initial weeks of battle and several top commanders were killed, leaving soldiers scattered and unguided. Under the RPF's new commander Paul Kagame (the future president), the troops withdrew to the Virunga volcanoes in the northwest of Rwanda. As news of the invasion spread, young men and women from across the region, and further afield, made the decision to join the ranks of the RPF, often travelling hundreds of miles to the military training camps

north of Rwanda. Those who had already had military training were welcomed.[19] However, in the early years, almost any man or woman who was
determined to fight was accepted into the RPF army, although some were
encouraged to take on roles within the political wing.

Many families struggled to accept the idea of their daughters becoming soldiers. Beatrice remembered the conversation with her father before
leaving for the front line:

> We discussed it. He said, 'Believe me, whatever you do, war is not for girls'. He
> supported us being engaged [in the movement], but not us going to war ... My
> father was involved in the RPF movement, [giving] contributions, organizing
> meetings, he was a [local] president, but he didn't want his daughter to be taken
> away from him.

In spite of her father's views Beatrice left anyway, confiding only in her
mother and younger brother. The majority of young women and men chose
to leave in secret, telling only close family members who would not try to
stop them. Alice confided in her mother, but received what she described as
a 'bad reaction':

> My mother removed her belt and put it down on the floor in front of the door
> and she said 'if you go beyond this rope, you will die'.

By throwing down her belt by the exit, her mother was effectively forbid-
ding Alice to leave. This tradition, known as *umweko,* was used by women in
precolonial Rwanda to stop their husbands fighting in wars that the women
believed to be foolish (Uwineza, Pearson and Fowley 2009: 15). By purpose-
fully disregarding the sign Alice showed that the cause was more important
to her than social conventions. This reiterates the message in the Ndabaga
legend that women were tacitly expected to rise up in exceptional circumstances, but might have to fight to do so.

Another determined young woman, Liliane, was instructed by her RPF
superiors to continue working in Uganda as a political *cadre* during the
invasion. Against orders, she travelled to the front line. Liliane was assisted
by soldiers who gave her a uniform, a gun and transportation. When she
reached the Rwandan border two days later, she recognized the voice of
her superior demanding to search the truck for her. Knowing there would
be trouble if she was caught, she jumped down and revealed herself. When
challenged, she asked, 'What is that [over there]?' 'Rwanda' was her superior's answer. She retorted, 'Look here, all these years I've been fighting for
my homeland. This is what I struggled for ... Give me peace.' She had never

been a soldier, but was determined to fight. Her bold insistence ultimately gained her the respect of her colleagues.

The RPF ensured that all troops clearly understood the ideology for which they were fighting. Initially, all recruits attended political school and soldiers received political-military training. The RPF carefully screened recruits and allocated roles to them according to their potential, skills and education. Clarisse, who had travelled by night on foot from the Zairian border to the training camp, explained her experience of selection:

> I'd expected to be in the military ... [to] help my brothers ... After the first train-ing, there were wise people who watched and judged where [to deploy you] ... I don't know how they chose me, but I remember the lines [of recruits], they'd say ... 'you go to political school', 'you return to your country, we need you there' or 'you, go to another country' ... What fascinated me was that wherever you ended up, you felt as if you were in the right place.

Similarly, Beatrice, who had defied her father, was also encouraged to become a political *cadre* as opposed to a soldier:

> [I expected] to fight, to go to the front. I came by plane to Entebbe ... I spent two weeks there in a training camp. First of all, they asked us to stay as [politi-cal] *cadres*, as there was so much to do: awareness raising, fundraising, cultural groups to organize. But I said to myself that ... I'd left school to go to the front; I could have been a *cadre* in Burundi, where I was born, but hadn't wanted to. I resolved to pursue my original idea [to become a soldier] and that's what I did.

These examples show that women could fight in the RPF army, but had to be determined to do so, as they were often encouraged to take on supporting roles. Again, this reveals the tension between the view that women should be protected and should act in ways typically seen to be suited to women, and the view that accepts that women may need to act outside their typical roles when exceptional circumstances so demand.

## Women's Experiences in the War Zone (1990–1994)

As we have just seen, the RPF did not especially encourage women to become soldiers and there was at times resistance to allowing them to join the army. Several hundred women did, however, fight on the front lines. The first were experienced soldiers who had served in the National Resistance Army (NRA) in Uganda. More women joined the RPF's army[20] over time,

responding to mobilization campaigns by political *cadres* in the regions surrounding Rwanda. The majority of female soldiers had no previous military
experience. This had implications for how women were able to rise up the
ranks in the military. Although women could be found in almost every rank
and role of the army, there were fewer women in positions of leadership;
the interviewees attributed this to the fact that a large proportion of female
soldiers were relatively inexperienced.

Larger numbers of RPF women served in the war zone as nurses or
in supporting functions such as welfare or administration. Mostly this was
under the remit of the medical wing or the political wing, although some
female soldiers held roles as secretaries or worked for the radio. All lived
the reality and dangers of war. Beatrice, a soldier in a non-combat role,
described her overwhelming memory of the war zone:

> The routine of war is bombings. Sometimes we would spend the whole day
> inside the shelters, with [iron] sheeting, like little houses. We also had trenches
> that we dug for when the bombing was intense. So we passed the days there.
> Sometimes, they bombed the whole day long ... We couldn't eat because we
> couldn't light the fire, because if you lit the fire, it could be seen. Sometimes we
> had to move quickly if it seemed like our camp had been discovered.

Women and men lived and worked in the camps together, although
where possible, women were provided with separate living quarters.
Otherwise, women and men shared camp chores as well as rare moments
of free time.

Once women had shown their determination to go to the war zone,
it appears that they were largely accepted and respected by their male
colleagues. The RPF specifically taught its members that women should
be treated as equals. As a result, women were expected to perform the
same duties as men. There was no ostensible special treatment. Beatrice
remembered:

> Women fought alongside men. They did the same exercises. One guy I served
> with ... recently said to me, 'Do you remember when you carried me on your
> shoulders when we were doing the exercises to evacuate the injured from the
> front? At that time you were so strong' ... I was. You couldn't tell me apart from
> the men!

Most of the women I interviewed affirmed that they felt they were
treated equally, saying they 'couldn't do different things'. Although some,
like Bernadette, admitted they would accept help when offered: 'War is
war. If you are being helped, I'm sure we would all appreciate it. It was very

hard'. Ambiguity in this comment lies in the fact that it was said by a woman who had become a commander. It betrays an additional fight that women faced as they attempted to overcome feelings of vulnerability linked to doing something that was not typically associated with their gender.

When I asked men how they perceived women in the war, all repeated that women were treated as equals. With further probing, some revealed that they believed physical strength set them apart. Jacques, a young soldier at the time, suggested to me that women were able to do '70 per cent of what a man could do'. Others explained that it was male soldiers who did most of the cooking because of the physical strength required to stir the enormous vats of *imvange* (beans mixed with maize), the RPF's staple diet. Similarly, men explained that women were not able to move artillery or march long distances carrying heavy equipment. On the other hand, women like Immaculée felt frustration that they were assumed to be 'weak' just because they were women. Immaculée believed that women had to prove themselves more than men to earn respect. She felt that if a woman made a mistake, men would say it was because she was 'only a woman', whereas, a man's error would be excused or explained away. This is a reminder that no matter how committed the RPF was to gender equality in the war, it would still take a long time to transform historic perceptions and behaviour.

Despite the RPF's discourse on women's equality, during the ceasefire of 1992, the RPF re-evaluated the role of women in the army. As a result, a special unit was created for female soldiers, named the Yankee Division. Women who had been on the front line were pulled back to join the division that operated behind the lines. Yankee had a full operational structure with female commanders, but never actually went to battle. Over several months, women were trained in practical skills such as nursing, sewing or carpentry. Several reasons were given for the creation of Yankee; when analysed, most come down to a desire to protect women. One motivation cited was to protect women from the dangers of conventional war (as opposed to guerrilla war), which was adopted as the RPF gained territory from 1992. New tactics necessitated greater physical strength and higher risks of capture and torture, and some people I interviewed suggested the women were removed from the front to avoid this. Secondly, ceasefires saw new young male recruits flood to join the army, meaning it was less necessary to deploy women to the front line. A further motivation given was to protect women from the risk of pregnancy, and to keep them away from the young male soldiers who had 'regained their energies'. For some women, it was a relief to be kept out of danger, but others were angry at being separated from their fellow soldiers. As battle resumed, the RPF redeployed the majority of women to non-combat supporting roles, although a few 'battle-hardened' women did return to the front line for the remainder of the war. No matter how much the RPF wanted to treat women as equals, when it came to dangerous situations, the men ultimately still felt a duty to protect the women.

Women worked hard to fulfil an important role in the war. Leaving their families, dedicating their futures to the movement and undertaking difficult and dangerous work in the war zone, the RPF women sacrificed themselves to the cause. Whatever their role, they contributed to gradually changing perceptions about women's capabilities, at least amongst the men and women they worked with. However, despite the fact that men could see their female colleagues' strength and tenacity first-hand, it did not appear to change their feeling of duty to protect women; this was revealed in many of the interviews with men. For the women, the war showed them that they were capable of much more than they had previously been led to believe. Those women who survived the war demonstrated that their wartime experiences had irrevocably changed their mindset, behaviour and attitudes, making them more confident of their abilities. The question was whether or not they would be accepted back into Rwandan society after the war.

## Life after War (1994 Onwards)

When the war ended in July 1994 it was a bittersweet victory. Since the invasion of 1990, Habyarimana's government had exacted reprisal killings against (mostly Tutsi) civilians in Rwanda, including women and children. Genocide was unleashed on 6 April 1994, killing up to one million Tutsi (and Hutu who opposed the regime). The nature of participation was complex and while thousands of women were victimized by sexual violence, others actively perpetrated genocide.[21] As the international community watched the massacres impotently, the RPF galvanized its forces to overthrow the genocidal government and end the four-year war.

The RPF women who returned to Rwanda following the genocide encountered death and destruction. It was a far cry from their parents' description of a promised land. Clarisse, a political *cadre*, explained her feelings upon her long-awaited return:

> We had dreamt of a country ... full of milk and honey ... [but] I entered a country that had been destroyed, a country of blood and tears.

All were shocked by the chaos that was left in the country. Espérence, an RPF leader, described her memory of the situation:

> The genocide threw us off balance completely. We had to reorganize because we encountered a totally abnormal situation. Suddenly one group kills the other like you've never seen. You find children dead, women, everybody, and [it's] just crazy ... You have children scattered. Even now when I say it I still get goosebumps ... They don't know where to go, they are wounded. And the country is empty, I tell you ... and there are so many dogs. We all took children into our families; you don't know how many, you don't know them. Sometimes you might not know their names.

Not only was the country in shatters, but for several years following 1994, insecurity was rife as genocidal militia led incursions into the western regions of Rwanda. Reconstruction would take many long years.

Women played pivotal roles in the country's reconstruction, undertaking tasks that many Rwandans still thought were not possible for women. In their thousands, they built houses, roads and hospitals whilst climbing ladders, milking cows and breaking myriad other stereotypes. For the first time in Rwanda's history, women participated in public works on a large scale. The people I interviewed attributed this to a number of factors. Firstly, the considerable gender imbalance after the genocide and war meant that women represented the largest body of potential workers and could not be ignored. Similarly, women (many of whom had been widowed) were obliged to work to ensure their families' survival. The RPF's wartime experience had given leaders confidence in the abilities of the female members, meaning that they were swift to give them new opportunities.

Upon taking power, the RPF appointed the first female mayor of Kigali, increased the percentage of women in parliament and created a separate Ministry for Women's Affairs (Burnet 2008: 367). Until that time, with the exception of the first female prime minister appointed in 1993, few women had played public roles under post-independence governments and public life had largely remained male-dominated. Under the RPF, although many women were given public roles, both at a national and local level, not all RPF women could be catered for. Some relied on their education to find jobs, while others found themselves unemployed. Women's futures were largely determined by their social status, experience, education and luck.

It was not until the very late 1990s or early 2000s that the situation of emergency could be said to have ended and a new phase in the country's reconstruction could begin. For some years following the end of the

war many female soldiers remained in the army. As women were gradually demobilized, many found that even with government support they
faced many challenges adapting to civilian life. Beatrice, an ex-soldier,
explained:

> Our families didn't know what had happened to us over the four years ... In a
> certain way we became killers to them because we had fought and as we had
> won the war. You don't win a war without killing.

Clearly, adapting to civilian life was very challenging, not just for the
women, but for their families. Women were quick to tell me that after the
war they married and had children.[22] There remained a social pressure on
women to marry and thus conform to tradition; this was a key way of rein-
tegrating into society.

In some ways, those who did not conform with stereotypes surrounding women's behaviour found it harder to be accepted by society. A
woman like Speciose, who had gained confidence as a consequence of her
wartime responsibilities with the RPF, felt excluded upon her return to the
community:

> Going to the front changed a girl's behaviour ... In Rwandan culture, a girl of
> twenty has behaviour everyone knows: she must be polite, she's afraid to par-
> ticipate and lives with her parents. But now, if you call me at midnight I'm no
> longer afraid, I could even go to Nyamirambo at night.[23] You can't spend four
> years in the forest and not change ... It was too hard afterwards. In Rwandan
> society, hearing that a woman was on the front, or was a soldier, was a scandal ...
> The first consequence was that men were afraid to talk to us.

There was a surprising tension between the initial euphoria that all who
participated (including women) were heroes and the harsh fact that many
women actually felt isolated. Beatrice put it into words:

> To a certain extent there is that marginalization, but it was not supposed to be,
> because we are called heroes.

While the war opened up opportunities for the RPF women, this was
only a small percentage of the Rwandan population and did not guarantee
long-lasting change in society's perceptions of women. Rather it was the
combination of the RPF's wartime experiences and the decimation of the
population by the genocide that meant that women continued to play an
important role in the public sphere after the war.

## Conclusion

The recruitment of women into the RPF's army is at once surprising and understandable. While it was not normal for women to join Rwanda's armies, there was some historic precedent for women assuming exceptional roles in exceptional circumstances. The RPF needed recruits for the army and political wing and could not exclude half the population; it was also aware of global trends towards gender equality. These elements, added to the sense of duty to Rwanda, all help to explain why thousands of women volunteered to join the RPF under dangerous circumstances. Determination and secrecy enabled women to break through social stereotypes and participate. The RPF educated its men and women on the importance of gender equality, and for the most part, women were treated as equals. Returning to civilian life after the war was always going to be challenging and indeed, many women married and started families as a way of fulfilling society's expectations. Whether the RPF's inclusion of women during the war alone would have had a long-lasting effect is difficult to judge. The genocide presented a subsequent exceptional circumstance that further challenged the 'traditional' role of women. As a result, women were able to assume different roles in society, some of which would historically have been male. The RPF experience of women contributing to the war undoubtedly led to the current focus on gender equality; the necessity of including women in reconstruction after the genocide guaranteed that this trend continued.

## Notes

1. http://news.bbc.co.uk/1/hi/7620816.stm (accessed 11 October 2013). In 2013, 64 per cent (2008: 56 per cent) of the lower-house parliamentarians were female: the highest proportion in the world. http://www.ipu.org/parline-e/reports/2265_A. htm (accessed 11 October 2013).
2. The issue of identity in Rwanda is delicate. In simple terms, the RPF was largely made up of people who would identify themselves as Tutsi, although it was open to all who opposed Habyarimana's regime and included some who would identify themselves as Hutu. President Habyarimana's government was Hutu-led and after he was killed, members of his party instigated the genocide against the Tutsi. I did not specifically ask my interviewees about identity, but it is likely that the majority would identify themselves as Tutsi. The majority had grown up in exile and had not visited Rwanda before the war.
3. *Cadre* refers to individuals working in the political wing.

4. This list of roles is not exhaustive; women are said to have been present in almost every role in the movement.

5. I conducted thirty interviews in English and French during March and April 2013. All direct quotations are from my audio recordings, with one exception taken from comprehensive notes. Translations are my own. I interviewed twenty-three women and seven men and gained additional insights from a further twenty informal discussions, mostly with men. Interviewees came from a range of backgrounds (having lived in a variety of countries pre-war) and social status. A disproportionate number had started or completed tertiary education; it is probable that less-educated women lived very different experiences before, during and after the war. My thanks to the Ndabaga Association, the RPF Secretariat and individuals who introduced me to interviewees.

6. Tutsi and Hutu cultures are said to be very similar.

7. Famous examples include Chief Nyirakigwene of Gitarama and Chief Nyirakabuga of Kibungo.

8. It is estimated that approximately five hundred and fifty thousand refugees fled Rwanda, leaving a total population of 7.4 million in the home country at the time (Prunier 1993: 122).

9. A term used during the genocide to refer to any Tutsi.

10. Popular Rwandan names are used as pseudonyms.

11. It was common for Rwandans living in Uganda to change their names to disguise their nationality.

12. Burundian pupils had to achieve over forty per cent in the secondary school entrance exams, whereas Rwandan refugees had to score in the range of eighty per cent to pass.

13. Alexis Kanyarengwe, a Hutu, was named president of the RPF during the war, demonstrating the movement's national as opposed to ethnic base (Reed 1996: 489).

14. For example, in Burundi, civil servants regularly contributed one-sixth of their salaries to the RPF.

15. Hutu, Tutsi and Twa all speak Kinyarwanda as their native language.

16. An estimated three thousand Rwandans fought in Museveni's NRA to overthrow Idi Amin: one quarter of the rebel army (Prunier 1993: 125).

17. The RPF force is estimated to have started with between four thousand and ten thousand soldiers, whereas the Rwandan national army increased from approximately five thousand to forty thousand soldiers (Reed 1996: 491).

18. President Museveni's involvement is much debated and whilst he did not openly support the RPF, it has been surmised that he tacitly supported his former comrades.

19. Women were not permitted to join the army in other countries of exile such as Burundi, Zaire, Kenya or Tanzania, so there were fewer female soldiers from these regions, especially initially.

20. The Rwandan Patriotic Front (RPF)'s military wing was called the Rwandan Patriotic Army (RPA). For consistency, I refer to the RPF throughout

the chapter; in military contexts RPF can be used interchangeably with RPA.
21. For example, President Habyarimana's wife, Agathe, is widely perceived to have been an architect of the genocide.
22. One study found that 57.9 per cent of female RPF ex-combatants married soldiers (Umutoni 2005: 24).
23. Nyamirambo is a neighbourhood in Kigali that could be described as similar to London's Soho.

## Bibliography

Burnet, J.E. 2008. 'Gender Balance and the Meanings of Women in Governance in Post-Genocide Rwanda', *African Affairs* 107(428): 361–386.

Government of Rwanda (GoR). 2010. *National Gender Policy*. Rwanda.

Kagame, A. 1954. *Les organisations socio-familiales de l'ancien Rwanda*. Brussels.

Kamukama, D. 1993. *Rwanda Conflict: Its Roots and Regional Implications*. Kampala, Uganda: Fountain.

Longman, T. 2006. 'Rwanda: Achieving Equality or Serving and Authoritarian State?' in G. Bauer and H.E. Britton, *Women in African Parliaments*. Boulder, Colorado: Lynne Rienner Publishers.

Mamdani, M. 2002a. 'African States, Citizenship and War: A Case Study', *International Affairs* 78(3): 493–506.

———. 2002b. *When Victims Become Killers: Colonialism, Nativism and the Genocide in Rwanda*. Princeton: Princeton University Press.

Maquet, J.J. 1961. *The Premise of Inequality in Ruanda*. Oxford: Oxford University Press.

Melvern, L. 2000. *A People Betrayed: The Role of the West in Rwanda's Genocide*. London: Zed Books.

Prunier, G. 1993. 'Elements pour une histoire du Front Patriote Rwandais', *Politique Africaine* 51(October): 121–138.

———. 1995. *The Rwanda Crisis: The History of a Genocide*. New York: Columbia University Press.

Reed, W.C. 1996. 'Exile, Reform, and the Rise of the Rwandan Patriotic Front', *Journal of Modern African Studies* 34(3): 479–501.

Rusagara, F. 2009. *Resilience of a Nation: A History of the Military in Rwanda*. Rwanda: Fountain Publishers.

Rwandese Patriotic Front (RPF). 1990. *Rwanda: Our Struggle for Democracy*. Rwanda.

———. 1994. *Rwanda: Background to Genocide*. Rwanda.

Turshen, M. and C. Twagiramariya. 1998. *What Women do in Wartime: Gender and Conflict in Africa*. London: Zed Books.

Umutoni, C. 2005. *A Study to Assess the Impact of Rwanda's Demobilization and Reintegration Program: On Female ex-Combatants and their Families*. Rwanda: Rwanda Demobilization and Reintegration Commission.

Uwineza, P., E. Pearson and E. Powley. 2009. *Sustaining Women's Gains in Rwanda: The Influence of Indigenous Culture and Post-genocide Politics*. Hunt Alternatives Fund.

Vansina, J. 2004. *Antecedents to Modern Rwanda: The Nyiginya Kingdom*. Oxford: James Currey.

**Hannah Spens-Black** is Programme Manager for a charity that supports rural communities in Ethiopia, Sudan and South Sudan. She lived in Eastern Africa intermittently over five years, which included three years living and working in Rwanda as project manager on international development research projects. In her early career, she qualified as a Chartered Accountant with the ICAEW and then worked as a theatre and festival producer in London. Hannah received her MSc in African studies from the University of Oxford. Her work as editor and art director includes *Rwanda the Rising Star 2003–2010* (GLCMC Kigali 2010).

# 8

# Women War Correspondents in 2013

## Glenda Cooper

As Israeli airstrikes once again hit Gaza City in November 2012, Phoebe Greenwood, a freelance journalist based in Jaffa, Tel Aviv, then heavily pregnant and working for *The Guardian* and *The Telegraph*, noticed something unusual as she sat writing her latest report in the lobby of the Al Deira Hotel (Barnett 2012). The hotel, a kind of unofficial newsroom for foreign correspondents, was full – but there was nothing strange there. Greenwood had been working with photographers Heidi Levine and Ewan Mohammed Darkhali. What struck Greenwood was the fact that the journalists surrounding her – from *The Sydney Morning Herald* to Sky Italia – were all women.

Not that Greenwood should have been surprised. After all, during the Libyan revolution of 2011 the first three reporters into Green Square, Tripoli were all women: Alex Crawford of Sky, Sara Sidner of CNN and Zeina Khodr of Al Jazeera English – yet their gender was something that some of the three involved felt was given undue focus. As Khodr put it:

> I was really shocked by the focus in Western media on female reporters – there's been nothing like that in the Muslim press. Surely we can both cover wars? – In fact some women are more brave; some men, some crews were definitely staying away from the front line.

So is it patronizing, irrelevant or sexist to mention the gender of war correspondents? Or can the fact that women appear more prominently at the forefront of media coverage of conflicts and revolutions be worthy of discussion?

Of course, women war reporters are nothing new: from Kathleen 'Kit' Blake Coleman covering the Spanish-American War in 1898, Margaret Bourke-White, Clare Hollingworth and Martha Gellhorn in the Second World War, to Kate Adie covering the Tripoli bombings and the late Marie Colvin who covered conflicts as diverse as Chechnya, Sri Lanka and Syria.

But many of the early correspondents had great difficulty in being taken to the front line; we have, says BBC correspondent Hilary Andersson, come a long way since Gellhorn had to hide in the bathroom of a hospital ship to avoid missing the D-Day landings (Andersson 2003). And while women correspondents may still be in a minority, their number is increasing – according to the Freedom Forum, during the first war in Chechnya nearly half the accredited reporters were women (*Journalists in Danger: Recent Russian Wars*, Freedom Forum, 1998, p. 307, cited in Seaton 2005). 'I think this high number of female correspondents in a conflict zone is a result of gender equality finally filtering down – making it totally normal for women to report from the front line', suggested Greenwood (Barnett 2012). And as jobs in journalism go, it can be a good one for women: the academics Marina Prentoulis, Howard Tumber and Frank Webster of City University have argued that women front line correspondents are actually less subjected to gender prejudices than other parts of the profession, because they face the same psychological and physical hazards as men. According to one female national newspaper journalist to whom Prentoulis, Tumber and Webster spoke for their paper *Finding Space: Women Reporters at War*, the reality was that:

> Everyone is reduced to an equal and there isn't tension between males or females ... no one would have ever said for example, 'we can't take you because you're a woman' ... you were just another reporter. (Prentoulis, Tumber and Webster 2005: 376)

Take for example, *Guardian* journalist Audrey Gillan. She was embedded in the second Gulf War with the Household Cavalry's Regiment D Squadron (a unit within 16 Air Assault Brigade, which does front line reconnaissance). The unit had initially said that it 'wished not to have women' (Gillan 2003: 8), but it changed its mind, and its soldiers completely accepted Gillan within the unit during their tour of Iraq; she also overcame her preconceptions about the soldiers, also known as 'squaddies'. Adapting to another culture was key:

> As they saw that I was prepared to muck in – and as part of a crew of five on a small vehicle, I had little choice but to take my turn at making the tea, heating

up the boil-in-the-bags or laying down people's 'doss bags', I was shouted at and ordered around – I simply became 'one of the boys'. Learning to swear like a trooper probably helped too. (Gillan 2003: 8)

Andersson described the 2003 Iraq war as a 'good war' for women (Andersson 2003: 20), with Christiane Amanpour for CNN, Emma Hurd for Sky, Andersson, Kylie Morris and Caroline Wyatt for the BBC and Cordelia Kreutzmar for GMTV all being given high-profile roles by their employers. She described the number of women war reporters as a 'vogue' and wrote at the time:

There is a well-entrenched belief at a high level of media management that audiences want to see and hear women on their screens. If press coverage of media deployments is anything to go by, women reporting wars also has an added 'wow' value. (2003: 20)

'Wow' value? Perhaps in the Iraq war, but when it came to the Libyan revolution executives were quick to say there was no deliberate attempt to foreground women reporters; Jon Williams, world news editor at the BBC says: 'This wasn't about male or female – it was about showcasing our best people'. In fact, in some cases perhaps it was more luck than deliberate action. Khodr, senior correspondent at Al Jazeera English, says she ended up in Tripoli purely because she was on the rota that week. And Crawford says she was sent back to Libya because of her previous experience in Zawiyah earlier in 2011, but believes that there were so many female reporters at the forefront of the reporting in other media organizations because:

I think they [news desks] did not realize how big a story it was going to be ... other organizations sent their big guns miles after the event. When I was leaving Libya and going to Tunisia, Ben Brown and John Simpson were going in – they are reporters you would expect in the starting line-up, but this time in the second line-up.

In Libya, the three women first into Green Square were all television correspondents as well: Lindsey Hilsum, Channel 4 News's international editor notes that the domination of the TV image has promoted the idea that Libya was reported by women:

The number of female correspondents reporting wars and other emergencies has been increasing over the years, but I don't really know why so much fuss [was made] about Libya. Maybe because Alex Crawford was so prominent, and the fact that she was doing live rolling TV news meant that people could see her in a dangerous place. No one watched live on TV as Marie Colvin's eye was shot in Sri Lanka. TV somehow makes it more powerfully obvious that the reporters are female.

Although women may have an increasingly high profile in war reporting, the truth is that the main difficulty for many women is getting the job in the first place. We have come some way since before 1970 when only six per cent of foreign correspondents were women (McAfee 2011). Crawford herself, a Royal Television Society award winner, took six years to win a foreign correspondent's role:

> I got turned down continually – it became a running joke in the newsroom how many times I got turned down; one friend said to me 'by now most people would have given up – they don't want you' but I kept on going and finally got it.

Those women who succeed in becoming foreign correspondents are a very specialized group, according to Anthony Feinstein and Mark Sinyor in a report for the Nieman Foundation for Journalism at Harvard. According to analysis of more than two hundred war reporters, they say that while two-thirds were male, those war correspondents who were female had several unusual attributes – they were less likely to be married (both compared to their male counterparts, and compared to journalists in general) and more likely to be better educated than male war correspondents.

Most intriguing was the gender parity the researchers found when it came to psychological problems or alcohol consumption, where the findings went against the grain of the normal gender divide: the women were no more likely to develop post-traumatic stress disorder, and they were just as likely to drink as the men (21 per cent of women versus 24 per cent of men exceeded standards of healthy drinking):

> The emerging profile of the female war journalist – more likely to be single and better educated than their male colleagues, no more vulnerable to PTSD, depression or overall psychological distress, and keeping up with the men when it comes to drinking – suggests they are a highly select group. It is not by chance that these women have gravitated to the frontlines of war. (Feinstein and Sinyor 2009)

Yet those who do succeed in the job still face frequent prurient discussion over their role in a way that their male counterparts do not: the key definition here often being whether or not they are a mother. As Andersson points out in her piece for the *British Journalism Review*, when Yvonne Ridley, then a reporter for the *Daily Express*, was arrested and detained in Afghanistan in 2001, her nine-year-old daughter Daisy's face was plastered all over the British papers. A national debate began about whether Ridley should have gone into a war zone when she had a young child; adjectives applied to her included 'daft' and 'glory hunting'. Andersson comments:

> Were the papers full of the plaintive faces of the children of any of the male journalists arrested, killed or injured in Iraq … ? No. That's because society still says that men are allowed to take risks because they can handle the situation, whereas women should be accepting their responsibilities at home. (Andersson 2003: 23)

Yet ten years on from Ridley, despite the admiration for the work in Libya of Crawford and others in the media, there has been a continuing debate about their marital/maternal status; this particularly affects those reporters who are mothers (such as Crawford) and who continue to put themselves in danger. In a 2011 Q&A session at the Edinburgh Television Festival discussing her reporting of Libya, Crawford says of questions over whether she should do this job as a mother of four:

> It's frankly really insulting and very, very sexist … I'm working alongside today the chief correspondent who's a man who's got three children and there will be no one who says what do you think you're doing, how awful, what are you doing to your children? No one, it won't even be raised as an issue and yet the stories that I do, [get] quite a lot of comment and a lot of criticism. (Crawford 2011)

Women who choose to work as war reporters still have to justify themselves. Christina Lamb, the award-winning *Sunday Times* journalist and author, who interviewed General Pinochet the day after she was released from hospital, where she had given birth to her son, and who was on the bus when Benazir Bhutto was assassinated, has said that she thinks motherhood has made her a better reporter. But she still talks of being 'a mother with a terrible secret in her wardrobe – a flak jacket' and that guilt is part of her life (Lamb 2005: 9). In a piece for the *Daily Mail*, Janine di Giovanni who has reported from Bosnia, Chechnya, Somalia, Rwanda, Iraq and Afghanistan, describes her decision to step back from war reporting in emotive terms:

> I knew having a child would mean I would miss lots of stories and would never again be the first one inside a city under siege or [to] get the first interview with a dictator. But I would have pages and pages of diaries filled with memories of [her son] Luka's first tooth and witness the first moment he walked. And no scoop is more satisfying than that. (di Giovanni 2011)

Even Crawford said, during her Edinburgh Q&A, that her children would prefer her to be a 'dinner lady' rather than a war correspondent. And Greenwood comments bluntly, saying that those of her colleagues who have children struggle because those children worry about their mothers while they are working in a conflict zone:

> It is really tough for dads too but there is just something different about poten-
> tially losing your mother on the front line of reporting. I know that being a
> mother and having that parental responsibility informs some of my journalist
> friends' decisions about where they place themselves during the conflict. Some
> will take fewer risks. (Barnett 2012)

But this debate was thrown into particularly sharp relief following the assault on CBS correspondent Lara Logan while covering the Egyptian revolution in Tahrir Square early in 2011.

Logan (a mother of two) came in for criticism that she had somehow 'deserved' to be assaulted. The academic Nir Rosen resigned from New York University after he tweeted that she had probably 'just been groped' (Hill 2011), and NPR had to remove countless offensive messages from their message boards (Memmot 2011) questioning whether Logan should have been reporting from Cairo in the first place.

As a result there were concerns that news organizations would be more reluctant to expose female journalists to possible danger, particularly of sexual assault, by reporting on the Arab Spring. A 2005 study for the International News Safety Institute found that, of the twenty-nine respondents who took part, more than half reported sexual harassment on the job (INSI 2005). The problem might be even bigger, since, in a piece for the *Columbia Journalism Review* in 2007, Judith Matloff argued that women often failed to report assault in case it stopped them from getting future assignments or hindered gender equality:

> The general reluctance to call attention to the problem creates a vicious
> cycle, whereby editors, who are still typically men, are unaware of the dangers
> because women don't bring them up. Survivors of attacks often suffer in lonely
> silence, robbed of the usual camaraderie that occurs when people are shot or
> kidnapped. It was an open secret in our Moscow press corps in the 1990s that
> a young freelancer had been gang-raped by policemen. But given the sexual
> nature of her injury, no one but the woman's intimates dared extend sympa-
> thies. (Matloff 2007)

Few women go on the record. Jenny Nordberg, a Swedish correspondent usually based in New York, was assaulted by a group of men while covering

Benazir Bhutto's return to politics in October 2007. Nordberg did not tell anyone about the attack, however, until she took part in a Committee to Protect Journalists report in 2011:

> 'I did not tell the editors for fear of losing assignments', she said. 'And I just did not want them to think of me as a girl. Especially when I am trying to be equal to, and better than, the boys. I may have told a female editor though had I had one'. (Wolfe 2012 cited in Ness 2012: 11)

Logan herself, however has since spoken out about her experience in Tahrir Square. In a foreword to a book on safety for women journalists printed by the International News Safety Institute (INSI) in 2012, the correspondent wrote as follows:

> I want the world to know that I am not ashamed of what happened to me. I want everyone to know I was not simply attacked – I was sexually assaulted. This was, from the very first moment, about me as a woman. But ultimately, I was just a tool. This was about something bigger than all of us – it was about what we do as journalists. That ancient tactic of terrifying people into submission or silence. (Cited in Storm 2012)

As Logan makes clear, danger must not be seen as a problem peculiar to female war reporters. Interviewed after Logan's assault, Jon Williams, international editor for the BBC, said that it would be naïve to see gender as irrelevant when deploying journalists to hostile environments but that 'changing [the] gender of the person doesn't eliminate the risk; it just makes it different ... The threat is there and real, how it manifests itself may be different for men and women but it doesn't eliminate the threat' (Connolly 2011).

The death of Marie Colvin in 2012 did not spark the usual controversy over whether female correspondents should be in war zones. This was for several reasons. First, the death toll of journalists in Syria (she was killed at the same time as French photojournalist Remi Ochlik, a week after Anthony Shahid of *The New York Times* died, and after five other journalists had been killed in the previous three months) meant that while Colvin's was perhaps the most high-profile death (arguably because she was a woman), the death of a journalist was sadly not unexpected. Second, as a childless, divorced woman, while there were various references to Colvin's private life and turmoils, the emotional frame of the mother-as-war-correspondent was absent, unlike the spotlight put on Ridley and Crawford referenced earlier. Added to that Colvin's quite extraordinary career and achievements – and her previous loss of an eye in Sri Lanka – meant that she was well-established as a journalist who had reported from, and narrowly survived, some of the world's most dangerous places. There was an old-fashioned Hemingway-esque legend about her obituaries: the wisecracking broad with the La Perla lingerie under the flak jacket. As a *Vanity Fair* profile after her death recalled, when reporting on an East Timor massacre in the city of Dili in 1999, she and two (female) Dutch journalists were the only ones who remained. 'Who's there? ... Where have all the men gone?' her editor in London asked. 'They just don't make men like they used to', she replied (Brenner 2012).

Colvin's gender may have meant she commanded front pages when she died; but for many journalists the suggestion is that, counter to what is often discussed, war reporting can be seen as safer for women than men. Prentoulis et al. point out that one male newspaper journalist they talked to stressed the advantages of being a woman, advantages that entail some potential tension with male reporters: 'I've been in situations, [where] there's only one place on the helicopter to go somewhere, and the chopper pilot thinks oh well, give it to the bird, the girl' (Prentoulis, Tumber and Webster 2005: 375).

This point is echoed by Lyse Doucet, chief international correspondent for the BBC who sees – the threat of sexual assault aside – less danger in general for women war reporters than their male counterparts, if not significant advantages:

> In most places I've worked, Western women have been regarded almost as a third gender. We aren't treated like the women of the place. We aren't treated like the men. But in traditional societies, where hospitality trumps ideology, we are almost always accorded the special privileges afforded to guests. In conservative societies, that also includes a belief that women need to be protected. (Cited in Storm 2012)

For Andersson, reporting from places like the Middle East, Asia and Africa, where fewer women hold prominent positions, the advantage can be that women are seen as harmless and less likely to be spies or aggressors than male journalists. And Alex Crawford agreed that women can be seen as less aggressive:

> Men find it easier dealing with women and are more likely to take against other men. It doesn't matter what you look like or your age; if you have half an ounce of charm and sociability, you can use that – not in a Machiavellian way but just in getting on with people, making friends ... and other females are obviously much more ready to talk to me than a strange foreign bloke.

In fact, Hilsum pointed out that there was a danger that one gender could be discriminated against as a result of difficulty in war reporting:

Often only women can talk to other women for cultural reasons ... It means women can get 100% of the story and men only part of it. But, as I've said before, I don't think this means men shouldn't be allowed to report wars. I think they have a contribution to make, even if they can't get the whole story.

Is the type of war reporting that we now see different though, because of the numbers of women journalists? Writing in *No Woman's Land*, the 2012 INSI report, Caroline Wyatt, the BBC's defence correspondent, mused on the time she spent reporting from Afghanistan in 2001:

Perhaps we brought a different perspective to the war: a little less focus on the bombs and the bullets, and more on what the end of the Taliban's rule in the north would mean for the families we met, and for their future. (Cited in Storm 2012)

The war correspondent Janine di Giovanni, writing in the *Daily Mail*, believes that in war situations the stories women cover mean that they are 'not equal to men':

We are often given the softer side of war to report, 'the female angle' so to speak, feeding into the stereotype that women are more 'caring' war reporters than men. (Di Giovanni 2011)

Interestingly di Giovanni's point is not new: Kit Blake Coleman talked of her disdain for editors trying to make her focus more on the human interest stories – dismissing this as 'guff' (Coleman cited in Ness 2012: 9). Yet many dispute that they cover 'guff' today. Andersson is wary of seeing women's reporting as different: 'Personally I believe women do add breadth to war reporting, but I don't think the point should be exaggerated. There are also many men who report with enormous depth and many women who don't' (Andersson 2003: 24). Khodr says of the stories she covered in Libya: 'We were covering battles; then we did the makeshift jail where people burned alive. It's going to be a while before we turn to the feature stories', while Hilsum said that she had interviewed far fewer women than usual: 'Women in Libya have largely been behind closed doors. They only came out on the streets in the last few days'. Talking of the work she did in Gaza City, Greenwood references the adrenaline surge that many war correspondents have commonly reported: 'Why would you want to be anywhere else other than in the eye of the storm? There is nothing better than reporting on the critical moments of our era' (Barnett 2012).

Jon Williams of the BBC points out that while Orla Guerin covered the plight of families in Misrata and the nurse in a Tripoli hospital, Ian

Pannell had done similar stories. Williams goes on to talk of a 'humanity and a personalization of the conflict' in both Guerin and Pannell's reporting, something that is backed up by the academic research. Prentoulis et al. argue that the shift towards human interest stories, encapsulated in the phrase 'the feminization of news', may be symptomatic of a broader cultural shift, moving towards a 'journalism of attachment'. They say:

> The latter, favoring more 'human' stories of civilian victims and some degree of emotional involvement, may be allowing women reporters more space for approaching war stories in their own way and, at the same time, allowing male correspondents to respond to the intensity of the war, without the 'macho' bravado often associated with the war correspondent. (Prentoulis, Tumber and Webster 2005: 377)

Lindsey Hilsum agrees that there is less distinction between male and female reporting in war these days:

> I think you'd be hard-pressed to find a consistent distinction between men's and women's reporting of wars and revolutions. But I would say that when a man does the weepy, human side he is regarded as empathetic and sensitive, but a woman may be perceived as 'not coping' if she shows emotion. So women broadcasters have to be very careful not to play into people's stereotypes.

And that perhaps is why images of female reporters have dominated the media agenda in recent times, in Libya, Syria and Gaza; not that there were women correspondents (there have been for decades) or that there were so many of them (unlikely to be statistically greater than normal). But in a world where we are used to a subjective, so-called 'feminized' approach to news, seeing Khodr and Crawford in their flak jackets and helmets having to shout their commentary over the sounds of bullets being fired, or hearing of Colvin's death in the middle of a bloody conflict just hours after she had appeared on television, we appear to be coming full circle. Just as men can report Williams' 'personalization of the conflict' without it being a shock, Crawford, Colvin, Greenwood et al. made clear that women can report in the traditional 'macho' way – and do it just as effectively.

### Acknowledgements

Some material from this chapter first appeared in G. Cooper (2011) 'Why Were Women Correspondents the Face of Coverage of the Libyan Revolution?', in R.L. Keeble and J. Mair (eds), *Mirage in the Desert? Reporting the Arab Spring* (London: Abramis). Unless otherwise referenced, the interviews carried out appear in that chapter.

## Bibliography

Andersson, H. 2003. 'The Wow Factor', in *British Journalism Review* 14(2): 20–24.

Barnett, E. 2012. *The Unique Advantage of Female War Reporters in Muslim Countries* (homepage of *The Daily Telegraph*). Available at http://www.telegraph.co.uk/ women/womens-life/9692810/The-unique-advantage-of-female-war-reporters-in-Muslim-countries.html (accessed 14 February 2013).

Brenner, M. 2012. *Marie Colvin's Private War, Vanity Fair*, August. New York.

Connolly, K. 2011. *Lara Logan Attack Turns Spotlight on Female Reporters* (homepage of BBC). Available at http://www.bbc.co.uk/news/world-us-canada-12510289 (accessed 14 February 2013).

Cooper, G. 2011. 'Why Were Women Correspondents the Face of Coverage of the Libyan Revolution', in R.L. Keeble and J. Mair (eds), *Mirage in the Desert? Reporting the Arab Spring*. London: Abramis.

Crawford, A. 2011. *Alex Crawford live Q&A at the MediaGuardian Edinburgh International Television Festival* (homepage of BskyB). Available at http://news.sky.com/ home/world-news/article/16058071 (last updated 27 August 2011; accessed 14 February 2013).

Di Giovanni, J. 2011. *Motherhood and Warfare: The Rise of Women Reporters on the Front Line* (homepage of *The Daily Mail*). Available at http://www.dailymail.co.uk/ femail/article-2031387/Motherhood-warfare-The-rise-women-reporters-line. html (accessed 14 February 2013).

Feinstein, A. and M. Sinyor. 2009. *Women War Correspondents: They Are Different in So Many Ways* (homepage of Nieman Foundation for Journalism at Harvard). Available at http://www.nieman.harvard.edu/reports/article/101967/Women-War-Correspondents-They-Are-Different-in-So-Many-Ways.aspx (accessed 14 February 2013).

Gillan, A. 2003. 'If You Cop It, Can We Have Your Radio?', *The Guardian*, 28 April. London.

Hill, K. 2011. *Nir Rosen's Tweets About Lara Logan Demonstrate the Problem of Twitter's Immediacy* (homepage of Forbes.com). Available at http://www.forbes.com/sites/ kashmirhill/2011/02/16/nir-rosens-tweets-about-lara-logan-demonstrate-the-problem-of-twitters-immediacy/ (accessed 14 February 2013).

INSI. 2005. *Women Reporting War* (homepage of INSI). Available at http://www. newssafety.org/images/stories/pdf/programme/wrw/wrw_finalreport.pdf (accessed 14 February 2013).

Lamb, C. 2005. 'My Double Life: Kalashnikovs and Cupcakes', *The Sunday Times*, 23 January. London.

Matloff, J. 2007. *Foreign Correspondents and Sexual Abuse: The Case for Restraint* (homepage of Columbia Journalism Review). Available at http://www.cjr.org/on_the_ job/unspoken.php?page=all (accessed 14 February 2013).

McAfee, A. 2011. 'The Trouble I've Seen', *The Guardian*, 16 April. London.

Memmott, M. 2011. *Why Have So Many Posts on the Attack on Lara Logan Been Removed?* (homepage of NPR). Available at http://www.npr.org/blogs/

thetwo-way/2011/02/16/133804167/why-have-many-comments-about-the-attack-on-lara-logan-been-removed (last updated 16 February 2011; accessed 14 February 2013).

Ness, A. 2012. *Women War Correspondents and the Battles They Overcame to Succeed,* All Theses and Dissertations (ETDs) Paper 742. Washington University in St Louis. Available at http://openscholarship.wustl.edu/etd/742/ (accessed 8 August 2015).

Prentoulis, M., H. Tumber and F. Webster. 2005. 'Finding Space: Women Reporters at War', *Feminist Media Studies* 5(3): 374–377.

Seaton, J. 2005. *Carnage and the Media: The Making and Breaking of News about Violence.* London: Allen Lane.

Storm, H. 2012. *On the Frontline with Female Reporters* (homepage of The Media Online). Available at http://themediaonline.co.za/2012/08/on-the-frontline-with-female-reporters/ (accessed 14 February 2013).

Wolfe, L. 2012. *The Silencing Crime: Sexual Violence and Journalists.* CPJ - Committee to Protect Journalists - Reports. Committee to Protect Journalists, 7 June 2011. Web. 18 April 2012. Available at http://cpj.org/reports/2011/06/silencing-crime-sexual-violencejournalists.php (accessed 8 August 2015).

**Glenda Cooper** is a lecturer and PhD researcher at the Centre for Law, Justice and Journalism, City University, London, looking at the changing coverage of humanitarian crises. Before that she worked as a journalist at a national level for more than a decade, including at the BBC, the *Independent, Washington Post, Daily Mail* and *The Daily Telegraph.*

# 9

# Talking Gender, War and Security at NATO

### Matthew Hurley

⚬⚬⚬

This study provides a reflection on how four military women, Celine, Nora, Grace and Anna, spoke about and conceptualized war, peace and security within the North Atlantic Treaty Organization (NATO).[1] These women were working, at various institutional levels, to mainstream a 'gender perspective' into NATO's operational planning as part of NATO's commitment to UN Security Council Resolution 1325 and the wider 'Women, Peace and Security' agenda. NATO defines a gender perspective as: 'Examining each issue from the point of view of men and women to identify any differences in their needs and priorities, as well as in their abilities or potential to promote peace and reconstruction' (NATO 2009: Appendix 1).[2]

The study of war is central to the discipline of international relations (IR), and yet the personal accounts of individuals (like those presented in this chapter) are often neglected, and women's voices and experiences of war in particular are often overlooked. It has been argued that 'IR does not conceptualise international relations as encompassing ordinary people and their experiences with the actors and processes it takes as canonical – states, markets, militaries, international organisations, security, development and so on' (Sylvester 2013: 61). Feminist researchers have challenged this imbalance; they draw attention to women's experiences, using gender to critique IR by placing the focus on the individual and their accounts of war, peace

(Tickner 1992, 2001; Enloe 2001, 2004, 2010; Steans 2006) and militarism (Sjoberg and Via 2010).

Women have always been involved in making and fighting wars, although these roles have often gone unacknowledged (Sjoberg and Via 2010: 5). However in recent years women's formal involvement and partici- pation in organizations of warfare, such as national militaries and by exten- sion international military organizations, has increased. As Sjoberg and Via identify, although these women 'remain a minority in all of these organiza- tions and are often prohibited from taking on certain roles of leadership or direct combat, women have been more active in the ... wars of the twenty- first century than at any documented time throughout history' (2010: 5). Speaking with these women at NATO offers an opportunity to discover how understandings of war can be gendered within military organizations, and also to consider the gendered nature of the institution itself. The presence of women within these masculine institutions challenges the strict division of masculine and feminine spheres of activity that traditionally defined their structure. Women represent what has historically been excluded from these institutions, therefore their presence 'makes visible the shapes and forms of gender power within such organisations' (Kronsell 2005: 285).

The accounts of Nora, Grace, Anna and Celine highlight how the ways in which these women talk (to me, a man)[3] about war and security are framed by the highly gendered nature of the institutional setting within which they are working – an organization of hegemonic masculinity (Connell 2005; Kronsell 2005), wherein NATO privileges militarized masculine norms and (re)produces binary notions of masculinity and femininity. What these accounts show is how 'ways of viewing' security are constructed around specific understandings of distinctly 'male' and 'female' perspectives, and how these perspectives can become associated with skills and competen- cies in war fighting and peace building perceived as particularly male, or particularly female.

## NATO and Military Masculinity

NATO is a complex organization. Established by the Washington Treaty in 1949, the current organization has twenty-eight European and North American member countries committed to collective military defence.[4] Following the collapse of the Soviet Union and the end of the Cold War, NATO has been involved in a number of military interventions. They include Bosnia and Herzegovina in the early to mid-1990s, Serbia and Kosovo (1999), Afghanistan (2001–2014) and the air campaign in Libya

(2011).[5] At its core NATO is a military organization comprised of the representatives of national military armed forces of member states and the political support structures they require. The national armed forces of NATO member states are still overwhelmingly male-dominated (Schjolset 2013). NATO draws upon the collective military resources of its member states in times of conflict. As an international military organization, built upon and for the purpose of waging war, NATO can be seen to embody what Annica Kronsell and others have called an 'institution of hegemonic masculinity' (Barrett 1996; Kronsell 2005) in that national 'military, defence and security related institutions have historically been "owned" by men and occupied by men's bodies' (Kronsell 2006: 111) – masculinity in this sense defines the norms of these institutions, and the language used to conceptualize war and security is in turn heavily masculinized (Cohn 1987).

These institutional norms are typified by forms of militarized masculinity, that include the construction of an ideal-type based around violence, aggression, heterosexuality and individual conformity to military discipline (Whitworth 2004: 16). Military organizations expend a great deal of time and resources constructing this ideal-type – what Cynthia Enloe describes as an 'ideology of manliness' (Enloe 2004: 16) – often starting with the basic training of troops that seeks to expel non-conforming men (Kovitz 2003) and to exorcise the 'feminine other' (Whitworth 2008: 121) from those who remain.

However, this is not to suggest that military masculinity is inherently uniform; like all masculinities there is variation within and similarities between categories of masculinity (Hearn 1996; Connell 2005). Indeed it can be argued that the ideal-type of militarized masculinity requires subordinate masculinities (associated more with 'feminine' characteristics) against which to define itself, and that these differences are manifest within the organization via unequal ranks and across multiple military occupations (Higate 2003; Kovitz 2003) and more recently with the inclusion of women into the armed forces. What is important here is that the construction of this ideal-type, through deliberate social practice, has a specific purpose; it is a means of operationalizing a unique mandate – deploying violence and waging war (Kovitz 2003: 9). As an organization that collectivizes national militaries for the purpose of waging war, NATO can be seen to be embodying a particular, internationalized form of military masculinity.

Understanding the construction of militarized masculinities is important within this chapter because the women interviewed often positioned themselves as women, articulated their experiences as women, and described war, peace and security in relation and in opposition to particular forms of masculinity that dominate the organization. It became clear that for Nora, Grace, Celine and Anna, men and women, as distinct groups within the organization, had very different understandings of war and security, and that the growing presence of women within the armed forces and the NATO structure was seen to challenge the dominant 'male view'. It is to these differences that I now turn.

## Viewing War and Security 'Differently'

One of the recurring themes to emerge in my interviews with Nora, Grace, Celine and Anna, was that men, more specifically military men, viewed warfare and the provision of security, differently from women. 'Men' in these accounts were often homogenized as a collective, their associated characteristics and qualities essentialized, representing the 'ideal-type' of militarized masculinity explained above. For them, this form of masculinity resulted in NATO viewing war and security in a specific way. In relation to this the women often spoke of a female viewpoint – one that was in turn homogenized and presented as a collective understanding.

For example, in the course of an interview with Celine, it became clear that for her, despite the presence of women, NATO remained a 'male organization'. As a result there was a distinct 'male point of view' that influenced understandings of war and security within the institution. Celine spoke of a male understanding of war and security that had traditionally neglected women's views and experiences. For her this was based around a conceptualization of war and security into different spheres – public and private:

> There is a saying, men die on the street and women die inside their houses. Now if you as a security force, if you as a man, want to work on security you make sure the street is safe, meaning that the men are safe. But women still die inside their houses.

Here, Celine draws attention to the space in which violence (and security) is experienced. For her, men are concerned with making the street safe, making the men (of the armed forces) safe. The security of the private space, of the home, is not considered. It is a conceptualization that privileges a traditional military understanding of where violence is perceived to take place – the street, the public realm. Violence within the home location, one occupied by women, remains unacknowledged and therefore invisible. For Celine the inclusion of women challenges this traditional understanding:

> I've been working for thirty years in the armed forces and I have experienced that women and men are not the same, our views have a different quality ... it's not just skills, it is also insights and ideas, the way of looking at things ... If

nobody tells them [military men] that women die inside the house, they will never see it as a problem.

Therefore, women's inclusion in the armed forces brings not only different skills to men, but also different perspectives and insights. For Celine, women will look at the security situation and define other women dying inside their houses as a problem; women understand security differently. This point of view was also expressed by Grace. When asked if she thought men and women viewed security differently she replied without hesitation, 'absolutely'. She went on to clarify:

> I think that females are much better at understanding what the UN has called human security. We, I think, are more likely to think when we go into a village within the military, to think, who are the people who aren't holding the rifles towards us? Let's think about the people on the other side of the compound that we can't meet, because they are going to be affected by what we do.
>
> We just think of things differently, not all of us obviously, just some, and some men are able to get it. But in the military the men are more focused on security, they view the security as the enemy side of it. Who is laying the IEDs? Who is it that is making it [the IED]? What is the network? They are not that bothered about females and children because they don't think that they can influence the people that are attacking you.

Here men define security in relation to the enemy. For Grace, incorporating a female perspective offers the possibility of a more holistic approach, talking to non-combatants, acknowledging the impact of war on those outside of the military compound defined loosely as 'human security'.[6] This is similar to Celine's public/private division of understandings of security. For military men, securing the public space from the enemy's Improvised Explosive Devices (IEDs) is prioritized. Women and non-combatants occupy a (private) sphere, where they are perceived to have no influence: they are not considered by military men to be of importance. However Celine and Grace claim that military women will consider this space.

Grace also draws attention to a difference in the way power is understood in areas of conflict. In her account power is understood in relation to the enemy. Power is defined within the context of men fighting other men. Civilian women are not understood to have power in this scenario and are constructed as passive actors – they cannot influence the security environment because they are perceived to be unable to influence the enemy. For Grace this was problematic, and the presence of women within the armed forces highlighted the need to reconceptualize where power lay within the communities that NATO was engaged with.

Anna was more cautious in expressing 'differences in thinking' between military men and women. However, she did identify a 'male perspective' that dominates within the armed forces, and that this perspective may not automatically take into account the different needs of men and women within areas of conflict. She stated that:

> I think that it is not necessarily that they [male military commanders] see security from a different perspective, but I think I help them to make sure that they see the different security needs that the people have out there ... like for instance, we had a road block issue a couple of months ago and I made sure that they saw how their plans affect the women ... there are mainly men at the road blocks and so soldiers mainly talk to men, which means that they only get the male perspective, they don't see the female perspective.

While Anna was keen to point out that she did not necessarily see the male commanders having a different perspective on security from her in general terms (i.e. the overall security goals of NATO as an organization), she does highlight that there is a need to draw attention to the 'female perspective'. She implies within her account that one particular view dominates: the male view and male security needs are privileged, male soldiers speak to male civilians. Again like Grace and Celine, Anna's female perspective is that her presence draws attention to these women – Anna helps the (male) military commanders to 'see security differently', to address concerns of civilian women that would otherwise be neglected.

This notion of the physical presence and physical difference of women within the military was also drawn upon by Nora. In her opinion the physical differences between men and women helped to highlight the difficulty some military men had in understanding certain aspects of security:

> In general if they hear someone talk about sexual violence, they say 'oh scary, we don't know what to do with that'. Not because they don't want to deal with it, but because they haven't done it before, it is quite new, and still this female thing is a little scary because they are after all men, you know what I mean? Let me take an example, I was on military exercises, a colleague and I were talking about things like this and she said: 'men have a problem handling things like this, everything that has to do with females, sexual things'. And you can make a very easy comparison, if you are on exercises and if the female officer says: 'oh I have my period, I have to go behind the trees' the men are like: 'oh just stay away from me'. I mean they have a problem with that, so how difficult is it to talk about sexual violence in war? Do you see the problem? It is something that they are not used to dealing with, you know it's female stuff – not because they don't want to deal with it, but because they don't fully understand it and they don't know what to do.

For Nora the fact that these men have difficulty in dealing with the menstruation of their female colleagues highlights the difficulty in their addressing sexual violence in war, as these are things that happen to women's bodies.[7] Here the difference between men and women, physically, becomes a way in which Nora attempts to understand and articulate the difficulty these men have in understanding, and conceptualizing, sexual violence in warfare and security provision. This account draws into sharp focus the minority position that these women (and their bodies) occupy within the military. However, what is evident is that the presence of these women disrupts the uniformity of the male-dominated organization.

## From Different Ways of 'Viewing' to Different Ways of 'Doing'

What became apparent during the interview process was that the inclusion of women into both national armed forces and their allied international organizations challenges traditional understandings of war, peace and security with NATO, up to a point. This process is furthered by NATO's engagement with UN Resolution 1325 and a dedication of institutional resources to focus on women, peace and security. Whilst all women spoke of some form of gendered differences in understandings and experiences of war and security, these differences were also seen to manifest themselves in particular female skills and ways of 'doing security', especially when discussing the role of female soldiers in NATO's involvement in Afghanistan.

NATO's protracted engagement in Afghanistan has, according to Nora, presented a challenge to NATO and opened up an opportunity to incorporate female skills and perspectives:

> NATO didn't plan for ten years ... that's the big lesson in Afghanistan, you can't do it all alone, you need to be innovative ... we never had a war like that ... I think they have struggled in Afghanistan, they see that they need something more.

The 'something more' for Nora was a female perspective. Nora spoke of 'female competencies' that were 'soft and hard-to-define things'. Interestingly, she found it hard to articulate exactly what these competencies were, and yet defines them as 'soft' in opposition to the 'hard' male competencies which included physical force and aggression. This again reinforced a distinctly male/female binary that ran throughout her interview.

For Nora, military men struggled to engage with these competencies, not for want of trying, but for lack of experience and the persistence of traditional understandings of war fighting. Security provision did not privilege these 'soft competencies', therefore male soldiers did not develop them and NATO's mission in Afghanistan has struggled as a result.

Grace was more specific in identifying a female skill-set that could be deployed within Afghanistan:

> I think that it was because NATO was involved in Afghanistan, I think that being involved in counter-insurgency has made them see the value of their females.
>
> I've noticed that these female engagement teams that the Americans use, the men would go up and talk to women and tell them things ... I think that the intelligence corps have realized that there is this difference between men and women and that women in some sort of intelligence role might have more to gain: in Afghanistan they can talk to women and men.

Here Grace identifies that NATO's struggle in Afghanistan has made the organization more receptive to particular female skills and competencies. This particular understanding of what the female perspective can bring to NATO operations is also being taken up at a policy and doctrine level, as well as in the training and education received by NATO soldiers. For example, in a position paper outlining why it makes 'sense' for NATO to adopt a 'gender perspective', the Civil-Military Co-operation Centre for Excellence states that:[8]

> For centuries, the army has been a male dominated organisation with a male culture. Competences such as being physically strong, mentally tough and decisive are selection criteria that are highly appreciated. Yet, the role of the armed forces has changed and other essential, more feminine, competences, such as close listening, mental endurance and empathising are now required. (CCOE 2008: 5)

The understanding of specific skills associated with men and women has also become enshrined in NATO doctrine:

> The experiences and skills of both men and women are essential to the success of NATO operations. Today's conflicts often require a comprehensive approach in terms of more tactful public relations, better and more extensive situational awareness, information operations, information gathering and intelligence production. Women in NATO-led forces can be an asset and an enabler, especially in activities of engagement with the local population. (NATO 2012: 11)

Within these accounts and policy documents specific skills, traits and characteristics have become associated with the female soldiers – listening, communication, compromise, empathy and information gathering have become a distinctly 'female' way of doing security – complementing the 'harder' competencies that the male soldiers are deemed to lack.[9] What was suggested by these women was that the changing nature of warfare – exemplified by the protracted conflict in Afghanistan – highlighted to the military command that traditional understandings of war fighting and security provision were insufficient. The 'value' of a distinctly female perspective and its associated skills (again, as something distinct and 'other') is beginning to be seen by NATO.

## A Note on Violent Women

In speaking to Nora, Grace, Celine and Anna I used a form of semi-structured interviewing. However, I was keen to let them lead the conversation, to discuss issues (around gender and security) that they deemed important. This led to rich accounts of professional and personal experiences of working on gender issues within NATO. However, it is worth reflecting briefly on what was left out of these accounts, what remained silent. As shown above, the narratives focused around notions of war, security and NATO's involvement in Afghanistan. What was absent from all of the interviews conducted was any notion of violence conducted by female soldiers and civilian women. In one respect this replicates most of the official doctrine and literature produced by NATO. This material emphasizes, almost exclusively, the positive (non-violent) contributions of women, often illustrated by pictures of smiling female soldiers holding children and integrating peacefully with the civilian population.[10] In one respect this is not surprising. NATO, like many military organizations, promotes a sanitized image of itself for public consumption. Violence and death do not feature prominently in NATO's account of itself – peace building and security provision are promoted over violence and war fighting.

These women's accounts can be seen as extensions of this. However, female soldiers are trained, like their male colleagues, to use deadly force, to deploy (state-sanctioned) violence to achieve desired aims.[11] Yet in the accounts offered to me during the interview process, female soldiers were framed as information gatherers and (relatively benign) interlocutors between the military and local population. With regard to civilian women, violence was something that was done to them (for example, in the form of sexualized violence); they were not conceived of as violent actors, or even to have the potential for violent behaviour.[12] That violence enacted by women was unspoken during the interviews can be read as a continuation of women's skills and competencies being conceptualized as 'soft', and that helps to position female soldiers as peacekeepers (Charlesworth 2008) or as civilian victims (Moser and Clark 2005), furthering the difference between women in the military and their war-fighting (violent) male colleagues.

## Conclusion – Essentialized Perspectives and Practices

The views of Grace, Celine, Nora and Anna – views of military women from within an international security organization – allow us to see how under-standings of war fighting and security provision are highly gendered. On the whole, despite the presence of women within national armed forces and at the international level, war remains a 'masculine enterprise' (Carter 1996) – men dominate the organizations of war, and the 'male perspective' identi-fied by these women is based upon traditional understandings of power and security arising from the experiences and expectations of men. However, the presence of women within these organizations disrupts this male domi-nance. Listening to how these women articulate a specific female view of security that is constructed in opposition to, and as a vital complement to men helps to expose the traditional masculine norms of the organization.

What these accounts demonstrated to me is how undoubtedly complex gender relationships between men and women can become reduced and highly essentialized within a military context. When these women spoke of security, a binary was established that placed the 'male' and 'female' views in opposition to one another. Some women seemed aware of this. Anna, for example, was reluctant to draw out specific differences in the way the military command viewed security in general terms – implying similarities in terms of a 'security perspective', but differences in terms of where that should be focused. Grace acknowledged that 'some men got it' and explicitly qualified her account of the 'female perspective' with statements such as: 'This makes me sound horribly essentialist, but I just think that we think of things differently'. She nonetheless reinforces a specific male/female divide within her accounts.

At one level, this is perhaps unsurprising – Celine, Nora, Grace and Anna's understandings and experiences have been shaped in relation to the military masculinity that their national armed forces and NATO continue to produce and privilege. In many ways the institution determines the char-acteristics of its men (and women), moulding individuals to its structures and ways of thinking through social discipline and training – these accounts reflect that process. Despite undergoing the same institutional training and military socialization as their male colleagues they simply do not reflect the dominant masculine norms of the institution, by virtue of being women. As a minority group within an institution of hegemonic militarized masculinity, their experiences and accounts become homogenized and reduced to represent the 'female perspective'.

As a consequence, specific characteristics and skills became attached to this perspective – listening, compromise, soft competencies. This binary understanding of male and female skills is becoming enshrined within NATO policy and doctrine as the organization develops a more 'comprehensive approach' to security following the struggles within Afghanistan and as it seeks to institutionalize a 'gender perspective'. I would argue that conceiving of male and female views and skills in this way is inherently problematic – variation and nuance within each 'category' becomes homogenized (even when it is acknowledged) and women's contributions, particularly to peace and security provision, become reduced and understood in limited terms (Charlesworth 2008) and ultimately run the danger of reinforcing gender stereotypes (De Groot 2001; Valenius 2007).

However, what speaking to these women shows is that their views are constructed in relation to and in opposition to a military masculinity that the organization has traditionally produced and privileged. Grace, Nora, Celine and Anna's accounts of differences between men and women, as they have seen and experienced them in the highly militarized and masculine context within which they work, offer an invaluable insight into the myriad ways that wars, and the organizations that fight them, are inherently gendered.

## Notes

1. As the group of women discussed within this chapter is small, the names provided are pseudonyms; details of specific job roles and areas of deployment are also omitted. This is in order to protect the anonymity of the women involved in the research.

2. This chapter represents a part of my wider research looking at NATO's engagement with United Nations Security Council Resolution 1325 on Women, Peace and Security (S/RES/1325, 2000), specifically NATO's attempt to mainstream a 'gender perspective' into military planning and operations. This process is analysed from a policy perspective (for example, NATO 2009) as well as by talking to individuals within the organization tasked with implementing those policies (Hurley 2014).

3. The participants in my research told me certain things, framed their work, their understandings of 'gender' and experiences of NATO in certain ways because I (and I as a man) was an audience for their stories. Had they been representing themselves to someone else (a female researcher for example) they

may have represented other aspects of their identity (Ackerly and True 2008: 703), told other stories about their experiences, spoke about 'men', 'women', 'gender' and 'security' in different ways (that drew upon a female commonality perhaps). Participants' perceptions of my identity were not limited to my sex; my nationality (white, British), my role as a civilian academic, someone who was non-military were also drawn upon by the participants. In this sense, the constructions and understandings of gender produced during the interviews were relational – co-constructed between me and the participant – formed in part by their perception of me 'as a man'. For more on the importance of a 'reflexive attitude' to research (especially in international relations) see Ackerly, Stern and True 2006; Ackerly and True 2008; Kronsell 2005; Tickner 2005; and for examples of the role of gender and perception in the interview setting, see Svedberg 2000; Pini 2005.

4. Article 5 of the North Atlantic Treaty states that 'an armed attack against one or more of them in Europe or North America shall be considered an attack against them all' (NATO 1949: Article 5).

5. See Cooper, in this volume.

6. While there are differing interpretations of the term 'human security', the UN 2005 World Summit defines it as: 'the right of all people to live in freedom and dignity, free from poverty and despair' and recognized that 'all individuals, in particular vulnerable people, are entitled to freedom from fear and freedom from want, with an equal opportunity to enjoy all these rights and fully develop their human potential' (UN 2005 (A/RES/60/1): Paragraph 143).

7. Within this particular account sexualized violence in war was spoken of as something that was primarily experienced by women and girls. Whilst women and girls continue to be disproportionately affected by sexualized violence, it is increasingly acknowledged that men and boys are also victims of sexualized violence. See Carpenter 2006; Sivakumaran 2007; Wood 2006.

8. The Civil-Military Co-operation Centre for Excellence (CCOE) is a NATO-accredited centre that provides training and education. Its mission statement declares that its purpose is to assist NATO, sponsoring nations and other military and civil institutions/organizations in their operational and transformation efforts in the field of civil-military interaction, by providing innovative and timely advice and subject matter expertise in the development of existing and new concepts, policy and doctrine, specialized education and training and contribution to the lessons-learned processes.

9. For examples of studies on the role of female peacekeepers, see Valenius 2007; Olsson, Skjelsbaek, Barth and Hostens, 2004; Olsson and Tryggestad 2001.

10. For an example of this, see NATO's briefing pamphlet entitled 'Women, Peace and Security' (NATO 2010).

11. There are national variations that determine the role of women in direct combat roles. For example, the United States lifted the ban on women to serving in 'front line' combat roles in January 2013. In the United Kingdom, the role of women in combat roles is currently under review.

12. For a detailed account of the role of women's violence in global politics and how this runs counter to inherited perceptions of the 'natural' role of women, see Sjoberg and Gentry 2007; Moser and Clark 2005; and for the role of violent military women and militarized femininity in Iraq, see Sjoberg 2007.

# Bibliography

Ackerly, B., M. Stern and J. True (eds). 2006. *Feminist Methodologies for International Relations*. Cambridge: Cambridge University Press.

Ackerly, B. and J. True. 2008. 'Reflexivity in Practice: Power and Ethics in Feminist Research on International Relations', *International Studies Review* 10(4): 693–707.

Barrett, F. 1996. 'The Organisational Construction of Hegemonic Masculinity: The Case of the US Navy', *Gender, Work and Organisation* 3(3): 129–142.

Carpenter, R.C. 2006. 'Recognising Gender-Based Violence against Civilian Men and Boys in Conflict Situations', *Security Dialogue* 37(1): 83–103.

Carter, A. 1996. 'Should Women be Soldiers or Pacifists?', *Peace Review: A Journal of Social Justice* 8(3): 331–335.

Charlesworth, H. 2008. 'Are Women Peaceful? Reflections on the Role of Women in Peace Building', *Feminist Legal Studies* 16: 347–361.

Civil-Military Co-operation Centre of Excellence (CCOE). 2008. 'Gender Makes Sense: A Way to Improve Your Mission', www.nato.int/ims/2008/win/opinions/gender_booklet_ccoe_v12.pdf (accessed August 2015).

Cohn, C. 1987. 'Sex and Death in the World of Rational Defence Intellectuals', *Signs* 12(4): 687–718.

Connell, R.W. 2005. *Masculinities*, 2nd edition. Cambridge: Polity Press.

De Groot, G. 2001. 'A Few Good Women: Gender Stereotypes, the Military and Peacekeeping', *International Peacekeeping* 8(2): 23–38.

Enloe, C. 2000. *Maneuvers: The International Politics of Militarising Women's Lives.* Berkeley: University of California Press.

———. 2001. *Bananas, Beaches and Bases: Making Feminist of International Politics*, 2nd edition. Berkeley: University of California Press.

———. 2004. *The Curious Feminist Searching for Women in the New Age of Empire*. Berkeley: University of California Press.

———. 2010. *Nimo's War, Emma's War: Making Feminist Sense of the Iraq War*. Berkeley: University of California Press.

Hearn, J. 1996. 'A Critique of the Concept of Masculinity/Masculinities', in M. Mac An Ghaill (ed.), *Understanding Masculinities*. Buckingham: Open University Press.

Higate, P. 2003. '"Soft Clerks" and "Hard Civvies": Pluralizing Military Masculinities', in P. Higate (ed.), *Military Masculinity: Identity and the State*. London: Praeger.

Hurley, M. 2014. 'Gendering NATO: Analysing the Construction and Implementation of the North Atlantic Treaty Organisation's Gender Perspective', PhD dissertation. Oxford Brookes University.

Kovitz, M. 2003. 'The Roots of Military Masculinity', in P. Higate (ed), *Military Masculinity: Identity and the State*. London: Praeger.

Kronsell, A. 2005. 'Gendered Practices in Institutions of Hegemonic Masculinity', *International Feminist Journal of Politics* 7(2): 280–298.

——. 2006. 'Methods for Studying Silences: Gender Analysis in Institutions of Hegemonic Masculinities', in B. Ackerly, M. Stern and J. True (eds), *Feminist Methodologies for International Relations*. Cambridge: Cambridge University Press.

Moser, C. and F. Clark (eds). 2005. *Victims, Perpetrators or Actors? Gender, Armed Conflict and Political Violence*, 2nd edition. London: Zed Books.

NATO. 1949. The North Atlantic Treaty, http://www.nato.int/nato_static/assets/pdf/stock_publications/20120822_nato_treaty_en_light_2009.pdf (accessed August 2015).

——. 2009. Bi-Strategic Command Directive 40-1: Integrating UNSCR 1325 and Gender Perspectives into the NATO Command Structure including Measures for Protection during Armed Conflict, http://www.nato.int/nato_static/assets/pdf/pdf_2009_09/20090924_Bi-SC_DIRECTIVE_40-1.pdf (accessed August 2015).

——. 2010. Briefing: Participation, Protection, Prevention, http://www.nato.int/nato_static/assets/pdf/pdf_publications/20120116_UNSCR_EN.pdf (accessed August 2015).

——. 2012. Bi-Strategic Command Directive 40-1: Integrating UNSCR 1325 and Gender Perspective into the NATO Command Structure, http://www.nato.int/issues/women_nato/2012/20120808_NU_Bi-SCD_40-11.pdf (accessed August 2015).

Olsson, L. and T. Tryggestad (eds). 2001. *Women and International Peacekeeping*. London: Frank Cass.

Olsson, L., I. Skjelsbaek, E. Barth and K. Hostens (eds). 2004. 'Gender Aspects of Conflict Interventions: Intended and Unintended Consequences', Final Report to the Norwegian Ministry of Foreign Affairs. Oslo: International Peace Research Institute, PIRO.

Pini, B. 2005. 'Interviewing Men: Gender and the Collection and Interpretation of Qualitative Data', *Journal of Sociology* 41(2): 201–216.

Schjolset, A. 2013. 'Data on Women's Participation in NATO Forces and Operations', *International Interactions: Empirical and Theoretical Research in International Relations* Vol. 39(4): 575–587

Sivakumaran, S. 2007. 'Sexual Violence against Men in Armed Conflict', *European Journal of International Law* 18(2): 253–276.

Sjoberg, L. 2007. 'Agency, Militarised Femininity and Enemy Others: Observations from the War in Iraq', *International Feminist Journal of Politics* 9(1): 82–101.

Sjoberg, L. and C. Gentry. 2007. *Mothers, Monsters, Whores: Women's Violence in Global Politics*. London: Zed Books.

Sjoberg, L. and S. Via (eds). 2010. *Gender, War and Militarism: Feminist Perspectives*. London: Praeger Publishers Inc.

Steans, J. 2006. *Gender and International Relations*, 2nd edition. Cambridge: Polity Press.

Sylvester, C. 2013. *War as Experience: Contributions from International Relations and Feminist Analysis*. Abingdon: Routledge.

Svedberg, E. 2000. 'The "Other" Recreated – A Relational Approach to East-West Negotiations', PhD dissertation. Lund Political Studies, Lund University.

Tickner, A. 1992. *Gender in International Relations: Feminist Perspectives on Achieving Global Security*. New York: Columbia University Press.

——. 2001. *Gendering World Politics: Issues and Approaches in the Post-Cold War Era*. New York: Columbia University Press.

——. 2005. 'What is Your Research Program? Some Feminist Answers to International Relations Methodological Questions', *International Studies Quarterly* 49: 1–21.

United Nations. 2000. Security Council Resolution 1325 – Women, Peace and Security (S/RES/1325/2000), http://daccess-dds-ny.un.org/doc/UNDOC/GEN/N00/720/18/PDF/N0072018.pdf (accessed August 2015).

——. 2005. World Summit Outcome (A/RES/60/1/2005), http://daccess-dds-ny.un.org/doc/UNDOC/GEN/N05/487/60/PDF/N0548760.pdf (accessed August 2015).

Valenius, J. 2007. 'A Few Kind Women: Gender Essentialism and Nordic Peacekeeping Operations', *International Peacekeeping* 14(4): 510–523.

Whitworth, S. 2004. *Men, Militarism and UN Peacekeeping: A Gendered Analysis*. Boulder: Lynne Rienner Publishers.

——. 2008. 'Militarised Masculinity and Post Traumatic Stress Disorder', in J. Parpart and M. Zalewski (eds). *Rethinking the Man Question: Sex, Gender and Violence in International Relations*. London: Zed Books.

Wood, E.J. 2006. 'Variation in Sexual Violence during War', *Politics and Society* 34(3): 307–342.

**Matthew Hurley** is a lecturer in sociology at Oxford Brookes University. His research interests include gender, international security and militarism, with a particular focus on the lived experiences of those within military organizations. His PhD explores the ways in which the North Atlantic Treaty Organization (NATO) engages with and implements United Nations Security Council Resolution 1325 on Women, Peace and Security.

# 10

# Military Masculinities and Counter-insurgency Theory and Practice in Afghanistan

An Uneasy Relationship?

**Rachel Grimes**

June 2007, Kandahar Air Field (KAF), in searing heat; I am squashing my body and the paraphernalia of war (rifle, helmet, body armour, pistol strapped to my upper thigh and bergen)[1] into a canvas seat on a U.S. Hercules aircraft. I am trying to adjust my body armour so that my breasts aren't crushed into my vertebrae during the flight. The obligatory bun net, holding my hair in a 1940s chignon, is trapped between the Velcro of the body armour and the red netting on the Hercules' 'seat'. None of this is helped by my Kevlar helmet, which wasn't designed for long hair, and is forcing my chin forward into the Osprey body armour, which now feels like a sumo wrestler resting on my sternum. I am so distracted by the array of factors conspiring against me having a 'comfortable' flight from KAF to Kabul, that I only subconsciously register the American soldier's conversation. He is sitting with his back to me. The red netting is the only barrier between us. In a loud voice he is bragging about how many women he will sleep with when he goes on leave the following week. I carefully twist around, trying to prevent my bun from collapsing or causing a self-inflicted broken sternum, attempting to see who could be so stupid. A soldier is animatedly telling his Afghan interpreter about his expectations for his leave period. It sounded like a sex-fuelled fantasy. The Afghan looks on in disbelief and is laughing with the soldier. I was in a predicament. The soldier was clearly doing the wrong thing. Talking about women with the Afghans is not advised. Conceited bragging about sexual relations with women is completely forbidden. But the moment passed. Thankfully, the aircraft growled into action, everyone on the Herc inserted their ear defenders to muffle the initial roar and then once in flight, the monotonous, heavy drone of the Lockheed Martin engines began. The conversation ended and everyone succumbed to the dusty heat, trying to sleep out the flight. To this day I am ashamed that I didn't reprimand the soldier.

* * *

The announcement by the British government that UK troops would be withdrawing from Afghanistan in 2014 left many observers debating the merits of the ongoing counter-insurgency (COIN) operation in Helmand Province, Afghanistan. Lack of tangible success was attributed to various factors. Some argued that there was too much corruption at the political level; Kilcullen argued that the support from Pakistan rendered it almost impossible to defeat the insurgents; others pointed to a lack of cultural understanding of the socio-political environment and a slowness to adapt as a learning organization (see Catigiani 2012; Kitzen 2012); while some blamed the lack of political will by the nations represented in the International Security Assistance Force (ISAF).

Here I consider the part that gender roles have played between 2005 and 2012 in military operations within Afghanistan. The British military's doctrine and conduct of operations will be examined and the expanded employment of servicewomen in Afghanistan will be considered from a gender perspective. While considerable work has been done regarding the utility of servicewomen in Peace Support Operations (PSO), there is negligible inquiry considering the role of military masculinities or the utility of servicewomen in roles such as Female Engagement Teams in the Afghan counter-insurgency.

For almost the last decade the United States and the UK were involved in countering the return of the Taliban and preventing other insurgents from undermining the development of the Afghan government. In 2003 both countries became part of the NATO-led ISAF operation. This was neither state-centric nor enemy-centric, but as General Richards points out, population-centric (2011: 15). The doctrine that guided Western armies and the tactics that were adopted in Afghanistan as part of counter-insurgency differed from conventional warfare tactics. Rather than a reliance on power, technology and holding ground, ISAF strove to win over the minds of the Afghan populace. This approach to operations included kinetic actions, such as lethal targeting of insurgents, but was essentially non-violent in outlook.

Effective counter-insurgency, commonly referred to as COIN, leads to political, economic and development functions as well as military activity. According to an academic, Nye, COIN distorts the once distinct boundary between the military and the civilian. He suggests that civilians are perceived as an extension of the feminine (2007: 418). This blurring of the battle lines confuses the hegemonic masculinity encouraged through a soldier's basic and pre-deployment training. My observation is that units that don't recruit women, typically the Combat Arms, are more likely to possess a heightened form of military masculinity. While I don't suggest there is a zero sum equation – the Combat Arms can only be employed in conventional warfare – there are some aspects of counter-insurgency that may be more challenging for these soldiers to embrace. Catigiani, an academic who spent time in Helmand, also noted that some soldiers were not completely at ease in 'COIN' operations (2012: 4).

The next section provides terms associated with COIN as defined by the military. I then consider how military masculinities have been created and perpetuated by the Combat Arms and will note where they have contradicted the doctrinal principles of COIN. Before concluding I will briefly identify a COIN dividend for servicewomen, and consider how military masculinities can be overcome for future military operations.

## Definitions and Terms

The U.S. Marine Corps's doctrinal publication on COIN states that an insurgency is an:

> organized movement aimed at the overthrow of a constituted government through the use of subversion and armed conflict. It is an organized, protracted politico-military struggle designed to weaken the control and legitimacy of an established government, occupying power, or other political authority while increasing its own control. (USMC 2007: 2)

For the UK military counter-insurgency is:

> [t]hose military, political, economic, psychological and civic actions taken to defeat the insurgency, while addressing the root causes. (MoD 2010: 1–4)

Kilcullen (2006) and Nagl (2005) emphasize the requirement to adopt a multifaceted approach that integrates and synchronizes diverse activities in one holistic approach in order to weaken the insurgent, while enhancing the government's legitimacy in the eyes of the local population. This approach to defeating an enemy, given the need for good relations with the population, requires soldiers to think and act in new ways.

To understand military masculinities as found on the ground in Afghanistan, it is necessary to be familiar with socially constructed Western masculinities and femininities. It is this social structure of gendered roles that has strengthened hegemonic military masculinity.

Hooper and Higate persuasively argue that masculinities and femininities are fluid and not fixed (Hooper 2001: 43; Higate 2003: 7). Instead they are a social construction that can change within cultural and societal domains. Military masculinities are therefore also constructed and changeable, but within the Combat Arms there is a resistance to any contemporary weakening of what it is to be a soldier. I agree with the academic Morgan, who suggests that to a significant extent:

> The warrior still seems to be a key symbol of masculinity ... in so far as masculinity continues to be identified with physicality then there are strong reasons for continuing to view military life as an important site in the shaping and making of masculinities. (1994: 168)

Enloe notes that in order to establish masculinities, Western femininities have been constructed in a binary and inferior relationship to them (2004: 5). The 'lesser' role of women, and by extension the roles of civilians, have been perpetuated within aspects of the military. Connell notes, 'one side of the polarity is devalued in culture and associated with weakness' (2010: 16). The military is not institutionally misogynistic but the presence of servicewomen is possibly contentious due to the social attributes that society has attached to women. In some way servicewomen undermine the concept of what it is to be a soldier.

The table below is a presentation by Hooper of the binary relationship between femininity and masculinity (2001: 43):

| Masculine | Feminine |
| --- | --- |
| Strong | Weak |
| Hard | Soft |
| Rational | Irrational |
| Tough | Tender |
| Mind | Body |
| Dominant | Submissive |
| Science | Art |
| Active | Passive |
| Competitive | Caring |

| | |
|---|---|
| Objective | Subjective |
| Public | Private |
| Independent | Dependent |
| Aggressive | Victim |
| War | Peace |
| Self | Other |

Within the military this binary view of gendered relations provides a psycho-logical conflict in military operations such as COIN. Afghanistan was a per-plexing blend of conventional and non-conventional warfare. Attempting to defeat insurgents while simultaneously promoting a liberal democracy through non-violent means. During two tours in Afghanistan I was able to witness this dichotomy of COIN. While the conduct of the soldiers was com-mendable, the psychological battle to adopt new, 'softer' soldiering skills was apparent.

## The Creation of Masculinities

Within the British Army women have been prevented from serving in the Combat Arms. According to the MoD this has been because they may distract their male colleagues or undermine operational effectiveness by lacking the same physical strength as their male cohort. This leads to another concern that as the female physique is less suited to the rigours of the infantry, the MoD has a 'duty of care' to prevent servicewomen becoming injured during their careers. These anxieties are reminiscent of Western attitudes towards women cultivated from the seventeenth century onwards. During the Enlightenment a greater division emerged between male and female participation in society. A key proponent for this male/female separation was the understanding and acceptance that the male was the breadwinner, with the responsibility to protect and support his family. Thus, according to Goldstein, separate spheres were developing whereby the male held the power while the female became dependent upon the male (2001: 21). Tickner argues that the public sphere was the domain of the military and foreign policy as well as economic and commercial enterprise (1992: 49). Legal restraints barring women's access from the public world led most women to be trapped in economic, social and cultural 'traditions', which gave rise to hegemonic masculinity while rendering the female role irrelevant. The private domain has habitually been devalued:

the historically established dominance of men in the public sphere and the restriction of women's identity, roles and prime social influence to the private sphere are fundamental to the construction of gendered identities and the perpetuation of unequal power relations. (Youngs 2000: 46)

Homosexuals were also viewed as the 'Other', as were non-white men and women. All were prevented from contributing to the public sphere. Homosexuality was criminalized and the colonies were viewed as a source of cheap labour. Enloe (2004: 31) suggests that, whilst not condoned by most militaries, homophobia and racism have at certain stages in military history contributed to the construction of the hegemonic warrior masculinity.

Psychoanalytical research conducted by Freud saw masculine power in society as a product of male neurosis and fear of castration, through a son's close relationship with his mother and father. The Oedipus complex, and Freud's case study of The Wolf Man, led him towards a theory of the patriarchal structure of society. This structure was reliant upon the strength and authority of the male over the female, competitiveness and an overreaction by men to the non-masculine/feminine.

The anthropologist Gilmore conducted global research questioning the international archetype of manliness comprising the essence of manhood. He concluded that in most states men were faced with the challenge of demonstrating their maleness through rites of entry, saying that 'so long as there are battles to be fought, wars to be won, some of us will have to act like men' (Gilmore 1990: 76).

## Military Training and the Development of Military Masculinities

Connell (2010: 212–213) and Goldstein (2001: 266–269) also argue that the masculinities involved in soldiering are socially constructed and reified by the military. From an early age, before a British male is recruited into the military he will have been subjected to media and cultural images of soldiering. Boys' games traditionally revolve around action and violence. The core concept of computer games appears to be focused around military scenarios. Military recruiting campaigns adopt catchphrases such as 'The Infantry Will Make You a Man', and play on gendered connotations. Goldstein argues that the military is accepted as providing 'the main remnant of traditional manhood' (2001: 265) and Barrett suggests that:

> Militaries around the world have defined the soldier as an embodiment of traditional male sex role behaviours. (2001: 77)

Civilian men are 'broken down' to become soldiers. Their civilian clothes are removed, hair is cut short, and through various tests (Hearn 1992: 46) and practices (Hale 2011: 2) they are moulded into soldiers. Military training takes place in unfamiliar locations that demand physical fitness, self-reliance, inner strength and camaraderie. However, if individuals can't perform as well as their peers there is little sympathy for them.

Lambert conducted a series of interviews with several serving infantry recruits. She was particularly interested in initial training:

> [F]rom week 1–15, it were just a total nightmare because they try and like break you and get the ones out that they don't like and the people they think they don't want. (Lambert 2007: 9)

As long as the recruits conform, pass their tests and impress the training teams they are accepted. During interviews Lambert noticed that to be in the team, and for the team to work, everyone had to be the same:

> Moreover, because of the emphasis on team work and the importance of sharing qualities rather than differing from each other, they [the soldiers] would alienate people who behaved differently or threatened the all-important cohesion integral to military culture. (2007: 11)

This contempt for people who don't fit is extended beyond the barracks and can include civilians, homosexuals and females. Nye states that '[m]ilitary training is meant to wrest the soldier out of the civilian and throw him into action' (2007: 430). One of the soldiers in Lambert's study said he felt his civilian friends could not understand what he had gone through. As well as being physically removed from civilians, the recruits viewed civilian men as being weaker than they were:

> In conveying what distinguishes a soldier from his civilian counterpart the soldier replied 'a pair of bollocks!'. (2007: 16)

In addition to exploiting historic social aspects of gender relations, military training encourages dominant leaders. This creates testosterone fuelled competition, both during training and throughout a military career. Complementing these traits is the requirement to be seen as solutions focused. To hesitate is to fail. Professor Anthony King observed that:

> During initial training soldiers are taught to retain the initiative; when they are confronted with the immediate presence of an enemy, it is better to do the

wrong thing decisively than to do nothing at all. Passivity always leads to defeat. (2009)

## The Necessity of the 'Other' within the Combat Arms

According to Goldstein a common feature of training is the use of humiliation and name calling: 'The epithets of drill instructors ... "faggot", "pussy" or simply "woman" left no doubt that not becoming a soldier meant not being a man' (2001: 265). Certainly I am aware that male soldiers beaten by servicewomen in physical tests receive verbal abuse by their colleagues, and when male soldiers are not performing well they have been referred to as a 'bunch of women', and the like. Being compared to women is a great insult for the soldiers. Frank Barrett's account of the multiple masculinities at play in the U.S. navy appears similar to Lambert's recruitment research. Barrett notes that the unifying theme between the varying (competitive) masculine roles in the U.S. navy was a shared negative attitude towards female navy personnel. From officers to sailors and from pilots to storemen, 'the association between weakness and women was reproduced' (Barrett 2001: 83).

In order to be a soldier there has to be an 'Other' to give meaning to soldiering. Within Afghanistan military operations demand traits traditionally associated with this 'Other', explains Khalili:

> At one level, COIN itself is presented as the opposite of a more mechanised, technologically advanced, higher-fire-power form of warfare. Given that the latter is often coded as hyper-masculine, the former is considered feminine. Second, the very object of COIN is the transformation of civilian allegiances and remaking of their social world. (2010: 1,473)

## Counter-insurgency in Afghanistan

The UK operates within the ISAF mandate which states that in order to carry out its mission:

> ISAF conducts *population-centric* COIN in partnership with the Afghan National Security Forces (ANSF) and provides support to the government and international community in security sector reform, including mentoring to the Afghan National Security Force (ANSF). The intention of this counterinsurgency strategy is to isolate extremists by building relationships with the Afghan people and the government. (NATO 2012)

Soldiers patrolling in Helmand routinely meet the local population, assist with development projects, attend *shuras*[2] and mentor the ANSF. The insurgent is indistinguishable from the civilian and blends in with the villagers. Taliban occasionally wear burqas (a type of overdress worn by women) in order to reduce the chances of being stopped and searched. That the insurgent lives and operates among the populace leads to the use of violent force in a pre-planned attack or in response to an attack – which is extremely difficult without causing collateral damage or civilian casualties.

## Theories and Counterinsurgency Doctrine

The British Army Field Manual (AFM 1/10 – see MoD 2010) provides principles and tactical frameworks for conducting COIN operations. Although not Afghan-specific, it was written in 2010 and was heavily influenced by the UK presence in Afghanistan. Kilcullen explains that:

> Doctrine is not only an idealized description of how things are done but is also an attempt to inculcate habits of mind and action that change organizational culture and behaviour. (2010: 20)

Kilcullen's reference to 'organizational change and behaviour' suggests that different military operations require different mindsets. Traditionally, soldiering has focused especially on destroying an enemy and dominating ground, which often involves Close Quarter Battle (CQB), shooting from a short range, fixing bayonets and hand-to-hand combat. The theoretical COIN principles given below point to a conceptual understanding of the human terrain at odds with the physicality of traditional soldiering. Below is a summary of the ten COIN principles as explained on the Soldiers' Card, an aide memoire:

| Political Primacy | Gain and Maintain Popular Support |
|---|---|
| Armed conflict should be driven by political motivation. The military aspect of COIN is a means to the political end. Galula, the French COIN theorist, argued that COIN is 80% political interaction and 20% military action. | This is the crux of the conflict between the insurgent and the counter-insurgent. Be a good guest. Treat people and their property with respect. Try to view your actions through their eyes. |

## Unity of Effort

Due to the variety of actors and means employed in COIN and being mindful that the military are not suitable for all tasks, there are a variety of actors involved. Ideally these different organizations should engage with each other and coordinate activity. Without Unity of Effort there is the risk of undermining and duplicating effort.

## Operate in Accordance with the Law

To remain credible and legitimate counter-insurgents must act in accordance with the law. This will distinguish NATO from the insurgents.

## Secure the population

With the population as the centre of gravity it also follows that the population must feel safe in order to side with the government and the counter-insurgents. Once an area is secured it should not be abandoned but left under the responsibility of the Host Nation security force.

## Neutralize the Insurgent

It is vital to separate the insurgent from his support system and the general population. Force is not the only way of neutralizing the insurgent. But, if force is employed, apply no more force other than what is absolutely necessary. Make every effort to reduce civilian casualties to the absolute minimum.

## Understanding the Human Terrain

With the population as the centre of gravity it follows that a detailed understanding of the people is essential. There is a lot to understand: culture, history, religion and politics – this is as important as being familiar with geographical terrain and knowledge of enemy capabilities and tactics. Causing cultural offence can undermine the mission.

## Integrate Intelligence

In counter-insurgencies information is usually more effective than firepower and is routinely built bottom-up. It is something we gather ourselves, through our own operations, through what we do.

## Prepare for the Long Term

COIN takes time, therefore a consistent and a coherent approach is vital. Everything must lead towards the end state, therefore longer-term plans are required at every level. Help the ANSF develop relationships with the local people.

## Learn and Adapt

Insurgents will continuously change their tactics. Learn and adapt more quickly than the enemy. Outsmart the insurgents and outpace their learning-cycle. Share the lessons that you have learned with your team, your commander and the Host Nation.

---

Aspects of military masculinities compete with the premises within these principles. 'Political Primacy' requires military leaders to stand by and watch the 'Other' (civilian leaders, other Government departments, etc.) dictate policy and give direction. Similarly a 'Unity of Effort' demands an acceptance that the military isn't the only show in town and that liaison with unlikely bedfellows from international and non-governmental organizations is necessary. Military and developmental organizations operate at different speeds and have different perspectives. The former expect and need quick results in order to 'win over the population', unlike the latter who understand that progress can be slow and requires time. 'Learn and Adapt' asks that the force make changes in how it operates, but in a hierarchical organization such as the military, introducing new concepts and accepting errors is challenging. The requirement to change may reflect mistakes by senior leadership who, owing to hegemonic military masculinities are unwilling to admit to errors. 'Prepare for the Long Term' necessitates military planners to design a plan that goes beyond their typical six-month tour duration. This could impact on opportunities to oversee a major operation. Key operations have been a defining moment for brigade staff, often leading to the award of medals. It is interesting to note that thus far medals have been awarded for acts of bravery in battle but, as Sgt Bob Seely notes, no one has been decorated for their part in developmental and non-kinetic projects (2011: 18).

The starkest contradictions between military masculinities and counterinsurgency doctrine are evident in the principles 'Understand The Human Terrain', 'Secure the Population' and 'Gain and Maintain Popular Support'. As retired Lt General Kiszley observed:

> In the eyes of the warrior, counterinsurgency calls for some decidedly unwarrior like qualities, such as emotional intelligence, empathy, subtly, sophistication, nuance and political adroitness. (2006)

Similarly the author of the U.S. COIN doctrine manual, General Petraeus, has been described by Khalili as embodying 'an emerging form of military masculinity, the "warrior-scholar"', whereby the hegemonic warrior combines academic, liberal sophistication with soldiering skills (2011: 1,471). This is a tough mantle for the average soldier in the Combat Arms to don. A British Commanding Officer, Lt Col. Kitson, explained in an interview with Catigiani that soldiers:

> [b]rought up on a diet of Ross Kemp and You Tube 'shoot 'em up' media coverage had difficulty in understanding the nature of the Helmand counterinsurgency campaign. (2012: 19)

## Principles of COIN that Challenge Military Masculinity

### Understanding the Human Terrain

Failing to understand what the military refer to as the 'human terrain' – that is the linguistic, political and cultural environment – can lead to misunderstandings, or worse, bring soldiers into conflict with the local population (MoD 2010: 3–4). During both tours of Afghanistan I witnessed how a lack of cultural understanding by NATO soldiers created friction with Afghan partners. In 2007 an infanteer, working as a mentor to the Afghan National Army (ANA), bought a towel with the Afghan flag emblazoned upon it from the Saturday market in Kandahar Airfield (KAF). Unbeknown to him, the flag included Koranic script, and when the ANA soldiers noticed this an argument ensued. The British soldier quickly apologized and the ANA soldiers gave him another towel. The incident was reported up the chain of command to prevent the same mistake being made. Then on another occasion, in 2012, American soldiers burnt copies of the Koran at Bagram Prison, after they had been ordered to dispose of them. Naïvely they thought that burning them was appropriate. Riots spread across the region, and NATO and the United States had to launch a large media response. Both incidents highlight the importance of cultural understanding and the need for soldiers to respect the 'Other'. A less dramatic example of cultural tradition clashing with a typical military outlook was apparent when several of my male friends complained that they had to hold hands with their Afghan partners during *shuras* and when walking.

### Educating Cultural Awareness

The MoD has invested in a new pre-deployment training package run by the Operational Training and Advisory Group (OPTAG), designed to enhance Afghan cultural awareness. For Catigiani, who visited OPTAG, the training remains kinetically focused (2012: 11). I sympathize with his view but feel that the British military has made a genuine attempt to train beyond the use of force. It is intent on teaching soldiers how to behave in a culturally unfamiliar country, and such cultural training should continue even after operations in Afghanistan have ceased.

At OPTAG Afghans teach UK soldiers what is socially and culturally acceptable and what will be viewed as a misdemeanour. To some, these efforts appear 'not to weaponize culture, but to culturize warriors'. Gonzales has been outspoken in his disdain of militaries using anthropologists while deployed on operations in Afghanistan. He has also noted the creation of a new military masculinity:

> Military interest in culture coincides with a broad shift within the Pentagon – the rise to power of a 'small band of warrior-intellectuals' in the post-Rumsfeld era. (2007: 17)

Cultural sensitivity is sold by these warrior-intellectuals as a battlefield tactic that will save lives. General Petraeus refers to cultural 'astuteness' and, according to Gonzales, some instructors have replaced 'sensitivity' with 'knowledge' (2007: 24). Soldiers are encouraged to focus on:

- • The importance of honour.
- • The role of women in Afghan society.
- • Courtesies and tradition.

### Honour

Honour is an intrinsic element in Afghan culture, especially in the Pashtun south where the code of Pashtunwali affects all aspects of life. Afghan men must never 'lose face', whereas British soldiers have been shaped by a training environment that uses humour and belittlement to teach lessons. Some Afghans have complained in polling surveys that they feel insulted by British humour and by the way they are treated. Swearing, crude jokes and a lack of religiosity strained the relationship between the ANSF and British troops. Although there are no statistics, anecdotally some insider attacks on NATO soldiers by ANSF members have been attributed to ANSF humiliation leading to a revenge attack on any NATO soldier.

### Treatment of Females

Afghan honour is interlinked with attitudes towards females, who should not be spoken to or seen by non-family members. For soldiers mentoring and living with Afghans this has been a challenging area. Soldiers receive and can purchase various 'lad's magazines' in Helmand. They also look at pornography. This aspect of military masculinity clashes with most Afghan sensitivities about women. There have been instances where soldiers have shared magazines and films with the ANSF, some of whom have been offended and angry. A military masculinity that objectifies women and revels in viewing inappropriate images of women is unhelpful in the face of conservative mores. During compound searches Afghans have been angered by the fact that non-family members have interacted with females.

### Courtesies

Connected with Afghan honour and the position of women in society are the traditions and courtesies that the Karzai government insist that NATO observe. Thus the conduct of night raids on compounds, understandably viewed by the Afghans as an affront on their privacy, was curtailed. But operating at night had given the patrols various tactical advantages and had produced several High Value Targets (HVTs). 'Going for raids during the day is like throwing a rock at a flock of birds', said a colonel during an interview with the academic Yousafzai (2012: 1). Hegemonic military masculinity predictably struggles to reconcile the importance of observing cultural sensitivities with military tactical planning and activity.

## Secure the Population

The principle focus for the security line of operation in COIN must be the protection of the population, rather than the security of the forces themselves, or attrition of insurgents (MoD 2010: 3–4). This principle requires a difficult balance between finding, fixing and striking insurgents and looking after the population. Soldiers are directed not to engage the enemy in built-up areas, as damaging mosques, schools or hospitals and killing or injuring civilians drives a wedge between the local population and ISAF and the Afghan government (GIRoA). In 2009 the number of Afghan civilian casualties rose dramatically. President Karzai made several inflammatory statements critical of ISAF's techniques. In response ISAF Commander, Gen. McChrystal, introduced a directive entitled 'Courageous Restraint', which implemented highly restrictive rules of engagement, requiring a passivity out of place in military masculinity. Khalili, like Gonzales, describes McChystal and Petraeus as warrior-scholars. Both have stated that the use of lethal force against insurgents operating amongst the civilian population can be counterproductive. But Courageous Restraint epitomized a theoretical clash of concepts. Tactical acumen, which is linked to military masculinities, was subordinated to the safety of the civilian population. Writing this down, I am surprised that Courageous Restraint met with such resistance. What is a military for if it can't protect civilians?

To the soldiers on the ground the practice of Courageous Restraint demonstrated that their superiors were not 'manly' and had forgotten what it was to be a warrior. During an interview a U.S. sergeant declared:

> I wish we had generals who remembered what it was like when they were in a platoon. Either they have never been in real fighting or they forgot what it was like. (Chivers 2010: 1)

All ISAF soldiers were encouraged to adopt Courageous Restraint by the introduction of a medal for refraining to use force. As one journalist asked:

> Will the idea of heroism that doesn't involve pulling the trigger catch on? I have my doubts. I think it's going to be difficult to get regular soldiers to buy into this concept – which goes against the heroic narrative so embedded in military culture. (Hastings 2010: 1)

As the majority of military medals are awarded for bravery and aggression, a medal bestowed on a soldier for not seizing the initiative or killing the enemy is likely to be viewed as a pusillanimous. A British soldier felt the policy had gone too far in favour of the insurgents:

> Our hands are tied the way we are asked to do courageous restraint. I agree that too many civilians were killed but we have got people shooting at us and we are not allowed to shoot back. Outrageous [sic] restraint is a lot easier to say. (Harding 2010)

Not responding to the insurgents undermines basic military training, where caution is viewed as 'feminine' and un-dynamic. The soldiers feel 'un-heroic' (Hastings 2010: 1) and that not responding appropriately (aggressively) makes them look 'weak' (Fox 2010). By 'Securing the Local Population' soldiers are making themselves more vulnerable and feel psychologically emasculated.

### Gain and Maintain Popular Support

Unless the government gains its people's trust and confidence, the chances of success will be greatly reduced (MoD 2010: 5–6).

AFM 1/10 suggests it is axiomatic that gaining the consent and tolerance of the local population will reduce support available to the insurgent, thus weakening the insurgency and demonstrating GIRoA's effectiveness. In a bid to gain consent of the population, GIRoA and ISAF embarked on political, security, social and economic initiatives. However, coordinating activities with civilian organizations, assisting with development projects, training the indigenous police force and mentoring GIRoA ministers is not routine military business and requires a mental attitude not normally associated with military masculinities.

### 'Non-Kinetic Influence Activities'

To complicate the conceptual environment, the insurgents did not conform to expected cultural behaviour. As Chin identified:

> The Taliban are making extensive use of modern communications to promote their cause. This is somewhat ironic, given they banned television when in power. (2010: 215)

The Taliban's use of modern technology led to a 'battle for the narrative', which forced the British military to expand and broaden non-kinetic activity through Influence Activity, which incorporates various 'soft' skills to win the hearts and minds of the population. Kilcullen explains that in a complex, multi-actor environment using non-violent methods of influence proves that 'control does not mean imposing order through dominance'; he goes on to justify/apologize for this approach:

> If this sounds soft, non-lethal and non-confrontational, it is not, the loser is marginalised, starved of support. (2006: 3)

Combat Arms soldiers were therefore expected to conduct Influence Activities (the use of media, the distribution of leaflets, posters and radio broadcasts, and key leader engagement through *shuras* with the community). Such tasks required soldiers to be able to think as an Afghan thinks. Putting themselves in the role of the 'Other' was new territory for soldiers possessing hegemonic, military masculinities. Sgt Bob Seely states:

> Influence has often been done unprofessionally by the military (two weeks on a poorly planned course compared with 20 years' training and practice for kinetic warfare). This has further deadened Influence's potential in the eyes of both commanders and soldiers. (2011: 19)

The non-violent approach of Influence Activities is in stark contrast to the traditional association with soldiering. When Duncanson described soldiers perceiving peacekeeping tactics as 'inferior, frustrating and less manly pursuits than real fighting' (2009: 68), she could have been describing how many view COIN.

## A COIN Dividend for Servicewomen

> When people are entering upon a war they do things the wrong way around. Action comes first, and it is only when they have suffered that they begin to think. (Thucydides, *The Peloponnesian War*)

The majority of British servicewomen are employed in Combat Service Support (CSS) regiments, logistics, human resources and as medics. Although it is highly unusual for servicewomen to be part of an infantry foot patrol, now they sometimes do participate, in order to search and converse with local women.

The concept of Female Engagement Teams (FETs) was developed to influence the 'other fifty per cent' of the population who wield influence over their sons and husbands (who are potential insurgents). Western militaries have belatedly recognized the shortcomings in not engaging with the female population and have introduced FETs in an ad hoc manner. Within the UK there is an insistence on placing FETS in the Defence Specialist Cultural Unit, but this is unhelpful. Culture within overseas patriarchal communities has a tendency to reinforce stereotypical views of the role of women and may therefore undermine attempts to empower local women.

There is more to a successful FET soldier than merely being female. The women who deploy with the teams have to be physically fit and able to understand how they can influence and help the local population. The role did not develop as successfully as it could have done in Afghanistan due to the insular outlook of military staff rather than the FETs but, since servicewomen can perform roles in host nations that their male colleagues are unable to, they were patrolling and operating in what were formerly exclusively male areas. More than their sex or their occupational skills, servicewomen are viewed as being imbued with characteristics and traits which make them more approachable and suitable to employ in operations 'amongst the people'. Those who decry such an essentialist perspective should consider the unique position servicewomen are in. I would argue they possess a better capacity to understand and empathize with the 'Other' in Afghanistan because they have been the 'Other' since basic training within the military.

According to McBride and Wibben, Afghans perceive servicewomen as different to their male colleagues:

> Many Pashtun men, far from shunning women, show a preference for interacting with females. They view them as a 'third gender'. As a result servicewomen are accorded the advantages, rather than the disadvantages, of both genders; they are extended the respect shown to men, but are granted the access to home and family normally reserved to women. (2012: 210)

The research conducted by 'Inclusive Security' for the NATO Committee on Gender Perspectives highlighted how local men in Sangin were willing to talk to female soldiers but not to male soldiers, which provided sound information that led to actionable intelligence (NATO 2011).

Afghanistan's COIN campaign, more than any peacekeeping operation or previous conventional war, enabled servicewomen to contravene traditional military norms dictating where they can operate. Since future military missions are likely to be in populated environments with the presence of men and women, initiatives such as the FETs should continue post Afghanistan. They will be particularly useful in preventing and responding to sexual and gender-based violence – an area which is now gaining traction with British politicians and even in the MoD.

## How to Accommodate Military Masculinities in Future Non-Conventional Warfare

Despite the increase in sales of male grooming products (CNBC 2014), military masculinities are unlikely to disappear from the battlefield. And nor should they. The Combat Arms, who, to me, encapsulate the essence of military masculinity, are the backbone of the British army. As the military resets itself for contingency operations post the cessation of combat operations in Afghanistan, the Combat Arms will be at the heart of the military contribution to UK security. But as the British Army realigns into a new structure (see 'Army 20/20') and becomes two forces – the Reactive and Adaptive forces – it is timely to suggest that recognition of the implications of military masculinities is necessary. Future tasks for the Adaptive force are likely to involve Combat Arms troops deploying globally to train overseas indigenous forces and to operate with cross-Whitehall departments. In order for them to build on the Afghan mentoring experience a course could be established that teaches how to mentor and includes references to gendered roles and military masculinities. So internalized is this military masculinity that it will involve a large leap of imagination to accept that it even exists. However, once its presence is understood then operating with indigenous forces and civilians in a non-kinetic environment will be easier.

## Conclusion

I argued that the Combat Arms has relied on Western essentialist sex-norms and has continued to exploit and mould hegemonic masculinities for its own survival. Historically, the soldiers selected to conduct population-centric operations have been those who have been trained to close with and kill the enemy. Elements of the Combat Arms have struggled to adopt the 'softer' aspects of COIN and its related practices. The principles, 'Understand the Human Terrain', 'Secure the Population' and 'Gain and Maintain Popular Support' would have been better fulfilled if it had been accepted that military masculinities influence military thinking and action. Of note, soldiers within the Combat Arms struggled to adapt to the policy of 'Courageous Restraint', and were reticent in becoming involved in 'Influence Activity'. The mentoring and training of the ANSF may have resulted in less friction and fewer insider attacks if soldiers had been made aware of their hegemonic masculinity. In order to conform to cultural sensitivities, the Combat Arms enrolled the assistance of servicewomen for patrols and mentoring tasks. Servicewomen have therefore been operating in spaces that traditionally have been exclusively male. The British Army's contribution to the government's Building Security Overseas Strategy (BSOS) specifically requires servicewomen to participate more in operations, and the FET project will probably build on the Afghan experience. Future military operations will require soldiers who can empathize with the 'Other'. Afghanistan has demonstrated that while soldiers are at ease with separating those they identify as the insurgent from the civilian population by using force, they have been less comfortable with the theoretical, 'soft' approaches of COIN doctrine. Who knows, perhaps if the bragging soldier on the back of the Hercules had been aware that he was the embodiment of a military masculinity he might have thought twice before sharing his plans for leave?

This chapter is based on my experience serving in the British Army in Afghanistan and in other missions over twenty years, backed up with documentary research. Now that the mission in Afghanistan has ended UK troops are no longer 'on the ground' in Helmand Province. Refreshingly I can write that the UK Ministry of Defence is considering how to develop a gendered perspective to military operations. Examples can be seen by 77 Brigade teaching a five-day 'Female Engagement' package to soldiers participating in the African Union's Mission in Somalia. British troops are now also teaching Peshmerga soldiers how to respond and support Yazede women who have escaped from Da'esh (Islamic State fighters) and are survivors of conflict-related sexual violence. I have been fortunate enough to be a Gender Field Advisor in the Democratic Republic of Congo and will deploy to New York to continue this role at a strategic level with the UN's HQ. These appointments have been endorsed by senior military officers – demonstrating that there is a growing recognition of the need for a gender perspective and for the expansion of servicewomen's roles in military operations and that military masculinity may not be appropriate in contemporary conflict. The role that gay soldiers can play in enhancing the Combat Arms' ability to be more inclusive and better able to operate amongst the 'Other' was beyond my study. However, comments made in October 2015 by the General commanding British Land Forces point to an acknowledgement that traditional military masculinity may be dated. In an interview with the *Financial Times*, the General said 'operational effectiveness is at the top of the pile' of reasons to recruit more gay and transgender people into the Army. He proposed that an emphasis on diplomacy, engaging with local populations and the need to understand 'human terrain' means the Army should recruit more broadly. (Farmer 2015). There is no doubt that the military is adapting and changing to the new character of conflict. The 'Other' is now being sought to enhance operational effectiveness.

## Notes

1. A bergen is a Disruptive Pattern Material (DPM) issued daysack.
2. A *shura* is a meeting where decisions are reached after consultation among a community. British soldiers frequently attended these meetings, occasionally frustrated at the time the meetings took to make a decision.

## List of Abbreviations

Army Field Manual – AFM
Afghan National Army – ANA
Afghan National Police – ANP
Afghan National Security Forces – ANSF
Counter-insurgency – COIN
Female Engagement Teams – FETs
International Security Force Afghanistan – ISAF
Ministry of Defence – MoD
North Atlantic Treaty Organisation – NATO
Peace Support Operations – PSO

## Bibliography

Associated Press. 2010. NATO Pushes 'Courageous Restraint', available at http://www.military.com/news/article/nato-pushes-courageous-restraint-for-troops.html (accessed 10 June 2012).

Barrett, F. 2001. 'The Organisational Construction of Hegemonic Masculinity: The Case of the US Navy', in S.M. Whitehead and F.J. Barrett (eds), *The Masculinities Reader*. Cambridge: Polity, pp. 77–100.

Catigiani, S. 2012. 'Getting COIN at the Tactical Level in Afghanistan', *Journal of Strategic Studies*, available at http://dx:doi.org/10.1080/01402390.2012.660625 (accessed 14 June 2012).

Chin, W. 2010. 'British COIN in Afghanistan', *Defence and Security Analysis* 23(2): 201–225.

Chivers, C.J. 2010. 'General Faces Unease among His Own Troops, Too', available at www.nytimes.com/2010/06/23/world/asia/23troops.html (accessed 5 September 2012).

CNBC. 2014. 'Real Men Don't Cry – But They Are Exfoliating', December, available at http://www.cnbc.com/2014/12/05/real-men-dont-cry-but-they-are-exfoliating.html (accessed 23 August 2015).

Connell, R.W. 2010. *Masculinities*. Cambridge: Polity Press.

Cornwall, A. and N. Lindisfarne. 1994. Introduction, in A. Cornwall and N. Lindisfarne (eds), *Dislocating Masculinity*. London: Routledge.

Duncanson, C. 2009. 'Forces for Good? British Military Masculinities on Peace Support Operations', available at http://core.ac.uk/download/pdf/278577.pdf (accessed 23 August 2015).

Dunne, T. and C. Schmidt. 2001. 'Realism', in J. Baylis and S. Smith (eds), *The Globalization of World Politics*. Oxford: Oxford University Press.

Egnell, R. 2011. 'Lessons from Helmand', *International Affairs* 87(2): 297–315.

Ehrenreich, B. 1999. 'Men Hate War Too', *Foreign Affairs* 78(1): 118–122.

Enloe, C. 1988. *Does Khaki Become You?* London: Pandora.

——. 2000. *Maneuvers*. London: University of California Press.

——. 2004. *The Curious Feminist*. London: University of California Press.

——. 2007. *Globalisation and Militarism*. Maryland: Rowman and Littlefield Publishers.

FCO, HMG. 2012. 'Building Stability Overseas Strategy', available at https://www.gov.uk/government/uploads/system/uploads/attachment_data/file/32960/bsos-july-11.pdf (accessed 4 June 2013).

Fox, R. 2010. 'Courageous Restraint', *The Guardian*, 24 June, available at www.guardian.co.uk//commentisfree/cifamerica/2010/jun/23/general-mcchrystal-britain-afghan-policy (accessed 5 September 2012).

Fukuyama, F. 1998. 'Women and the Evolution of World Politics', *Foreign Affairs* 77(5): 24–40.

Gilmore, D.D. 1990. *Manhood in the Making: Cultural Concepts of Masculinity*. New Haven: Yale University Press.

Goldstein, J.S. 2001. *War and Gender*. New York: Cambridge Press.

Gonzales, R. 2007. 'The Dangerous Militarisation of Anthropology', available at http://www.antropologi.info/blog/anthropology/2007/the_dangerous_militarisation_of_anthropo (accessed 23 August 2015).

Hale, C.H. 2011. 'The Role of Practice in the Development of Military Masculinities', *Gender Work and Organisation* 19(6): 699–722.

Harding, T. 2010. 'Courageous Restraint – Putting Troops' Lives at Risk', available at www.telegraph.co.uk/news/worldnews/asia/afghanistan/7874950/Courageous-restraint-putting-troops-lives-at risk.html# (accessed 3 September 2012).

Harrison, D. 2003. 'Violence in the Military Community', in P. Higate (ed.), *Military Masculinities, Identity and the State*, Westport: Praeger, pp. 71–91.

Hastings, M. 2010. 'Afghanistan: "Courageous Restraint" the New Catch Phrase', available at https://michaelhastings.wordpress.com/2010/05/12/afghanistan-courageous-restraint-the-new-catch-phrase/ (accessed 5 September 2012).

Hearn, J. 1992. *Men in the Public Eye*. London: Routledge.

Hearn, J. and D.L. Collinson. 1994. 'Theorising Unities and Differences between Men and between Masculinities', in H. Brod and M. Kaufman (eds), *Theorizing Masculinities*. London: Sage Publications.

Higate, P. 2003. '"Soft Clerks" and "Hard Civvies": Pluralizing Military Masculinities', in P. Higate (ed.), *Military Masculinities: Identity and the State*. Westport: Praeger, pp. 27–43.

Hooper, C. 2001. *Manly States*. New York: Columbia University Press.

Khalili, L. 2010. 'Gendered Practices of Counterinsurgency', *Review of International Studies* 37: 1,471–1,491.

Kilcullen, D. 2006. 'Twenty-eight Articles of Counterinsurgency', available at http://smallwarsjournal.com/documents/28articles.pdf (accessed 10 June 2012).

———. 2010. *Counterinsurgency*, Oxford: Oxford University Press.

King, A. 2009. 'Why We're Getting it Wrong in Afghanistan', available at http://www.prospectmagazine.co.uk/magazine/getting-it-wrong-in-afghanistan/ (accessed 7 September 2012).

Kiszley, J. 2006. 'Learning about Counterinsurgency', *Military Review* March-April 2007, USMC, p. 5.

Kitzen, M. 2012. 'Western Military Culture and COIN: An Ambiguous Reality', *Scientia Militaria, South African Journal of Military Studies* 40(1): 1–24.

Kuehnast, K., C. de J. Oudraat and H. Hernes (eds). 2011. Chapter 2, *Women and War: Power and Protection in the 21st Century*. Washington DC: US Institute of Peace Press, pp. 17–28.

Lambert, C.H. 2007. 'The Development of British Military Masculinities through Symbolic Resources', *Culture and Psychology*. Dublin: Geary Institute.

McBride, K. and T.R. Wibben. 2012. 'The Gendering of COIN in Afghanistan', *Humanity* 3(2): 199–215.

Ministry of Defence (MoD). 2010. *Army Field Manual Countering Insurgency*, vol. 1, part 10. London: The Stationery Office.

Morgan, D.H.J. 1994. 'Theatre of War: Combat, the Military, and Masculinities', in H. Brod and J. Kaufman (eds), *Theorizing Masculinities*. London: Sage.

Morgan, W. 2010. 'Afghanistan's Green Zone', available at http://atwar.blogs.nytimes.com/2010/07/29/afghanistans-green-zone/ (accessed 12 June 2012).

Nagl, J. 2005. *Learning to Eat Soup with a Knife*. Chicago: The University of Chicago Press.

NATO. 2011. 'How Can Gender Make a Difference to Security in Operations', available at http://www.nato.int/issues/women_nato/index.html (accessed 15 June 2012).

———. 2012. 'ISAF's Mission in Afghanistan', available at http://www.nato.int/cps/en/natolive/topics_69366.htm (accessed 8 June 2012).

Nye, R.A. 2007. 'Western Masculinities in War and Peace', *The American Historical Review* 112(2): 417–438.

Richards, D. 2011. 'Introduction to Contemporary Insurgency', in D. Richards and G. Mills (eds), *Victory Among the People*. London: RUSI.

Seely, B. 2011. 'Winning Through the People', *The British Army Review* 152: 17–29.

Segal, L. 1992. 'Sex as Domination', in S.M. Whitehead and F.J. Barrett (eds), *The Masculinities Reader*. Oxford: Blackwell Publishers, pp. 100–112.

Smith, M.L.R. 2012. 'A Tradition That Never Was – Critiquing the Critique of British COIN', *Small War Journal*, available at http://smallwarsjournal.com/jrnl/art/a-tradition-that-never-was (accessed 4 September 2012).

Smith, R. 2006. *The Utility of Force*. London: Penguin.

———. 1998. '"Unacceptable Conclusions" and the "Man" Question: Masculinity, Gender, and International Relations', in M. Zalewski and J. Parpart (eds), *The 'Man' Question in International Relations*. Oxford: Westview Press.

*The Times*. 2012. 'Taliban Flee Wearing Burqas', available at http://www.timesof malta.com/articles/view/20120417/world/Taliban-flee-wearing-burqas.415876 (accessed 12 June 2012).

Thucydides. 441 BC. *The History of the Peloponnesian War*. London: Penguin Classics.

Tickner, J.A. 1992. *Gender in International Relations*. New York: Columbia University Press.

USMC. 2007. *Counterinsurgency Field Manual*, 3–24. Chicago: The University of Chicago Press.

Whitehead, S.M. and F.J. Barrett. 2001. 'The Sociology of Masculinity', in S.M. Whitehead and F.J. Barrett (eds), *The Masculinities Reader*. Oxford: Blackwell Publishers.

Whitworth, S. 2007. *Men, Militarism and Peacekeeping*. New York: Lynne Rienner.

Youngs, G. 2000. 'Breaking Patriarchal Bonds', in M.H. Marchand and A.S. Runyan (eds), *Gender and Global Restructuring*. London: Routledge, pp. 44–58.

Yousafzai, S. 2012. 'US Hands Over Night Raids', available at http://www.thedailybeast.com/articles/2012/04/08/u-s-hands-over-night-raids-to-afghan-forces-with-possible-consequences.html (accessed 5 September 2012).

**Major Rachel Grimes** has served with the British Army for twenty years; she has been deployed to Northern Ireland, Bosnia, Iraq and Afghanistan, and most recently with the United Nations in the Democratic Republic of Congo. She obtained an MSc in International Relations and Gender from Bristol University in 2012. When not overseas or studying she enjoys fell-running races, cross-country skiing and listening to 'The Archers'. Her companion of ten years is a German Wirehaired Pointer, Gus, who is well versed in UNSCR 1325.

# Index

www.ingramcontent.com/pod-product-compliance
Lightning Source LLC
Chambersburg PA
CBHW070926030426
42336CB00014BA/2558